# The Classic Guide to GARDENING

# The
# Classic Guide
# to
# GARDENING

## Frank J. Scott

AMBERLEY

First published 1870
This edition first published 2016

Amberley Publishing
The Hill, Stroud
Gloucestershire, GL5 4EP

www.amberley-books.com

Copyright © Amberley Publishing, 2016

British Library Cataloguing in Publication Data.
A catalogue record for this book is available from the British Library.

ISBN 978 1 4456 5170 5 (print)
ISBN 978 1 4456 5171 2 (ebook)

Typesetting and Origination by Amberley Publishing.
Printed in the UK.

# Contents

# Preface

A pastime that has blossomed over thousands of years, gardening has been enjoyed wherever man has made his home. With the emergence of the first civilisations, wealthy individuals began to indulge in gardens created for purely aesthetic reasons – the most famous of these, of course, being the Hanging Gardens of Babylon. Though the Hanging Gardens remain the sole Wonder of the Ancient World whose existence has not been established beyond doubt, they are seen as the ultimate romanticised ideal of an Eastern garden; a perfected vision of engineered harmony in nature.

Writing here in 1870, Frank J. Scott's classic American text outlines how those on more modest incomes could cultivate their environment and, though they may not quite be able to match Babylon, the people of Batavia, Baton Rouge and beyond could, in Scott's own words, partake in 'the arts of suburban-home embellishment'. Covering everything from outbuildings and fences to lawns, paths and trees, Scott provides the reader with all the information they need to create their very own suburban oasis. Great emphasis is placed on the importance of finding that 'happy medium between extravagance and parsimony', and the pioneering landscape architect's work supports the notion that one does not need to break the bank in order to beautify the house and home: a belief that rings as true today as it did nearly 150 years ago.

Over the course of those 146 years, gardening has evolved alongside society, with technological breakthroughs and trends in fashion continually reshaping the leisure activity. Despite this, the basic principle remains the same – people want to enjoy the environment in which they live; to see flowers bloom and leaves fall, and to hear birds sing and bees buzz. Today, gardening is a major industry – millions spend their weekends cultivating land, whether it be in a traditional private garden, atop a roof or on an allotment. Scott's influence continues to be felt to this day, and he remains one of the great leaders of garden design, standing alongside such luminaries as Andrew Jackson Downing and Grace Tabor.

# Introduction

The landscape, forever consoling and kind,
Pours her wine and her oil on the smarts of the mind.

*Lowell*

The aim of this work is to aid persons of moderate income, who know little of the arts of decorative gardening, to beautify their homes; to suggest and illustrate the simple means with which beautiful home-surroundings may be realized on small grounds, and with little cost, and thus to assist in giving an intelligent direction to the desires, and a satisfactory result for the labors of those who are engaged in embellishing homes, as well as those whose imaginations are warm with the hopes of homes that are yet to be.

It is more than twenty years since the poetical life and pen of A. J. Downing warmed the hearts of his countrymen to a new love and zest for rural culture. In the department of suburban architecture, the work so charmingly begun by him has been carried forward by Vaux and a host of others, whose works are constantly appearing. But in the specialty of decorative gardening, adapted to the small grounds of most suburban homes, there is much need of other works than have yet appeared. Downing had begun in the books entitled *Cottage Residences and Cottage Grounds* and *Country Houses*, to cover this subject in his peculiarly graceful as well as sensible style; but death robbed us of his pleasant genius in the prime of its usefulness. Since his time, many useful works have appeared on one or another branch of gardening art, but not one has been devoted entirely to the arts of suburban-home embellishment. The subject is usually approached, as it were, sideways – as a branch of other subjects, architectural, agricultural, and horticultural – and not as an art distinct from great landscape-gardening, and not embraced in floriculture, vegetable gardening, and pomology. The busy pen of the accomplished Donald G. Mitchell has treated of farm embellishment with

an admirable blending of farmer-experience and a poet's culture, but he has given the farm, more than the citizen's suburban lot, the benefit of his suggestions. Copeland's *Country Life* is a hand-book grown almost into an encyclopaedia of garden and farm work, full of matter giving it great value to the farmer and horticulturist. Other works, too numerous to mention, of special horticultural studies, as well as valuable horticultural annuals, have served to whet a taste for the arts of planning as well as planting. Some of them cover interesting specialties of decorative gardening. It is a hopeful sign of intelligence when any art or science divides into many branches, and each becomes a subject for special treatises. But books which treat each of some one department of decorative gardening, should follow, rather than precede, a knowledge of the arts of arrangement, by which, alone, all are combined to produce harmonious home-pictures, and for precisely the same reason that it is always best to plan one's house before selecting the furniture

– which, however good in itself, may not otherwise suit the place where it must be used.

The term landscape-gardening is misapplied when used in connection with the improvement of a few roods of suburban ground, and we disavow any claim, for this work, to treat of landscape-gardening on that large scale, or in the thorough and exhaustive manner in which it is handled by the masters of the art in England, and by Downing for this country. Compared with the English we are yet novices in the fine arts of gardening, and the exquisite rural taste even among the poorer classes of England, which inspired glowing eulogiums from the pen of Washington Irving thirty years ago, is still as far in advance of our own as at that time. British literature abounds in admirable works on all branches of gardening arts. Loudon's energy and exhaustive industry seem to have collected, digested, and illustrated, almost everything worth knowing in the arts of gardening. But his works are too voluminous, too thorough, too English, to meet the needs of American suburban life. Kemp, in a complete little volume entitled *How to lay out a Garden*, has condensed all that is most essential on the subject for England. But the arrangements of American suburban homes of the average character differ so widely from those of the English, and our climate also varies so essentially from theirs, that plans of houses and grounds suitable there are not often adapted to our wants. There is an extent and thoroughness in their out-buildings, and arrangements for man-servants and maid-servants and domestic animals, which the great cost of labor in this country forces us to condense or dispense with. Public and private examples of landscape-gardening on a grand scale begin to familiarize Americans with the art. The best cemeteries of our great cities are renowned even in Europe for their tasteful keeping. But more than all other causes, that wonderful creation, the New York Central Park, has illustrated the power of public money in the hands of men of tasteful genius to reproduce, as if by magic, the gardening glories of older lands. But public parks, however desirable and charming, are not substitutes for beautiful homes, and with observation of such public works, and of examples of tasteful but very costly private grounds in many parts of the country, there comes an increasing need of practical works to epitomize and Americanize the principles of decorative gardening, to illustrate their application to small grounds, and to effect in miniature, and around ordinary homes, some of their loveliest results. Some of the most prized pictures of great landscape painters are scenes that lie close to the eye; which derive little of their beauty from breadth of view, or variety of objects; and yet they may be marvels of lovely or picturesque beauty. The halfacre of a suburban cottage (if the house itself is what it should be) may be as perfect a work of art, and as well worth transferring to canvas as any part of the great Chatsworth of the Duke of Devonshire.

Of the millions of America's busy men and women, a large proportion desire around their homes the greatest amount of beauty which their means will enable them to maintain, and the minimum of expense and care that will secure it. It is for these that this work has been prepared. It is not designed for the very wealthy, nor for the poor, but principally for that great class of townspeople whose daily business away from their homes is a necessity, and who appreciate more than the very rich, or the poor, all the heart's cheer, the refined pleasures, and the beauty that should attach to a suburban home.

In planning home-grounds, a familiarity with the materials from which the planter must choose is requisite to success in producing a desired effect. This work, therefore, embraces descriptions and many illustrations of trees and shrubs, and is intended to be full in those matters which are of most interest to unscientific lovers of nature and rural art, in their efforts to create home beauty; such as the expression of trees and shrubs, as produced by their sizes, forms, colors, leaves, flowers, and general structure, quite independent of their characteristics as noted by the botanist. The botanical information incidentally conveyed in the names and descriptions of trees, shrubs, and flowers, has been drawn, it is hoped, from the best authorities, but, for any errors that may be found in them, the author asks the kind indulgence of the more scientific reader.

# 1
## Art and Nature

All nature is but art unknown to thee;
All chance, direction which thou canst not see.

*Pope*

The prevalent idea that the best decorative gardening is simply an imitation of pleasing natural scenery, is partially incorrect. If an imitation of Nature were the only aim, if she were simply to be let alone, or repeated, then a prairie, a wild forest, an oak-opening, a jungle, or a rocky scene, would only need to be inclosed to seem a perfect example of landscape gardening. All these forms of Nature have their peculiar beauties, and yet these very beauties, when brought into connection with our dwellings, are as incongruous as the picturesqueness of savage human life in streets or parlors. All civilization is marked by the touch of the arts which have subjugated the ruder elements in human and vegetable nature to mould and re-arrange them. We are not made to be content on nature's lower levels; for that spark of divinity within us – Imagination – suggests to us progress and improvement, and these are no less natural than existence. The arts which make life beautiful are those that graft upon the wildings of nature the refinements and harmonies which the Deity through the imagination is ever suggesting to us.

Decorative gardening had reached a high degree of perfection among ancient nations before the art now known as Landscape Gardening had its origin, or rather the beautiful development which it has reached in England within the last three centuries. The art which reproduces the wildness of rude nature, and that which softens the rudeness and creates polished beauty in its place, are equally arts of gardening. So too are the further arts by which plants and trees are moulded into unusual forms, and blended by studied symmetries with the purely artificial works of architecture. All are legitimate, and no one style may say to another, 'Thou art false because thou hast no

prototype in nature,' since our dwellings and all the conveniences of civilized life would be equally false if judged by that standard. However diverse the modes of decorative gardening in different countries, all represent some ideal form of beauty, and illustrate that diversity of human tastes which is not less admirable than the diversity of productions in vegetable nature.

That may be considered good gardening around suburban homes which renders the dwelling the central interest of a picture, which suggests an intention to produce a certain type of embellishment, and which harmoniously realizes the type intended, whether it be a tree-flecked meadow, a forest glade, a copse belted lawn, a formal old French garden, a brilliant parterre, or a general blending of artfully grown sylvan and floral vegetation with architectural forms.

Not to reproduce the rudeness of Nature, therefore, but to adapt her to our civilized necessities, to idealize and improve, to condense and appropriate her beauties, to eliminate the dross from her vegetable jewels, and give them worthy setting – these are the aims of Decorative Gardening.

# 2

# Decorative Planting: What Constitutes It?

He who sees my park, sees into my heart!

*Prince Puckler to Bettina Von Arnim*

The objects sought in Decorative Planting are various. The simple pleasure of working among and developing beautiful natural productions is one; the desire to make one's place elegant and attractive to others' eyes, and therefore a source of pride to the possessor, is also one of the strongest objects with many. To have a notably large variety of flowers, shrubs, or trees, is a very common form of planting enthusiasm, and the passion for some special and complete display of certain species of flowers (florists' hobbies) is another. Finally, and highest of all, is the appreciation of, and desire to create with verdant Nature, charming effects of sunlight and shadow, or lovely examples, in miniature, of what we call landscapes. Decorative Planting should have for its highest aim the beautifying of Home. In combination with domestic architecture, it should make every man's home a beautiful picture. As skillful stonecutting, or bricklaying, or working in wood, does not make of the artisan an architect, or his work a fine art, so the love of trees, shrubs, and flowers, and their skillful cultivation, is but handling the tools of the landscape gardener – it is not gardening, in its most beautiful meaning. The garden of the slothful, overgrown with weeds and brambles, could not have been much more ugly to look upon than many flower-gardens, in which the whole area is a wilderness of annuals and perennials, of all sorts and sizes and conditions of life, full of beautiful bloom if we examine them in detail, and yet, as a whole, repulsive to refined eyes as a cob-webbed old furniture museum, crammed with heterogeneous beauties and utilities. Such gardens cannot be called decorative planting. They are merely bouquet nurseries of the lowest class, or botanical museums. Neither the loveliness of flowers, nor the beauties of trees and shrubs, alone, will make a truly beautiful place,

unless arranged so that the special beauty of trees, plants, and flowers is subordinated to the general effect. An attempt to make good pictures by haphazard applications to the canvas of the finest paint colors, is not much more sure to result in failure than the usual mode of filling yards with choice trees, shrubs, and flowers. It is as easy to spoil a place with too many flowers as to mar good food with a superfluity of condiments. The same may be said of a medley plantation of the finest trees or shrubs. Numbers will not make great beauty or variety; on the contrary, they will often destroy both. That is the best art which produces the most pleasing pictures with the fewest materials. Milton, in two short lines, thus paints a home:

> Hard by a cottage chimney smokes,
> From between two aged oaks.

Here is a picture; two trees, a cottage, and green sward – these are all the materials. Unfortunately the 'two aged oaks', or their equivalents, are not at hand for all our homes.

Has the reader ever noticed some remarkably pleasant old home, where little care seemed taken to make it so, and yet with an air of comfort, and even elegance, that others, with wealth lavished upon them, and a professional gardener in constant employ, with flowers, and shrubs, and trees in profusion, yet all failing to convey the same impression of a pleasant home? Be assured that the former (though by accident it may be) is the better model of the two. A well-cut lawn, a few fine trees, a shady background with comfortable-looking out-buildings, are the essentials, and walks, shrubs, and flowers, only the embellishments and finishing touches of the picture. Only the finishing touches – but what a charm of added expression and beauty there may be in those perfecting strokes! How a verdant gateway arch frames the common walk into a picture view; how a long opening of lawn gives playroom for the sunlight to smile and hide among the shadows of bordering shrubs and trees; how an opening here, in the shrubs, reveals a pretty neighborhood vista; how a flower-bed there, brightens the lawn like a smile on the face of beauty; how a swing suspended from the strong, outstretched arm of a noble tree attracts the children, whose ever-changing groups engage the eye and interest the heart; how a delicate foliaged tree, planted on yonder margin, glows with the light of the afternoon sun, or with airy undulations trembles against the twilight sky, till it seems neither of the earth or the sky, but a spirit of life wavering between earth and heaven!

Let us, then, define Decorative Planting to be the art of picture making and picture framing, by means of the varied forms of vegetable growth.

# 3

# What Kind of Home Grounds Will Best Suit Business Men, and Their Cost

Nature is immovable and yet mobile; that is her eternal charm. Her unwearied activity, her ever-shifting phantasmagoria, do not weary, do not disturb; this harmonious motion bears in itself a profound repose.

*Madame Michelet*

It is always a difficult matter to keep the happy medium between extravagance and parsimony. This uncertainty will be felt by every business man of moderate means who begins the expenditures about a suburban home. All men, who are not either devoid of fine tastes, or miserly, desire to have as much beauty around them as they can pay for and maintain, but few persons are familiar with the means which will gratify this desire with least strain on the purse. Two men of equal means, with similar houses and grounds to begin with, will often show most diverse results for their expenditures; one place soon becoming home-like, quiet, and elegant in its expression, and the other fussy, cluttered, and unsatisfactory. The latter has probably cost the most money; it may have the most trees, and the rarest flowers; more rustic work, and vases, and statuary, but the true effect of all is wanting. The difference between the two places is like that between the sketch of a trained artist, who has his work distinctly in his mind before attempting to represent it, and then sketches it in simple, clear outlines, and the untutored beginner, whose abundance of ideas are of so little service to him that he draws, and re-draws, and rubs out again, till it can hardly be told whether it is a horse or a cloud that is attempted. If the reader has any doubt of his own ability to arrange his home grounds with the least waste expenditure, he should ask some friend, whose good taste has been proved by trial, to commend him to some sensible and experienced designer of home-grounds.

It may be set down as a fair approximation of the expense of good ground improvements, that they will require about one-tenth of the whole cost of the buildings. Premising that the erection of the dwelling generally precedes the

principal expenses of beautifying the grounds, this amount will be required during the two years following the completion of the house. If the land must be cleared of rocks, or much graded, or should require an unusually thorough system of tile-drainage, that proportion might be insufficient, but if the ground to be improved is in good shape, well drained, rich, and furnished with trees, a very much smaller proportion might be enough, and almost the only needful expense, would be that which would procure the advice and direction of some judicious landscape gardener. As a good lawyer often best earns his retainer by advising against litigation, so a master of gardenesque art may often save a proprietor enough, to pay for all that will be needed, by advising him what not to attempt.

But it is on bare, new grounds, that there will be most room for doubt of what to attempt. The man who must leave his home after an early breakfast to attend to his office or store business, and who only returns to dinner and tea, must not be beguiled into paying for the floral and arboricultural rarities that professional florists and tree-growers grow enthusiastic over, unless the home members of his family are appreciative amateurs in such things. Tired with town labor, his home must be to him a haven of repose. Gardeners' bills are no pleasanter to pay than butchers' and tailors' bills, and the satisfaction of paying either depends on the amount of pleasure received, or hoped to be received, from the things paid for. A velvety lawn, flecked with sunlight and the shadows of common trees, is very inexpensive, and may be a very elegant refreshment for the business-wearied eye, and the manner in which it is kept will affect the mind in the same way as the ill or well-ordered house-keeping of the wife. But the beauties and varied peculiarities of a fine collection of trees, shrubs, and flowers require a higher culture of the taste, and more leisure for observation, than most business men have. All women are lovers of flowers, but few American ladies are yet educated in that higher garden culture – the art of making pictures with trees, lawn, and flowers. Without this culture, or a strong desire for it, it is best that the more elegant forms of gardening art should be dispensed with, and only simple effects attempted. Now a freshly mown meadow is always beautiful, and a well-kept lawn alone produces that kind of beauty. But the meadow or lawn, without a tree, is tame and monotonous. Large trees are necessary to enliven their beauty. A well-built house, with broad porch or veranda, may enable one to get along very comfortably without the shade of trees to protect its inmates from the excessive heat of the sun, but the play of light and shade in the foliage of trees, and upon the lawn, is as needful food for the eye as the sunny gayety of children is to the heart. These two things, then, are the most essential to the business man's home – a fine lawn and large trees. The former may be produced in a year; the latter must be bought ready grown on the ground. No amount of money spent at nurseries will give, in twenty years, the dignified beauty of effect that a few fine old trees will realize as soon as your house and lawn are completed.

But, unfortunately, the mass of men are obliged by business necessities, or other circumstances which are imperative, to build on sites not blessed with large trees. To enable them to make the most of such places, it is hoped that the succeeding chapters will point the way.

There is one hobby connected with removing from a city house to one 'with some ground around it', which has been happily caricatured by some modern authors. We refer to the enthusiastic longing for fresh vegetables 'of our own raising'. A wealthy citizen, who had been severely seized with some of these horticultural fevers, invited friends to dine with him at his country-seat. The friends complimented his delicious green corn. 'It is capital, I'm glad you appreciate it,' said he; 'it is from my own grounds, and by a calculation made a few days since I find that the season's crop will cost me only ten dollars an ear'. Certainly this is an extreme case, but among the expensive luxuries for a business man's home a large kitchen garden is one of the most costly. Grass, and trees, and flowers, give daily returns in food for our eyes, seven months of the year, and cost less; yet many good housewives and masters spend more in growing radishes, lettuce, peas, beans, and even such cheap things as cabbages and potatoes, than it would cost to buy, just as good articles, and maintain, besides, a lawn full of beauties. Vegetable gardening is a good and profitable business on a large scale, but on a small scale is not often made so, except by the good Dutch women, who can plant, hoe, and market their own productions, and live on the remainders. The kitchen garden does more to support the family of the gardener than the family of the proprietor, and it is respectfully suggested that the satisfaction of having one's table provided with 'our Patrick's' peas and beans is not a high order of family pride. The professional gardener, who does the same business on a much larger scale, and vends his vegetables at our doors, is likely to grow them cheaper and just as good as we can grow them.

But in the matter of fruit, it is different. There are some fruits that can only be had in perfection ripened on the spot where they are to be eaten. All market fruit-growers are obliged to pick fruit before it is ripe, in order to have it bear transportation and keep well. We cannot, therefore, get luscious ripe fruit except by growing it, and we advise business men of small means and small grounds to patronize the market for vegetables, but to grow their own strawberries, raspberries, peaches, and pears; at least so far as they may without making the beauty of their grounds subordinate to the pleasures of the palate. The eye is a constant feeder, that never sates with beauty, and is ever refining the mind by the influence of its hunger, but even luscious fruits give but a momentary pleasure, and that not seldom unalloyed by excess and cloying satiety. Nature is more lavish of her luxuries for the eye than of those for the stomach, and, in an economic point of view, it will be wise to take advantage of her generosity. To this end, it may be profitably borne in mind that pleasing distant or near views of country or city, of trees or houses, of sea or stream, which cost nothing to preserve or keep in order, are the best picture investments that can be made, and to make charming verdant frames for these pictures as well as little 'cabinet pieces' of your own for your neighbors to look in upon, will call into play the best skill in gardenesque designing.

To make the most of common and inexpensive materials requires the same culture of the eye and the mind, as the manipulation of the rarest. To produce an effective picture with a single color requires the same talent that would produce only more brilliant effects with all the colors of the palette. The most needed advice to novices in suburban home-making is this: if you can afford to spend but little on your grounds, study with the greater care what beauty outside of them can be made a part of the outlook from them; do not introduce anything which will convey the impression that you desire to have anything look more expensive than it really is; dispense with walks and drives except where they are required for the daily comfort of your family; eschew rustic ornaments, unless of the most substantial and un-showy character, and in shadowy locations; avoid spotting your lawn with garish carpentry, or plaster or marble images of any kind, or those Lilliputian caricatures on Nature and Art called rock-work, and, finally, by the exquisite keeping of what you have, endeavor to create an atmosphere of refinement about your place, such as a thorough lady housekeeper will always throw around her house, however small or plain it may be.

As the wife and family are the home-bodies of a residence, the business man of a city who chooses a home out of it should feel that he is not depriving them of the pleasures incident to good neighborly society. During his daily absence, while his mind is kept in constant activity by hourly contact with his acquaintances, the family at home also need some of the enlivening influences of easy intercourse with their equals, and should not be expected to find entire contentment in their household duties, with no other society day after day than that of their own little circle, and the voiceless beauty of grass, flowers, and trees. A throng of arguments for and against what is vaguely called country life suggest themselves in this connection, some of which are treated of in the following chapter, in which suburban and country homes are contrasted. The former, as we would have them, involve no banishment from all that is good in city life, but are rather the elegant culmination of refined tastes, which cannot be gratified in the city; the proper field for the growth of that higher culture which finds in art, nature, and congenial society combined, a greater variety of pleasures than can be found in the most luxurious homes between the high walls of city houses; a step in advance of the Indian-like craving for beads, jewelry, and feathers, which distinguishes the city civilization of the present day. Choosing a home out of the city simply because it can be secured more cheaply than in it, is not the kind of plea for a suburban life which we would present, yet we urge that at a given cost of home and living it yields a far greater variety of healthful pleasures, and a fuller, freer, happier life for man, woman, and child, than a home in the city.

# 4
# Suburban Neighborhoods Compared with Country Places

'Twas town, yet country too; you felt the warmth
Of clustering houses in the wintry time.

*George Eliot*

Landscape gardening, on a grand scale, in this country, is only to be accomplished in public parks and cemeteries. Parks of considerable extent, as private property, are impracticable, by reason of the transient nature of family wealth, in a republic where both the laws and the industrial customs favor rapid divisions and new distributions. Attempts to make and keep great private parks are generally conspicuous failures. Some of the old family parks on the Hudson River, and a few in other parts of the country, may be thought of as exceptions, but they are exceptions which rather prove the rule; for most of them are on portions of manorial grants, held under almost feudal titles, which have remained in the same families through several generations, simply because they are held under laws which present a jarring contrast with the general laws of property which now govern in most of the States. Great fortunes cannot be lavished perennially for half a century to keep them up, where fortunes are so seldom made or kept in families of high cultivation – the only ones which are likely to be led by their tastes, or qualified by their education, to direct such improvements successfully. It is from this lack of cultivation, and from sheer ignorance of the fine arts, the great expenditures and the generations of patient waiting for results, which are all necessary to produce such works, that so many wealthy men stumble and break their fortunes in ridiculous attempts to improvise parks. It would be well for our progress in Landscape Gardening that this word park, as applied to private grounds, should be struck out of use, and that those parts of our grounds which are devoted to what feeds the eye and the heart, rather than the stomach, should be called simply Home-grounds,

and that the ambition of private wealth in our republic should be to make gems of home beauty on a small scale, rather than fine examples of failures on a large scale. A township of land, with streets, and roads, and streams, dotted with a thousand suburban homes peeping from their groves; with school-house towers and gleaming spires among them; with farm fields, pastures, woodlands, and bounding hills or boundless prairies stretched around; these, altogether, form our suburban parks, which all of us may ride in, and walk in, and enjoy, and the most lavish expenditures of private wealth on private grounds can never equal their extent, beauty, or variety.

A serious inconvenience of extensive private grounds, or parks, is the isolation and loneliness of the habitual inmates of the house – the ladies. Few, even of those who have a native love for rural life, can long live contented without pleasant near neighbors. A large family may feel this less than a small one. Those who have the means, the health, and the disposition to entertain much company at home, will escape the feeling of loneliness. But much company brings much care. It is paying a high price for company when one must keep a free hotel to secure it. To do without it, however, soon suggests to the ladies that fewer acres, and more friends near by, would be a desirable change, and not knowing the facility with which the happy medium may be reached, they are apt to jump at the conclusion that, of the two privations –

life in the country without neighborly society, or life in the city without the charms of Nature – the latter is the least. Thousands of beautiful homes are every year offered for sale, on which the owners have often crippled their fortunes by covering too much ground with their expenditures. Instead of retiring to the country for rest and strengthening recreation, they have added a full assortment of losing and vexatious employments in the country to their already wearisome but profitable business in the city. It is the ambition to have 'parks' (young Chatsworths!) – to be model farmers and famous gardeners; to be pomologists, with all the fruits of the nursery catalogues on their lists: in short, to add to the burden of their town business the cares of half a dozen other laborious professions, that finally sickens so many of their country places after a few years' experience with them. There is another large class of prosperous city men who have spent their early years on farms, and who cherish a deep love of the country through all their decennial rounds of city life; who have no fanciful ambitions for parks; whose dreams are of hospitable halls, broad pastures, and sweet meadows, fine cattle and horses. It is a less vexatious mesh of ambitions than the preceding, but one that requires a very thoughtful examination of the resources of the purse and the calls that will be made upon it, before purchasing the model farm that is to be. And we beg leave to intrude a little into the privacy of the family circle, to inquire how long will the wife and daughters be contented with isolation on ever so beautiful a farm; how long before the boys will leave home for business or homes of their own, and how long, if these are dissatisfied, or absent, will the 'fine mansion' and broad fields, in a lonely locality, bring peace and comfort to the owner? That there are men and families that truly fill, enjoy, and honor such life, it is good to know, but they are cluster-jewels of great rarity.

Our panacea for the town-sick business man who longs for a rural home, whether from ennui of the monotonousness of business life, or from the higher nature-loving soul that is in him, is to take country life as a famishing man should take food – in very small quantities. From a half acre to four or five acres will afford ground enough to give all the finer pleasures of rural life. The suburbs of most cities, of from five to fifty thousand people, will have sites at reasonable prices, within easy walking distance of business, where men of congenial tastes and friendly families may make purchases, and cluster their improvements so as to obtain all the benefits of rural pleasures, and many of the beauties of park scenery, without relinquishing the luxuries of town life.

In the neighborhood of large cities, horse and steam railways, and steamers, transport in a few minutes their thousands of tired workers to cheerful villages, or neighborly suburban homes, environed with green fields and loveable trees. To be thus transported from barren city streets to the verdant country is a privilege for which we cannot be too grateful. But, if we are to choose a suburban residence for the whole year (not migrating to a city home or hotel with the first chills of November), it is a serious matter to know whether there is a good hard road and sidewalk to the home. City life, with its flagging, and gas lights, and pavements, comes back to the imagination *couleur de rose* when your horses or your boots are toiling through deep mud on country roads. This is bad enough by daylight; at night you might feel like stopping to bestow a benediction on a post that would sparkle gas-light across your path. Now the moral which we would suggest by thus presenting the most disagreeable feature of suburban life, is this: to go no farther into the country than where good roads have already been made, and where good sidewalks have either been made, or, from the character or growth of the neighborhood, are pretty sure to be made within a short time. Some persons must, of course, be pioneers. Those who locate in a new suburban neighborhood expect to buy their lots enough cheaper than the later comers to compensate for the inconveniences of a sparse neighborhood. But, in playing pioneer, one must be pretty sure that followers are on the track, for 'hope deferred maketh the heart sick.' One of the greatest drawbacks to the improvement of suburban neighborhoods is the fact that many persons own long fronts on the roads who are not able to make the thorough improvement of roads and sidewalks in front of their grounds which the new-comers, located beyond them, require. This should have been foreseen by the new-comers. Having chosen their homes with the facts before them, they must not complain if some poor farmer or 'land-poor' proprietor is unable to improve for their benefit, and unwilling to sell at their desire. In choosing a suburban home, the character of the ownerships between a proposed location and the main street or railroad station should be known, and influence to some extent one's choice.

The advantages cannot be too strongly urged, of forming companies of congenial gentlemen to buy land enough for all. Select a promising locality, divide the property into deep narrow strips, if the form of the ground will admit of it, having frontages of one, two, or three hundred feet each, according to the means respectively of the partitioners, and as much depth as possible. A depth four times as great as the frontage is the best form of suburban lots for improvement in connection with adjoining neighbors. Lots of these proportions insure near neighbors, and good walks and roads in their fronts, at least. Acting together, the little community can create a local pressure for good improvements that will have its effect on the entire street and neighborhood. In subsequent chapters we propose to show how such neighbors may improve their grounds in connection with each other, so as to realize some pleasing effects of artistic scenery at a comparatively small expense to each owner. Even the luxury of gas in our suburban houses and roads is quite practicable in the mode of dividing and improving property which we have recommended, and with good roads, sidewalks, and gas, added to the delightfulness of rural homes, no healthy-hearted family would wish to have their permanent home in a dark and narrow city house. Our cities would gradually become great working-hives, but not homes, for a majority of their people. It may be said that such homes as we speak of, in the suburbs of great cities, would be simply village residences. It is true, but they would be villages of a broader, more generous, and cosmopolitan character than old-fashioned villages. Post-offices, shops and groceries, butchers, bakers, blacksmiths, shoemakers, and laborers of all kinds must be near by, and a part of our community, or there would be no living at all, but where a large, and probably the most wealthy, part of the inhabitants go daily to the city centre to transact business, the amount of traffic carried on in the village or suburban centre will not be large enough to seriously injure the general rural character of the vicinity. The stir of thrifty industry is in itself refreshing, and the attractions of lecture, concert, and dancing halls, and ice-cream resorts, cannot be dispensed with.

We believe this kind of half-country, half-town life, is the happy medium, and the realizable ideal for the great majority of well-to-do Americans. The few families who have a unanimity of warm and long-continued love for more isolated and more picturesquely rural, or more practically rural homes, are exceptions. The mass of men and women are more gregarious. Very poetical or reflective minds, or persons absorbed in mutual domestic loves, find some of their deepest pleasure in seclusion with Nature. But the zest even of their calm pleasures in the country is greatly heightened by frequent contrasts with city excitements, and by the company of sympathetic minds, who enjoy what they enjoy. A philosophic Frenchman, who lived much alone, was once asked by a lady if he did not find solitude very sweet. He replied, 'Indeed, madam, when you have some pleasant friend to whom you can say, "Oh, how sweet is solitude."' A suburban home, therefore, meets the wants of refined and cultivated people more than any other.

# 5
# Building Sites and Ground Surfaces

Having, in the chapter on 'Suburban Neighborhoods Compared With Country Places', suggested the most desirable proportions for suburban lots, we propose in this to consider building sites with reference to their tree-furniture, their natural surfaces, and the better ways of improving them. But it may not be superfluous to repeat, that where the form of the lot can be determined by the purchaser, a proportion where the depth is from three to four times as great as the frontage is usually the most desirable.

A varied surface is, of course, a great desideratum; yet, for quite small grounds, abruptness or picturesqueness is seldom compatible with the high keeping that is essential near the dwelling. Occasionally, in rocky situations, or on the border of a running brook, such sites may be charmingly harmonized with the practical requirements of the dwelling and outbuildings; but they are exceptional. The great mass of house sites are smooth swells or levels.

Trees already grown are invaluable. To have them, or not to have them, is, to speak in business phrase, to begin with capital or without it. As capital draws to itself capital, so trees are magnets of home beauty, towards which domestic architecture, the gardener's arts, and varied family enjoyments are most naturally attracted. But there are trees whose age and habits of growth are not such as to give them high value. Forest trees, which have attained a lofty height, are not only dangerous in proximity to a dwelling, but are also likely to maintain a sort of living death when their contemporary trees are cut from around them – putting forth their leaves annually, it is true, but dying limb by limb at their summits, and scattering on the ground their dead twigs and branches. No grandeur of lofty trunk can mitigate the danger from spring winds or summer tempests that may bring its crushing weight upon the house and its inmates. But trees which have grown broadly in open ground, and lashed their arms and toughened their fibres in the gales of half a century, may be relied on to brood protectingly over a home,

and few among these are more loveable in blossom, shade, and fruit, than fine old apple-trees. There is another class of trees which have little beauty as environments of a dwelling. We refer to 'second-growth' trees, which have grown thickly together, and which, though valuable for their shade, form rather a nursery of rough poles, with a valuable mass of foliage over them, than an ornamental grove. Rough woods are quite too common in this country, and too rude in all their looks and ways, to be welcomed to our cultivated homes as we welcome the civilized and polished members of the tree family. But such dense groves of second-growth trees usually have many specimens among them well worth preserving, and which, if twenty feet high or upwards, will better repay good nursing and care than any young trees that can be planted to fill their places. The proprietor of such a building site is much more likely to err, however, in leaving too many than too few, and the thorough cutting out of the grove, which a landscape artist will insist on, may seem like wholesale slaughter to the owner.

Trees which have grown up singly, or in groups of a few only, exposed on all sides to the full glow of the sun and air, are worth more than a whole catalogue of nursery stuff for immediate and permanent adornment. It is surprising how little additional price most purchasers are willing to pay for lots that are enriched by such native trees, while they willingly expend ten times their cost in the little beginnings of trees procured from nurseries. One fine-spreading tree, of almost any native variety, is of inestimable value in home adornment. Few exotic trees are so beautiful as our finest natives, and nothing that we can plant will so well repay the most lavish enrichment of the soil to promote its growth as one of these trees 'to the manor born'. In locating a house with reference to fine trees already growing, it is much better to have them behind, or overhanging the sides, than to have them in front; the object being to make them a setting, or frame-work, for the house; to have the house embowered in them, rather than shut out behind them.

Let us now consider some different forms of ground surfaces.

Ground which rises from the street, so that where it meets the house it is about on a level with the top of an ordinary fence at the street line, is a good form of surface. This rise should not, however, be on a plane from the street boundary to the dwelling. The lawn, and whatever is planted, will show to much better advantage if the rise takes the form of the arc of a circle, as shown in Fig. 1, section A, on which the front steps of the house are indicated at *a*, the front fence at *b*, and the street sidewalk at *c*.

Or, for increasing the apparent extent of the ground, the curve rising more rapidly near the fence may be an improvement, as shown in section B, of the same cut.

Sections C and D of Fig. 2 illustrate three less common, and perhaps more elegant forms for ground surfaces next to the street. Back of the fence, at

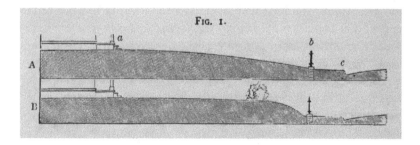

Fig. 1.

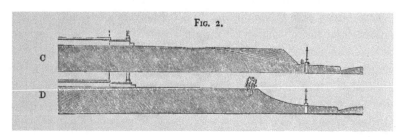

Fig. 2.

*a*, is a strip of ground, level with the sidewalk, not more than a foot wide, which should be kept free from grass by the hoe. The grass at the bottom of the terrace slope can then be trimmed to a line parallel with the fence. The effect is very pretty, and as it would be difficult to keep grass neatly cut at the bottom of such a slope so near the fence, this plan saves labor. The lower line on section C of the same cut shows a form that may be substituted for the terrace slope, and at D is another form more gardenesque than either.

It is surprising how much larger grounds look which show such surfaces than those which are on a plane, level with the street. A quick rise from the street has the disadvantage, when the distance from the house to the gate is short, of requiring steps to gain the rise near the gate. Though no serious objection in summer, they are often dangerous in winter, especially to old people. In towns, a choice between such surfaces is frequently necessitated by the grading of a street a few feet below the level of adjacent lots. These should never be walled next to the street the full height of the excavation. The cuts just described illustrate appropriate modes of shaping the surface of the ground next to the street where the grade has not cut more than four feet below the general level at the street line. Grass slopes, behind light fences, are not only much cheaper than stone walls, but add more to the beauty of the grounds.

Fig. 3 shows a more elegant treatment of the same sort of surface for a deeper and larger lot. Here a space, at least wide enough to swing a scythe easily, is left between the fence and the first grass terrace. It must not be less than six feet wide, nor more than one-sixth of the distance from the fence to the house steps. Another grass terrace around the house is shown at C. Two terraces of this kind are as many as any ordinary place will bear. To break a small lawn into a multiplicity of terraces is a sure means of spoiling it. This form of surface is well adapted to be carried around three sides of a

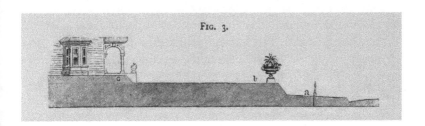

Fig. 3.

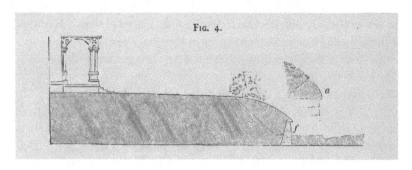

FIG. 4.

block embracing several residences, the fronts of which should be from 80 to 150 feet from the street, and the lower grass plat at a from 10 to 20 feet wide.

Fig. 4 shows two forms of treating a bank made by a deeper street-cut – say from six to eight feet. Owners frequently wall such street lines the whole height of the cut. No more foolish expenditure can be incurred, both in an economic and artistic point of view. It is difficult to make such a wall that will resist the enormous pressure of the earth when frosts disintegrate, and heavy rains soften it. If constructed so that it can resist for years this interior pressure, it must be by the expenditure of a sum of money that might create ten times the beauty if expended in other ways. A solid wall from two to three feet above the sidewalk level is as high as we would advise on street lines from which it is intended that grounds shall show their beauty. On Fig. 2, sections C and D, where the street cut is three or four feet, the ground-slope down to the sidewalk, as shown by the formal terraces, and the lower line, on section C, is more pleasing than any wall.

But for the deep cut illustrated by Fig. 4, it is an open question whether, as some kind of fence will be necessary, a partial wall, as at *f*, may not effect that object, and produce the best form of ground surface. It will be seen by the enlarged section a that the coping of the low wall (say 3 feet) is to be cut so as to make its outer surface a continuation of the sloping bank above. This will make a pretty effect, and no other fence will be required, but the wall must be of great strength. The lower line, being merely a sloping bank of grass, would require another kind of fence, and to be treated as at *a*, Fig. 2.

Fig. 5 is intended to illustrate the prettier effect that may be produced by making use of small inequalities of the ground, instead of grading to a uniform slope. It does not show just the surface it was intended to show, but will suggest to the observer the greater possibility of pleasing effects than on a uniform plane.

FIG. 5.

Where a natural elevation for a house occurs a few rods from the street, with an intervening level between it and the street, it is usually better to preserve its form, than to grade down and fill up to bring the whole lot to what some persons are pleased to term 'a correct grade'. Fig. 6 (overleaf) illustrates what is meant; the natural surface is a graceful form, and the most capable of decorative effect.

Though rising ground is usually more valued than that which is below the level of the road, it is not always more desirable. If a dwelling-site has its main walks to the doors on a level with the street, and a part of the ground lower, but relatively higher than other grounds farther back, the location may be capable of more beautiful effects than a plain swell. A bird's-eye view over small grounds is so rare that any approach to it is a pleasing novelty, and the opportunities to obtain such effects should be made the most of. The most lovely views the world can boast are narrow valleys seen from adjacent hills. Figs. 7 and 8 (overleaf) are sections showing pleasing forms of surfaces below the level of the street, but overlooking lower ground farther back.

A building site may even be much lower than its street entrance, as in Figs 7 and 8 (overleaf) where the level of the road is shown at *a*, on the condition already named, that the ground in its rear be still lower relatively. A cottage in the spirit of the Swiss style, in such a locality, would be quite appropriate, or, indeed, any style in which the roof lines are both prominent and graceful. It is essential, however, that the house site should not have the appearance of being in a basin, much less be so in fact; for the latter would be a miserable inconvenience in wet weather, and the mere supposition of such a situation would make the site seem undesirable even if the soil and drainage were perfect. Such locations should not be basins with reference to the surrounding land, however dry the soil, as in that case the damp evening and morning air would settle in them. But if the rear ground, as

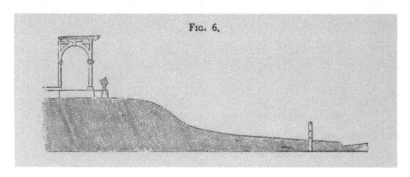

FIG. 6.

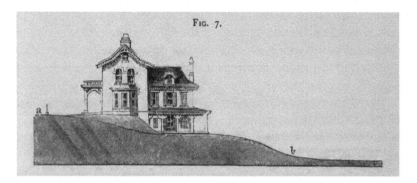

FIG. 7.

shown in Figs. 7 and 8, is the bank of a stream or valley, down to which the damp cool air will flow, then such sites may really be freer from morning and evening damps than much higher ground which is not high relatively to other ground near by.

A form of ground surface is especially desirable, for small lots, on which side-hill houses, blending the character of city basements and village cottages, will look well. Fig. 7 represents one form that might be suggested for such a site, and Fig. 9 a mode of treating the ground of a town lot which is below the street level.

In Fig. 7, nearly all of the lot is supposed to be behind the house, the front being connected by a short, straight walk with the street, and by a diverging curved walk with the basement entrance on the rear plateau, where it is supposed the kitchen and dining-room are located.

Fig. 9 illustrates the treatment of a corner lot, around which the streets have been graded considerably above the lot surface. Instead of filling the lot to the street level, it should be treated as here shown, and there is no

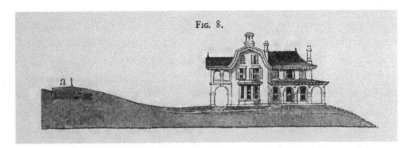

FIG. 8.

FIG. 9.

question that the house is not only better, but the ground improvement is far more pleasing than it could have been made on a level with the street.

After all, the vast majority of building sites are pretty nearly level surfaces, and if we will but learn to develop all the beauty that such are capable of, there will be little cause to envy the possession of more varied surfaces. Most of the designs which follow will be for such places, as they can be planned with more certainty of being useful to a great number of persons. Varied surfaces require such thorough knowledge of each peculiarity of the ground, the drainage required, the difference of levels, the nature of the trees, or rocks, or water, that may be upon it, that their features must not only be seen, but carefully surveyed and platted, in order to be planned to advantage, and even then the skill of an artist-gardener will be essential to their judicious improvement, unless the proprietor is a person of unusual taste in such matters. Many persons involve themselves in useless expenditures on such sites from misdirected zeal for improvement, and ignorance of what not to attempt. Uneven sites also necessitate greater skill in the architect, in adapting the house to the ground. It is by such adaptations, happily executed, that the difference between architects of fine native taste and culture, and mere routine designers, is occasionally illustrated. And the same faculty for the happy adaptation of one mode of planting or another to suit different ground surfaces, to develop the best effects of existing trees, to turn a rock or a brook to the best account, is that which distinguishes the artistic from the commonplace planter.

## DRAINAGE

The absolute necessity of deep sub-soil drainage is known to all intelligent agriculturists and gardeners, but on the supposition that among our readers are town-bred people who have not had occasion to become well-informed in even the rudiments of horticulture, we will state broadly, that deep and thorough sub-soil drainage is the most essential of all preparations for the growth of trees and shrubs; without which neither care nor surface enrichment of the soil will develop their greatest beauty. Many valuable shrubs cannot survive the winters of the middle States in imperfectly drained soils, which in those deeply drained and cultivated are hardy and healthy. In Chapter XVIII, on the philosophy of deep drainage and cultivation, and the treatment of half-hardy trees and shrubs, to which, in this connection, the reader's attention is earnestly invited, the results of drainage are more fully treated. The same causes which make the most thorough drainage of the soil a pre-requisite to success in growing half-hardy trees, act with equal efficiency to give fuller health and greater vigor to those which are hardy. The white oak may continue to grow, in a slow and meagre way, in a soil filled during most of the year with superfluous moisture, but if that same soil were deeply and completely drained the annual growth would be doubled, and the increased abundance and finer color of the foliage becomes as marked as the difference between an uncultivated and a well-tilled field of corn. A lilac bush growing in a soil cold with constant moisture a little below the surface, will develop only surface roots; and having no deep hold in the soil, its main stems will hang to one side or another with a sort of inebriate weakness. But if the soil is dry, deep, and porous, when the plant is set out, the roots strike down deep and strong, the stem will exhibit a sturdy vigor, and the top a well-balanced, low-spreading luxuriance, never seen in cold undrained soils. Even willows, much as they love a moist soil, are much more healthy and symmetrical when planted in well-drained than in wet places; their peculiarity being to flourish best where their roots can find water by seeking it, as an animal goes to a stream and stoops to drink, but not by standing in it perpetually. Trees requiring much moisture, which grow close to streams or wet places, usually have their finest development when standing several feet above the level of the water in ground that is perfectly drained by the proximity of a watercourse, and which at the same time affords the roots an opportunity to drink at will when deep enough.

No thorough gardener, or intelligent planter, is content with surface or open-ditch drainage. It is always insufficient, bungling, and untidy. The most perfect drainage is that formed by a gravelly soil underlaid with coarser gravel to a considerable depth. This is Nature's sub-soil drainage, and it is a well-known fact that soils but meagrely supplied with vegetable and mineral food for plants – 'poor soils' as they are often called, when judged by their appearance rather than their results – will yield better annual returns in crops than the richest undrained lands. Where Nature has provided this sub-soil drainage, other drains may not be necessary, but there are few localities where the sub-soil is so perfect as to render artificial drainage superfluous. Where cellars are found to be always dry, though not provided with drains, the natural drainage may be considered perfect, but it will not do to infer that because one spot is dry, without drains, that another a hundred feet from it, on a different altitude or exposure, is equally favored; though large districts of country are occasionally found where good natural drainage is the rule, and springy sub-soils the exception. The writer has observed some very suggestive phenomena illustrating the relative efficiency of sub-soil and surface drainage. On the same slope of one large field, where the soil is a friable clay, one half the field had been sub-drained with lines of tile thirty feet apart and three feet deep, and the surface left level between them; the other half was plowed into 'lands', or ridges of the same width, sloping down to ditches in the middle which were two feet below the level of the highest ground between them. After heavy rains the surface of the open-ditch part of the lot always glistened with moisture and was sticky for several days, although the descent was so rapid that the water seemed to run off immediately. On the sub-drained part, level as it was, the surface always had a dry spongy appearance, was free from superfluous moisture, and ready to be worked and pleasant to be walked upon in half the time required to dry the sticky surface of the other part of the field. The advantage did not stop here. The porous character given to the soil by the formation of innumerable and invisible channels in a vertical direction down through the earth to the drains below, had such a tendency to lighten the ground that it became much more capable than the harder-surfaced soil to resist drouth, and was just as much moister in very dry weather as it was dryer in wet weather. This is in consequence of the fact, well known to cultivators, that the more porous and deeply worked a soil is, the greater is its power of absorbing moisture from the atmosphere in times of drouth. In sandy soils with clay substratum the effect of drainage is quite as striking in its effect on the growth of plants and trees as in clayey lands, though not so necessary for comfort in walking upon, or working the soil. A wet sandy soil is more apt to be cold and sour than a clayey soil, notwithstanding its more comfortable surface, and the sandy loams known as 'springy', which have veins of quicksand not far below the surface, are those which most need drainage, and which are most difficult to drain well.

The top of a hill, or a steep hill-side, is as likely to need subsoil drainage as the bottom of a valley. It is the nature of the subsoil in each case, that renders drains necessary or superfluous, and not the relative altitude of the location. Land surveyors are familiar with the fact that swamps are most numerous in the neighborhood of summit-levels.

Tile and other earthernware pipes are the best materials for common drains, and for garden and suburban lot drainage, should be put down from three to four feet below the surface. Professional drainers, or tilers, who use long narrow spades and hoes can put down drains four or five feet deep with a small displacement of soil, and so rapidly that it is not an expensive operation to drain thoroughly a half-acre or acre suburban lot by a series of drains not more than twenty feet apart, provided there is a sewer or other good outlet near by. Persons who are about to build on suburban lots which require drainage, should have the work done in connection with the house main drain, which is usually deep enough to be used as a trunk drain for the land, and all the needful connections can be made to better advantage when planned and executed at one time, than when pipes must be found and tapped for subsequent connections. When the work is done, the exact locality of the main drain, and all its connections, should be marked with blue ink on a general plan of the house and grounds.

Rats, mice, and moles frequently make their nests in tile-drains when there is no water in them, and may stop them completely. If the mouths of drains are always immersed in water, or if there is a constant flow of water through them, there will be little danger from this cause. But the best precaution is to fill one-third or one-half the depth of the ditch above the tile with coarse gravel around the tile, and broken stone, brick, or coal-clinkers above, putting a layer of sod over all. The deeper drains are located, the less danger there is of their becoming nests for these animals, and the greater the fall, and the amount of running water, the more certain will they be to keep clean and serviceable.

Where tile is used in a soil that has veins of quicksand opening in the sides of the ditch, it should be laid on a board bed, and surrounded and covered with straight straw, and then with coarse sand (which is not quicksand) or gravel on top of the straw; otherwise the quicksand will get into, and clog the drain.

There is considerable choice in tiles. One should be willing to pay a little extra for those which are unusually straight and smooth, as well as hard. In good clay-beds the round tile, which are a trifle the cheapest, answer very well, but the 'sole-tile' – those which have a flat bottom and a round or egg-shaped tube – are better for most kind of works, the latter being the most perfect form of all. For house-drains of considerable importance, glazed pipes, which fit into each other with collars around the joints, are preferable. These, however, are not used so much for land drainage as for conduits of waste water from the house. Where it can be done so as not to create any offensive odor, all the water wastage from the house which contains fertilizing ingredients should be conducted to some reservoir, where, by mixing it with dry earth, or diluting it with pure water, it may be returned to the land.

# 6
# Dwellings, Outbuildings, and Fences

You shall see a man,
Who never drew a line or struck an arc,
Direct an Architect and spoil his work,
Because, forsooth, he likes a tasteful house!
He likes a muffin, but he does not go
Into his kitchen to instruct his cook;
Nay, that were insult! He admires fine clothes,
But trusts his tailor! Only in those arts
Which issue from creative potencies
Does his conceit engage him.

*Holland's Katrina*

So many excellent works have been published of late years on cottage and villa architecture, and so many competent architects are to be found in our large towns and cities, that it seems almost an unpardonable offence against propriety in our day for any one to build an unsightly cottage or mansion. If the reader contemplates building a house, we pray him to lose no time in obtaining and carefully reading some of these works, and if he finds in them a plan and exterior that meet his wants, let him entrust no illiterate carpenter with their execution, but employ some competent architect, who will furnish all the drawings, not only of the dwelling itself, but of the stable and all the outbuildings. There is no better evidence of a vulgar taste, or an exhausted purse, than to see dwellings of some architectural pretension and expensive finish, with rude outbuildings, having no resemblance in style to the house, and seeming, by their incongruity, to say to every passer – 'You see we are but poor relations.' Decorating the street-front of the house only, or robbing the outbuildings to add finery to the dwelling, belongs to the same class of mistakes as that of the ostrich, which, in flying from danger, seeks a place in

which to thrust its head only, and there thinks itself safe and unseen. Do not our friends, who think their outbuildings of little importance, reveal their foolishness in the same way?

There is an unfortunate tendency among our countrymen who are building houses, to be willing victims of some fashionable mania pertaining to architectural styles; so that different eras of style in domestic architecture can be distinctly traced throughout our country by a multitude of examples of what were, in their day, called houses in 'the classic styles', and their Doric, Ionic, and Corinthian varieties; houses in 'the Gothic style', with its rustic Norman, Tudor, Elizabethan, and Castellated varieties; houses in 'the Italian style', with bracketed, Romanesque, Lombard and Swiss varieties, and lastly, those least grotesque, but often clumsy forms for small houses, 'the French or Mansard-roof style'; a title that does not even assume to designate a style of architecture for an entire house, but fore-dooms a dwelling to be designed for the purpose of sustaining a certain fashionable hood of roofs. Hardly do we begin to adapt one style or another to our needs in building, with a tolerable degree of fitness and good taste, before some supposed new style, or novel feature of an old style, intrudes itself as 'the fashion', and straightway builders throughout the breadth of our land vie with each other in numberless caricatures of it. That new, or rather unfamiliar old styles are constantly being made known to us by beautiful photographic prints and engravings of the most remarkable existing architecture, is certainly cause for congratulation, but the misfortune is that we use them as if their mere novelty, in whatever form adopted, and the fact of their being the latest mode, were alone sufficient evidence of their fitness and tastefulness. We forget the vast difference there is between obeying the behests of fashion in those things which pertain to articles of apparel that are usually worn out by the time the fashion changes, and building houses that must stand for many years, and which, if not designed so as to be truly and pleasingly adapted to the use intended, without any reference to the prevailing mode, will remain objects of ridicule for all the period of their duration after their style has ceased to be fashionable.

There is no style the mere adoption of which will secure a tasteful house; while a truly competent architect may design admirable houses with entire disregard of the formulas of established styles, as well as by the careful study and adaptation of them. The style should be in the brain and culture of the designer, and not in the age or associations of certain imported forms, which he may be requested to duplicate. But architects usually have their preferences in styles. They will be likely to succeed best in those which they like best. One will study Gothic more thoroughly than Italian forms, and will therefore design more tastefully in the spirit of the former. Another will excel in Italian, or classic forms, and another still, with more cosmopolitan culture and creative art, with the taste to produce harmonious proportions, and with care to make a thorough adaptation of the means to the end, may develop most tasteful and appropriate designs with little reference to set forms.

The persons for whom a house is to be designed are usually the best judges of their own domestic wants, and will generally furnish an architect with the rough floor plans of what they desire. Good architects will studiously conform to their wishes pertaining to the distribution of interior comforts, in such plans, but when it comes to the matter of choosing a style, they should be as little trammeled as possible, save in its expense. That architects occasionally mislead those who are about to build, by lower estimates of the cost of executing their designs than what proves to be the actual cost, may be true, but we have found that such complaints are apt to come from those who had not given the architect a full and frank statement of their wants and their limitations; and oftener still from those who have merely consulted with an architect, obtained a few sketches, and his rough guess of the cost of what the proprietor says he wants, and endeavored to save the further cost of full sets of drawings and specifications, from which alone an architect can make a true estimate. Then, after working up their plans with builders to whom the work is entrusted or contracted, and altering and adding as the work progresses, if they find the total cost to be much greater than the cost suggested by the architect, the latter is charged with the fault. The fact is, that when a man fancies he can be his own architect, his imagination is excited by the possibility of achieving a great many pleasant results by his own peculiarly fortunate talents, and in endeavoring to realize one after another of his desires, the building enthusiasm draws him so gradually, and by so many unseen currents, into the maelstrom of expense, that he rarely realizes, until too late, the quality of his conceit and extravagance. We believe that the employment of an honest and qualified architect will always be an economy to the employer, and that to dictate to him the adoption of any particular style because just then it happens to be the rage, is a pretty sure way to secure his poorest, instead of his best designing.

Another matter that we would most earnestly impress on all persons about to build is this: that, when it is the intention to employ an architect, he should be given months, instead of days, to mature his designs. We would always doubt the competence of that architect who prides himself on throwing off designs in a hurry. Long practice, and plethoric portfolios, may greatly facilitate the rapidity with which good designs can be matured, but it is nevertheless true that all designs which are at all original in character, and at the same time tasteful and harmonious, are the result of many sketches, and careful comparisons, corrections and eliminations, which can only be made when ample time is given. Dwelling-houses of moderate cost are the most difficult, in proportion to their cost, of all forms of architectural designing, and specifications for them the most tedious and embarrassing. A court-house, or city-hall, that costs a hundred thousand dollars, will give an architect no more thought, nor tax his creative faculties so much, as the designing of an original and tasteful suburban dwelling costing not more than one-tenth that sum. It is therefore very desirable that those who wish to have houses of enduring beauty should give themselves and their architects ample time to mature the plans.

There is a world of expression in the character of outbuildings that is little thought of or understood in this country, notwithstanding their mere conveniences are carefully considered. A stable and carriage-house should be one of the attractive, home-looking features of every place large enough to require them, and, if properly built and taken care of, no more to be shut out of sight than your house chimneys. What more pleasing sight than to glance over a smooth lawn, under trees, or through vistas of shrubbery, to the sunlit open space around the carriage-house door, where the horse in the brightly-polished 'buggy' stands neighing for you, or the children are clustered around 'our pony' – while doves are cooing in their little house above, and martins and swallows twitter about the eaves, up to which luxuriant grape-vines clamber. Ah, the children are at home there! One has not learned the art of enjoying home till he knows how much of beauty and delight there may be in the domestic work-places, and buildings set apart for the animals that serve us. The English are much more generous in their tastes in this respect than we. An English lady shows her stable, her horses, cows, pigs, and poultry, with the same pride and affection for her animal retinue that she has in leading you through the beauties of her lawn and flowers.

The stable, the wood-shed, the well-house, the tool-room, and all needful back buildings, should be made with as much reference to good taste in their design as the dwelling, and should all have the same general architectural character. The style and keeping of all these will have more to do with the home-look and general elegance of a suburban residence than any amount of ponderous or superfine carpentry, masonry, or interior decoration.

## COLOR

The color of houses and outbuildings is a subject in which fashion has ranged widely in different directions. Twenty-five years ago, white, white, white, everywhere and for everything, was 'the American taste'. Suddenly the absurdity of being always dressed in white struck the great public, and parrots of fashion everywhere echoed remarks about 'garish white', 'neutral tints', 'subdued tones', till a mania seized whole communities to paint wooden houses, cottages and all, 'to imitate brown stone'! Everything of wood was dismally darkened and sanded, and brick sombrely stuccoed and 'blocked off', as if we were ashamed of our best materials, and must needs conceal them. Our homes, before sepulchrally white, and garishly brilliant, were then crocked and blackened with bogus stone colors. The most beautiful and necessarily most pleasing of all colors for window-blinds, which harmonizes with nearly every neutral tint, and with all natural objects – ever-beautiful green – the tenderest and most welcome of all colors to the delicate eye, was thrust aside even by the cultivated taste of Downing, and in its place dull brown blinds, and yellow blinds, and verdigris-bronze blinds, were the fashion and 'in taste'. Common sense and common eyesight have been too strong for such a fashion to endure long, and green again greets our grateful eyes on cottage, villa, and mansion windows. After the rage for dark colors, the reaction carried many back to white again, but on the whole the color of our houses is greatly improving.

In choosing colors, the proprietor needs to guard himself from himself. If he desires some color different from any which the neighborhood affords an example of, let him beware of trusting to his own selection of paints in the pot, or from a specimen patch on the house. Both will deceive him. Colors which appear to have no character at all on small surfaces, are often beautiful when applied to an entire building; while the tints which please us best in samples may be rank and vulgar on broad surfaces. After giving a general idea of what is wanted, to a skillful painter, it is better to leave the exact shade to him, or to your architect. They may fail to meet your wishes exactly, but console yourself with the reflection that had you made the selections, the result might have been worse! Between dwelling, outbuildings, fences, garden decorations, etc., there should be a strong similarity of tone, though the depth of color may differ materially. A gray or cool drab-colored house should not have a warm brown color for its outbuildings. A cream-colored house should have its outbuildings of some darker shade, in which yellow is just perceptible as one of its constituent parts. In places where they are much shaded by trees, the outbuildings may, without impropriety, be the color of the dwelling, provided the latter is some un-showy neutral tint. Shading parts of the buildings with different colors is practiced with beautiful effect by good painters, but the proprietor is here again warned not to trust to his own skill in choosing colors.

## FENCES

We are at a loss how to convey just ideas of the choice that should be made among the infinite variety of fences in our country without writing an illustrated essay. For country, or large suburban grounds, it is safe to say, except where hedges are maintained, that that kind of fence is best which is least seen, and best seen through. But in towns our fences must harmonize with the architecture and more elegant finish of the street, and therefore be sufficiently well-designed and constructed to be in themselves pleasing objects to the passer-by. The great desideratum is to answer this requirement, and at the same time to adopt some design that will least conceal the lawn and other beauties beyond or behind it. Our fences should be, to speak figuratively, transparent. Now what will make a comparatively transparent fence is a matter much more difficult to decide than the reader will suppose. Where iron fences can be afforded, it is easy to affect the desired result, but they are so expensive that wood will long continue to be the main fence material even in towns. Where something really elegant can be afforded, an architect's services should be called into requisition as much as for the residence design. A fence may be as fine a work of art as any other construction, but the architect ought to bear in mind that it should not unnecessarily conceal the beauty it encloses. Among the less expensive kinds of fencing, we will mention a few of the forms generally used. First, and most common of all fences claiming to be ornamental, is the plain picket fence, made of strips set vertically the whole height of the fence, and from one and a half inches square to one inch by three. All picket fences shut out a view of the ground behind them until one is nearly opposite the pickets, as completely as a tight board fence of the same height. An old and ornamental form of picket fence is that composed of three horizontal rails, with two equal spaces between; one set of pickets being short, and terminated in points above the middle rail, while every other one rises through the top rail in the same way. This gives double the space between the pickets on the upper half of the fence, where a transparent fence is most indispensable. It is the best, and also one of the most expensive of the old forms of wooden fences, and the only kind of picket fencing that should be tolerated for enclosing ornamented grounds.

Fences formed of horizontal rather than vertical pieces are preferable, and the openings between the bars should be as wide as insurance against animals will permit. A substitute for the old-style of picket fences, now much used, is composed of boards sawed so that their openings form ornamental designs. These are adopted from German designs for cheap balconies and veranda guards, for which purposes they are well adapted and beautiful, but for front fences they are even more objectionable than pickets, because they bar more completely the view of what is behind. To unite strength, beauty, and 'transparency', is the object to be gained. What wooden fences will best do this, we must leave to the reader's ingenuity and good sense to decide. Those who build most expensively do not necessarily secure the most tasteful places, and in fencing there is much opportunity to let thought balance money. Some very pretty rod-iron fences are now made, both vertical and horizontal, which are much cheaper than woven wire or cast-iron, but both of the latter being always at hand or ready made for those who have the means to use them, will probably continue to increase in use. The tasteful forms in which iron fences are generally made, together with their indestructible character, will continue to make them more and more desirable. Were it not for the shameful freedom given to animals in many town and village streets, such fences might be made so much lower and more open than now, as materially to lessen their cost. If the reader will turn to the vignette at the head of this chapter, he will see a form of iron posts and rods well adapted to a suburban place.

We would suggest that all fences, not of a massive character, should have an open space under them, so that a scythe may pass clear through. No person should consider his grounds well kept unless the sidewalk in front or around his premises, is as neatly kept as the part within the enclosure. An open space under the fence, through which the blade of a scythe may glide, greatly facilitates the mowing of the lawn on both sides of the line.

For large suburban places, we would suggest that a sod fence, with light posts, and one or two horizontal bars above it, may be made both elegant and sufficient as a street protection. Fig. 10 represents a section of the fence proposed, the dotted line a a being the natural surface. The sod should be laid with a slight inclination downwards towards the centre of the fence, so that rains striking the sides will have a tendency to soak into, instead of being shed from them. If the sods are of a soil retentive of moisture (and most soils

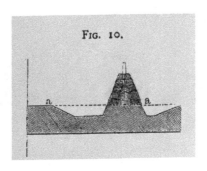

FIG. 10.

which grow a good sod are), the sides of the fence, if kept well mowed, will make a beautiful low green hedge. In very dry weather, of course, such fences would suffer and turn brown, though even then they will not be unsightly if their form is good. If water and watering facilities are at hand, they may be kept bright at all seasons. The little hollows at either side must also be kept shaved close, and will add to the beauty of the yard by giving a slight roll in the surface all around the outside boundary. The bottom and sides of the hollows should be made so that a hand mowing-machine can run upon them easily. The right side of the section was intended to represent a single slope, and the left side a hollow with a level bottom, and the slope carried farther off. The latter is the better manner. On Fig. 11, several bottom-lines are shown to suit different requirements in making fences of this kind. The sod fence may be made altogether on top of the natural surface, but as its height would be greater, it might be too serious an obstruction to views of the grounds. Lowering the ground on both sides will generally give the earth and sod required for such a fence, and make the needful height for protection against animals without barring a view of the grounds. If jumping animals are to be guarded against, it may be well to insert posts at regular distances for bars across their tops, as shown in the same cut, and to use vertical pickets, say a foot or more long, through the bars.

A picket line is more of a terror to animals than a horizontal fence of the same height, and the pickets may be so small and wide apart as not to intercept views upon the lawn within. Where cattle are not allowed in the street, a single bar or rail, running from post to post, within three or four inches of the top of the sod, with ornamental iron points screwed to the top, will make a pleasing enclosure. There is a great variety of such castings to choose from. Some of the narrower patterns of woven-wire fencing would have an

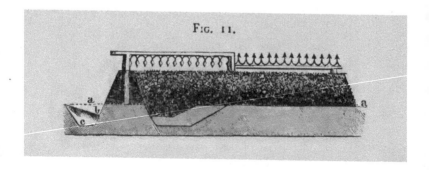

Fig. 11.

admirable effect on low sod fences. The reader's ingenuity will doubtless suggest various ways of improving these hints concerning sod fencing, but it must be borne in mind that fences of this character are unsuited to the use of those who do not feel disposed to give them the constant care which is required to keep a lawn in order, and in those semi-civilized towns where hogs are allowed at large, they are of course impracticable. Where it is desired to have the sod fence sufficiently high to be a good protection against cattle, without any posts or bars above them, it is best to make the additional height by larger and deeper excavations on each side, or on the side on which the height is most needed. A straight slope like that at *b*, Fig. 11, is easily made and kept clean with a scythe or machine, but the lower double lines can be used, where a higher fence is needed, provided the level on the bottom is wide enough to allow the use of a scythe or hand-mowing machine. As such ridges of turf are peculiarly exposed to injury from excessive cold, it is recommended, in districts where evergreen boughs, especially hemlock, can be procured, that the top of the turf be covered late in the fall. Such twigs can be neatly interlaced, with little trouble, under the bar above the turf, so as to form an evergreen hedge through the winter, and the snow that will lodge in them will protect the bank from constant heaving by freezing and thawing in the winter and early spring, and give the grass additional vigor when the time comes to uncover it.

These sod enclosures are ill-suited to form front fences in village neighborhoods, and are suggested solely for places of large extent, and with rural surroundings.

With regard to live hedges, some cautions are needed. The practice of hedging one's ground so that the passer-by cannot enjoy its beauty, is one of the barbarisms of old gardening, as absurd and unchristian in our day as

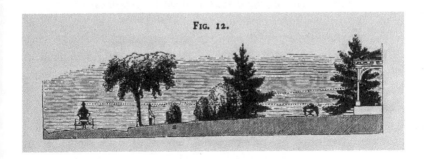

Fig. 12.

the walled courts and barred windows of a Spanish cloister, and as needlessly aggravating as the close veil of Egyptian women. It is not well, generally, to plant live hedges on the street fronts of a town or suburban residence. On larger places they are very useful and beautiful as separating screens between the decorated ground and the vegetable garden, or hiding portions of outbuildings, or as a protection for fruit yards against injurious winds, but as a street fence for town or suburban residences they should be made use of but rarely. There are other places enough where we may avail of all their beauties. Fig. 12 shows a section of front grounds and street with a hedge on the street line. It will be seen that the line of view from the eye of a man on the sidewalk, over the top of the hedge, isolates him as completely from the view of the grounds as a jail wall, and even from a carriage, in the middle of the street, one can see but little more.

A word, in conclusion, about gateways and gate-posts. Showy posts of carpentry or masonry, which are not of solid wood or solid stone, or which are made higher than the general character of the fence calls for, are apt to seem pretentious. A gateway, whether for a carriage road or a walk, should always be marked in some way, so that one will know at a glance, and at some distance, just where the entrance is. This is generally and properly done by making the gate-posts conspicuous, either by their size or their finish. But it is easy to overdo, by giving them a cheap showiness or massiveness disproportionate to their importance. Stone is far more beautiful than any other material for posts, and for the gateways of walks should be used in simple forms and of single blocks, if it can be afforded. Or, after making a suitable foundation of cheaper stone, the part above ground may be a single block of sufficient weight not to be jarred on its foundation by the ordinary use of the gates. It is not necessary that the two gate-posts be alike. The one upon which a gate is swung requires to be far heavier than the one into which it latches, and it will not be 'out of taste' to make the size of each conform to its use, and to economize by making one heavy post instead of two. Children will swing on gates in spite of all warnings, and the gates must be hung so that they will bear the strain. To insure this solidity, great weight is required, or else the post must be very thoroughly bedded in the ground. There is much less strain on the post into which the gate catches, and therefore no need of making it of the same weight and expense. In making the suggestion that it is not necessary to have the opposite posts of the gateway fac-similes of each other, it must not be understood that there is any impropriety in it, but only that the means are best adapted to the end when the one which is most heavily taxed shall be provided first to meet the calls upon it. For gateways on drives it is not always practicable to obtain single blocks of sufficient weight to resist the constant strain of a long gate. Single gates being preferable to double ones for this purpose, the posts to which such gates are hung should have marked importance, and may, with propriety, be of block masonry, or of brick, with stone caps and binding layers, and it must not be forgotten that mere height and size, for the purpose of rendering them conspicuous, is not the true object, but that weight and tasteful forms are required. The facility with which slender wood posts can be encased with heavy shells of carpentry, has had a bad influence in substituting showiness for solidity; yet it is also true that much real beauty of form and effect is obtained by casing posts with joiner's work, at a small expense compared with what is required by the use of heavy timber or stone. Each man's necessities and culture must be the law to himself in this matter. The post in the vignette at the head of this chapter is a fair example of a simple and unpretending form of stone post. There are few matters in which the taste of the proprietor, or his architect, may be more pleasingly illustrated than in the designs for stone gate-posts. In putting in posts of wood or single blocks of stone deep in the ground, the hole around them should be filled with sand, and especial care should be used to have the bottom firm and solidly bedded before filling more than a few inches; the top of the stone should then be fastened in place by braces until the filling is completed. It is desirable that the part of a stone below the surface of the ground increase in size like a wedge, with the largest end down, for if the stone is the reverse in form, that is to say, a wedge with the point down, it then forms a shoulder against which the earth in swelling, as it does by freezing, will inevitably heave the post upwards. Iron gate-posts, arched over like those shown by Fig. 184, and covered with wire, are charming for village-lot entrances, though less expressive of solidity and homeliness than stone. Even for an iron fence, the contrast between the low massiveness of well-designed stone gateways, and the lightness of iron work, is quite pleasing. And if these stone posts are used only for gateways (and we think it better not to use them anywhere on a front except for gateways and street corners), they become the most prominent feature of the street front. There is no end to charming architectural combinations for gateways, but it will not do on a place which has not otherwise a highly architectural character, to 'make it up' on the gateway.

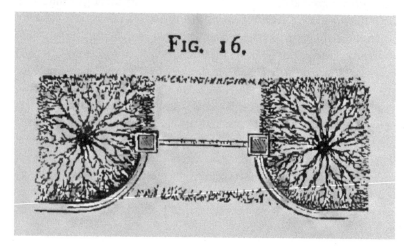

On places where solid constructive decorations cannot be afforded, we advise the use of topiary work, by which is meant the fanciful forms sometimes given, by cutting and trimming, to verdant arbors, thickets, trees, and hedges. There are many species of evergreens which may be planted on each side of the gateways of ordinary foot-walks so as to be made into charming arches over the entrance. With patience and annual care, these can be perfected within about ten years, but they will also afford most pleasing labor from the beginning, and the infantile graces of the trees, which are year by year to be developed into verdant arches, will probably afford quite as much pleasure in their early growth as in their perfected forms. In the descriptions of the trees which are suitable for this kind of topiary work, the mode of managing them will be noted in detail. We here introduce the same cuts to give a hint of the effect intended, though, when well grown, such arches are far more beautiful than our engraving can even suggest. Fig. 13 shows a pair of hemlocks planted inside of a gateway, and grown to a height of 10 to 12 feet, and only trimmed on the inside. Fig. 14 shows the effect at the end of ten years – the tops of the two trees having been twisted together so as to grow as one tree over the centre of the arch, and all parts trimmed year by year to the form illustrated. Fig. 15 shows the effect that may be produced from the same trees by permitting the main stems to keep their upright direction, and forming the arch by encouraging and uniting the growth of the inner branches at the proper height.

Where evergreens are to be planted for this purpose, the fence should curve inwards to the gate, as shown by the transverse section (Fig. 16), so that trees designed to form the arch can be planted on a line with the posts, and two or three feet from them. All this topiary work may be a substitute for expensive gateways, or it may, with equal propriety, be introduced as an accessory decoration, where the posts are not of a massive, or highly ornate character. In the latter case, whatever beauty of design and workmanship has been wrought out in stone should not be deliberately concealed by such forms of verdure.

# 7
## Neighboring Improvements

Small is the worth of beauty from the light retired.

*Tennyson*

There is no way in which men deprive themselves of what costs them nothing and profits them much, more than by dividing their improved grounds from their neighbors, and from the view of passers on the road, by fences and hedges. The beauty obtained by throwing front grounds open together, is of that excellent quality which enriches all who take part in the exchange, and makes no man poorer. As a merely business matter it is simply stupid to shut out, voluntarily, a pleasant lookout through a neighbor's ornamental grounds. If, on the other hand, such opportunities are improved, and made the most of, no gentleman would hesitate to make return for the privilege by arranging his own ground so as to give the neighbor equally pleasing vistas into or across it. It is unchristian to hedge from the sight of others the beauties of nature which it has been our good fortune to create or secure, and all the walls, high fences, hedge screens and belts of trees and shrubbery which are used for that purpose only, are so many means by which we show how unchristian and unneighborly we can be. It is true these things are not usually done in any mere spirit of selfishness: they are the conventional forms of planting that come down to us from feudal times, or that were necessary in gardens near cities, and in close proximity to populous neighborhoods with rude improvements and ruder people. It is a peculiarity of English gardens, which it is as unfortunate to follow as it would be to imitate the surly self-assertion of English travelling-manners. An English garden is 'a love of a place' to get into, and an Englishman's heart is warm and hospitable at his own fire-side; but these facts do not make it less uncivil to bristle in strangers' company, or to wall and hedge a lovely garden against the longing eyes of the outside world. To hedge out deformities is well, but to narrow our own or

our neighbor's views of the free graces of Nature by our own volition, is quite another thing. We have seen high arbor-vitae hedges between the decorated front grounds of members of the same family, each of whose places was well kept, and necessary to complete the beauty of the other and to secure to both extensive prospects! It seems as if such persons wish to advertise to every passer, 'my lot begins here, sir, and ends there, sir', and might be unhappy if the dividing lines were not accurately known. 'High fences make good neighbors', is a saying often repeated by persons about walling themselves in. The saying has some foundation in fact. Vinegar and soda, both good in their way, are better kept in separate vessels. If a man believes himself and his family to be bad neighbors, certainly they ought to fence themselves in, thoroughly. Or if they have reason to believe their neighbors are of the same sort, they may well be sure of the height and strength of the divisions between them. But we prefer to imagine the case reversed, and that our neighbors are kindly gentlemen and women, with well-bred families, who can enjoy the views across others' grounds without trespassing upon them. These remarks are intended to apply to those decorative portions of home-grounds which, in this country, and especially in suburban neighborhoods, are usually in front of the domestic offices of the house. The latter must necessarily be made private and distinct from each other. One of the most fertile sources of disagreements between families having grounds opening together, are incursions of boisterous children from one to another. Now it is suggested that children may be trained to respect and stop at a thread drawn across a lawn to represent a boundary, just as well as at a stone wall. Every strong high barrier challenges a spirited boy's opposition and enterprise, but what costs no courage or strength to pass, and a consciousness of being where he don't belong, generally makes him ashamed to transgress in such directions. A well-defined line will, in most cases, be all that is necessary. This may be simply a sunk line in the grass, as shown at *a*, Fig. 17, or it may be a row of low, small cedar or iron posts, with a chain or wires running from one to another, or some very low, open, and light design of woven-wire fencing; anything, in short, which will leave the eye an unbroken range of view, and still say to the children, 'thus far shalt thou go, and no farther.' If parents on both sides of the line do their duty in instructing the children not to trespass on contiguous lawns, less trouble will result from that cause than from the bad feelings engendered by high outside boundary walls that so often become convenient shields to hide unclean rubbish and to foster weeds.

An interesting result, that may be reached by joining neighboring improvements, is in equalizing the beauties of old and new places. Suppose B has bought an open lot between A and C, who have old places. The grounds of A, we will suppose, are filled, in old village style, with big cherry trees, maples, lilacs, spruce trees, roses, and annuals, and C's grounds may have a growth of noble old trees, which had invited a house to make its home there. Between the two is Mr B's bare lot, on which he builds a 'modern house', which is, of course, the envy of the older places. But Mr B and his family sigh for the old forest trees on the right, and the flowers, and verdure, and fruit trees on the left. Not having them to begin with, we advise him to make a virtue of necessity, and cause his neighbors to envy him the superior openness and polish of his own grounds. A has a yard cluttered with the valuable accumulations of years; a fine variety of trees, shrubs, and flowers; yet nothing shows to advantage. The shade, the multiplicity of bushes, the general intertanglement of all, make it very difficult to grow a close turf,

Fig. 17.

*a*

and keep it mown as a lawn. Mr B, on the other hand, can begin, as soon as his ground is enriched and set to grass, to perfect it by constant cutting and rolling till it is a sheet of green velvet. Cut in the lawn, here and there near his walks, small beds for low and brilliant flowers may sparkle with sunny gayety; at the intersection of walks, or flanking or fronting the entrances, low broad-top vases (rustic or classic, as the character of the house or their position may require) may be placed, filled with a variety of graceful and brilliant plants. In two or three years, if Mr B shall thus have made the most of his open ground, ten chances to one both of the neighbors will be envying the superior beauty of the new place. It will, probably, really be the most charming of the three; not, however, by virtue of its open lawn alone, but by the contrast which his neighbor's crowded yard on one side, and the forest trees on the other, serve to produce. Each of their places forms a background for his lawn; while, if the three places are allowed to open together, his lawn is a charming outlook from the shades of theirs. *Neither one of these places would, alone, make landscape beauty; yet the three may make chaining combinations from every point of view.* Every home needs some fruit trees, and a shadowy background, or flanking, of noble forest trees, which Mr B would desire to have started as soon as possible, but with such adjoining improvements as we have described, he should preserve the distinctive elegance of his front grounds, and leave them as open and sunny as possible. If, however, B's bare lot stood unflanked by old trees or old places, then his aim should be materially changed, and a few large trees, and some shrubbery, would enter into his designs for planting. Though farther on we shall endeavor to impress again the necessity of restraint in choosing but few among the thousands of trees, shrubs, and flowers that are offered to every planter, it is appropriate that, in this chapter on Neighboring Improvements, we should also suggest to planters how very few of all the sylvan and floral treasures that beautify the surface of the globe, each one's half-acre or five acres can comfortably accommodate. As every city has its hundreds or thousands of good and charming people, whose acquaintance we may never have time to make, we very sensibly confine our companionship to a few congenial families, in whose intimate friendliness we have much more pleasure than if we were to 'spread too thin' in efforts to embrace an entire community. Just so with the populous best society in the community of trees, to whose members the citizen is about to be introduced. He had better abandon the idea of domesticating them all into his home circle. He may even leave scores of the best families out entirely, and still have all that he can well entertain and cultivate. But by means of neighborhood association in improvements, the neighborhood, as a whole, may furnish examples of almost every kind of vegetable beauty that the climate admits of. Suppose, for instance, that a dozen neighbors, known as A to L respectively, have each an acre to devote to decorative planting. Laid out in the old way, with the stereotype allowance of evergreens, deciduous trees, and shrubs, they would, as plantations, have but little more interest after one was seen than duplicate copies of a book that we have done with. But if A shall conclude to make the pines and birches his specialty, and procure all the varieties that are pleasing to the eye, which grow well in our climate, and arrange them around his home under the direction of some intelligent planter who knows the best locations for each, he will find, at the end of ten years, that his place will be a distinguished one. He will have about fifty varieties of hardy pines to choose from, among which from ten to twenty are trees of great beauty, and the beautiful birches will sparkle among them as well set jewels. The pines will embrace a variety of sizes and forms, from the graceful and lofty white pine of our forests, and the much larger pines of California and Oregon, down to interesting bushy dwarfs, which do not exceed the lilac in size. Making a specialty of the pine and the birch families will not prevent A from having a due proportion of open lawn, and a small variety of the finest flowering shrubs and flowers, proportioned to the size of his lawn.

Now we will suppose Mr B is his next neighbor, and that he chooses to make the maple tree his specialty. No one familiar with the almost endless number of varieties of the maple, foreign as well as native, with all their diversity of growth and wealth of foliage, with their spring loveliness and autumn glories, their cleanliness and their thrift, can for a moment doubt the beauty that might be produced under proper management on Mr B's acre. A few trees, but a few, of more irregular outlines, should be admitted as a foil to the compacter maples.

Next Mr C must choose his favorites. Supposing his house to be of some unpicturesque style, he may take the different species and varieties of the horse-chestnut, *Æsculus*, and the common chestnut, *Castanea*. At certain seasons of the year his place would be unrivalled in display of flowers and foliage.

If D will take the oak, he will not find his acre large enough to accommodate one-half of the hardy and beautiful varieties which are natives of his own country alone. But as the oak is rather slow in developing its best traits, Mr D would be wise to find a site for his specialty on which some varieties of oak have already attained good size.

The elms, with some other trees that contrast well with them, will furnish a beautiful variety for E.

Mr F may make trees of gorgeous autumn foliage his specialty, and, while surrounded by some of the loveliest of spring and summer trees, may have his place all aglow in September and October with the dogwood, the liquidamber, the pepperidge or tupelo, the sassafras, the sugar, scarlet, and Norway maples, the scarlet oak, and many others.

If G will make a specialty of lawn, shrubs, and flowers alone, among a thousand beauties he can hardly fail to make an interesting collection.

H may have a predilection for spruces, hemlocks, and spiry-top trees, and make the evergreens of those forms, and the deciduous trees that harmonize with them, his specialty. But care must be used not to render the place gloomy with their too great abundance. (Spiry-topped evergreens, like the balsam fir or Norway spruce, are rather impracticable to make entire plantations of on any place. Their forms are too monotonous, and their shadows too meagre, to be used with the same careless profusion near a dwelling that we may employ broadly overhanging trees, like the elms, oaks, pines, and maples. Such evergreens are planted quite too much already; many fine places having been rendered most gloomy by their great abundance. A specialty of this kind would, therefore, be 'stale and unprofitable', unless made with great skill.)

I will not have any species in particular, but loves those trees, of whatever species, which spread low and broadly, but clear above the lawn; like the apple-tree, the mulberry, the horse-chestnut, the catalpas and paulonias, the white oak, the beech, and some varieties of the thorn.

J admires the classic formalities of the old French style of gardening, and prefers trees and shrubs that will bear clipping well, and grow naturally or artificially into symmetric and formal shapes; with straight walks and architectural decorations. In close neighborhoods, and on well-improved streets, architectural gardening is the most elegant of all, but requires much money for constructions, which, if not thorough and tastefully complete, were better not attempted.

K wishes a place full of graceful forms, and will use those trees which will best carry out his idea. His walks must be serpentine; his trees weeping varieties, both deciduous and evergreen, of which the variety in form and character is such as to enable him to make a most picturesque as well as graceful collection.

L has a special admiration for trees of exotic or tropical appearance, and *if his soil is deeply drained, rich, and warm*, the magnolias, catalpas, paulonia, mulberries, and ailanthus, with some evergreens of rounded forms, will make an interesting collection. (By deeply-drained, we do not mean the draining of a foot below the surface, but at least four feet, so that the large roots of trees will be invited to penetrate into the substratum, which is never cold to the freezing point, and from which the roots of trees form conductors to the branches above, and thus serve to modify the rigors of the upper air by the warmth of the earth below the frost. If one will but think of the difference in winters' coldest days, between riding all day with warm blocks to the feet, or without them, he can appreciate the argument for inviting trees to root deeply in the earth's warm substratum.)

We have here named a dozen places, with each a specialty. Now, it is to be clearly understood that the nature of the locality, the form of the ground, the peculiarities of the soil, and the architecture of the house, are all to be taken into consideration before deciding what species of planting to make the specialty of any one home. It would be ridiculous to plant weeping willows on a dry, bald site, or gloomy balsam firs on a sunny slope, or a collection of spiry evergreens alone on a level lawn, or in juxtaposition with masses of round-headed trees, like maples and horse-chestnuts. All the surrounding circumstances must govern the choice, and neighbors should consult together with competent advisers, as far as practicable, before determining what each will plant, so as to make contiguous grounds harmonize, as well as add to the variety of each other's grounds.

To be repeating the same round of common favorite trees in one place after another, on a fine suburban street, is to lose much of the varied beauty which would result from each planter making thorough work in some one specialty of arboriculture. To employ an artist in landscape gardening to design all the places that adjoin each other, with reference to a distinctive characteristic for each, and a happy blending of the beauty of all, would, of course, be the most certain way to secure satisfactory results. It will be found, as we grow more intelligent in such matters, that it is quite as essential to the beauty of our home-grounds to commit their general arrangement to professional artists, and to be as absolutely restricted to their plans, as it has been in the management of cemeteries. So long as each lot-owner can plant and form his lot to suit himself alone, whatever his taste may be, such grounds will be but a medley of deformities. To insure a high order of beauty in neighboring improvements, all planting must be done under some one competent direction. The result of this is seen in our beautiful modern cemeteries. A similar subordination of individual fancies to a general plan, in a community of neighboring grounds, may develop like results.

## STREET TREES

The subject of street trees comes properly under the head of neighboring improvements. It might be inferred, from the modes of planting recommended in the preceding pages, that a variety of trees will be recommended for one street in preference to a single sort. On the contrary, the effect is much better, on a straight street or road, to have an avenue composed of a single species of tree only. To attempt the varieties of park scenery on an avenue is as much out of place as to compose a park of straight rows of trees. There ought to be but one variety of street tree on the same block, at least, and the longer the continuity is kept up the nobler will be the effect. Street trees are usually planted quite too close together. For wide avenues (where alone such great spreading trees as the elm, sycamore, silver maple, and silver poplar should be planted), from thirty to fifty feet apart is near enough, and thirty feet is the least distance that any street trees should be planted from each other. The finest deciduous trees are those already most commonly planted – elms, maples, and horse-chestnuts. The white pine is a noble street tree, very little used. It deserves to be, but as it must be planted of smaller size than the deciduous trees, in order to do well, and therefore requires box protection during a greater number of years, it should only be planted where such protection is sure to be given. No trees should be planted in streets which do not come early into leaf, or which have disagreeable blossoms, or which bear nuts or eatable fruit, or the leaves of which are subject to worms, or do not drop promptly and dry after the first severe autumn frosts. The different varieties of the maple, the horse-chestnut, the weeping elm, and the English and Scotch elms, all unite to a great extent the best qualities for street trees. The linden is peculiarly subject to worms, and should not, therefore, be planted in streets. The elm, near the sea-coast, is also infested by a species of worm, which does not, however, seem to be very annoying in the interior. The tulip tree, or white wood, is rather difficult to transplant, and not adapted to any but a rich warm soil, but, once established in such a soil, it makes an elegant street tree. The oaks grow too slowly to be popular, and many of them have not a cheerful expression in winter. The willows generally have thin leaves, which rot where they fall, and therefore make the walks filthy under them in autumn. The poplars all have blossoms, or cottony seeds, that are annoying. Among the foreign maples, the Norway and the sycamore maples are well adapted to street planting, but not superior to the sugar maple. If we were to name six species of trees to choose from for the street, they would be the American weeping elm, the Scotch or Wych elm, the horse-chestnut, the sugar, Norway, or sycamore maples, the weeping white birch, and, in light, warm soils, the white pine.

Charming effects may be produced by planting such trees as the weeping birch at long intervals, to break the monotony of heavier-formed trees by the delicate sprightliness of their foliage in summer, and their brilliant white-barked spray when the trees are leafless. We know no reason why several varieties of the birch would not make admirable avenues for streets which are too narrow for elms, and in which maples and chestnuts make too deep a shade.

In conclusion, we will venture to suggest an innovation for town streets which are occupied for residences alone, and upon which there is little travel in vehicles. The roadway on such streets is often needlessly wide, and trees planted on the sidewalk on both sides of the road, expand their tops so as to obstruct a view of the street, and so close to the house that their beauty cannot be seen. It is recommended that such streets have but one row of trees, and that in the middle of the road, where a strip of grass, six feet wide or more, would give them a pleasing setting. As this width of grass cannot be spared from many town sidewalks, but can be from the roadways, the plan may occasionally be used to advantage.

# 8

# Materials Used in Decorative Planting

There are no vegetable productions in Nature which, when thoroughly observed and understood, are not beautiful. Few plants are more beautiful than the thistle. Most weeds will elicit our admiration if their forms, growth, and structure are carefully noticed. Even bare rocks give pleasure to the eye, and their vastness and ruggedness awaken emotions of sublimity, as sun, moon, or darkness light and shadow them. A lightning-shivered pine, projecting from a mountain side, makes a striking point in a painter's landscape, and serves to heighten, by contrast, the smooth-featured loveliness of a valley below it.

Yet the thistle would give more pain than pleasure as a pot or border plant. What we call weeds are only so because some other plants unite more beauties, or give more pleasurable returns for cultivation. We reject the former, because we cannot have all, and therefore choose their betters. The shivered pine, though pleasingly picturesque up among the rocks, would give more pleasure added to the wood-pile than to the front yard of the citizen, and the rocky beauties of mountain scenery are sometimes those of which the poet says,

'Tis distance lends enchantment to the view.

The noble exhilaration of climbing and roaming over mountain scenery is a charm not so much of their beauties, seen near by, as of the tonic air, and tonic exercise, and bounding blood, and glow of pride to be above some part of the world and to look down upon it.

Tennyson thus nobly contrasts the mountain with the valley:

Come down, O maid, from yonder mountain height;
What pleasure lives in height (the shepherd sang),
In height and cold, the pleasure of the hills?

But cease to move so near the heavens, and cease
To glide a sunbeam by the blasted pine,
To sit a star upon the sparkling spire,
And come! for Love is of the valley;
let the torrent dance thee down,
To find him in the valley; let the wild
Lean-headed eagles yelp alone, and leave
The monstrous ledges there to slope, and spill
Their thousand wreaths of dangling water-smoke.
That like a broken purpose waste in air;
So waste not thou: but come; for all the vales
Await thee; azure pillars of the hearth
Arise to thee; the children call, and I,
Thy shepherd, pipe; and sweet is every sound,
Sweeter thy voice, but every sound is sweet;
Myriads of rivulets hurrying through the lawn,
The moan of doves in immemorial elms,
And murmuring of innumerable bees.

We turn from where we stand upon the mountain, not so much to look at
the vast and rugged forms around us, as upon the lovely scenery at its base;

scenes where the hand of Art has set its impress on the works of Nature, and added human interests to their normal beauty.

Mountain and picturesque scenery is something which can neither be transplanted nor successfully imitated, and is, therefore, rarely within the pale of decorative gardening, as applied to the grounds of townspeople. Great mossy boulders, little ledges, and stony brooks, are now and then natural features of suburban sites, and should be prized for the picturesque effects and variety of interest that may be made with them. The paltry artificial rock-works that mar so many otherwise pretty grounds, need scarcely be mentioned, as the sight of them must necessarily make their proprietors feel as dissatisfied with their effect as the animal who essayed to don the garb and imitate the roar of the lion was with his success. It is not intended, however, to condemn those rock-works which are unobtrusively placed, for the purpose of growing to better advantage certain favorite plants, but only 'rock-work' which is built for exhibition.

What, then, are the materials which every one may command, and which can be combined in town and village grounds to realize the greatest and most permanent pleasure? We will name these:

Of Nature's gifts – Earth, Grass, Trees, Shrubs, Flowers, Vines, and Water; of Art's productions – Houses, Walks, Roads, Fences, and all the needful accessories of dwellings for cultivated people. Let us briefly sketch what are the essential characteristics of Nature's materials.

Earth – Of the Earth we demand, for decorative planting, that she shall be rich, and her bosom smooth and flowing; that, whether varied in surface by billowy inequalities, or formed to less interesting slopes or levels, the surface lines shall always be smooth, and free from all rough irregularities.

Grass – This is the most lowly, the simplest, and the loveliest element to be used in the adornment of home. A chapter will hereafter be devoted to it under the head of The Lawn. Here its essential use and beauty is defined to be a close-fitting green robe thrown over the smooth form of the earth, through which every undulation is revealed, and over which the sunlight will play as upon velvet, and the shadows of environing objects be clearly outlined as upon a floor.

Trees – The beauty of trees is in the endless variety of their forms, their coloring, the contrasts of light and shade in the depths of their foliage, and their shadows, which play with the sunlight and moonlight on the grass beneath them. The latter is one of their greatest charms, but one which the smoothness of the ground and grass has much to do in developing. There is also a noble fascination in viewing the grand trunks of large trees towering over our heads, their rough branches projected in bold defiance of gravitation, swaying listlessly in quiet air, toying with gentle breezes, or lashing the air in proud defiance of its ruder gales.

Shrubs – These are to small places the lowly representatives of what trees are to the park, and more: for there are few trees which we value for their flowers, while most ornamental shrubs are covered at some season with a bloom of glowing colors, and adorned with the same luxuriance of leafage that clothes the best trees. They are the mainstay after grass for the adornment of pleasure grounds of small extent. The variety to choose from is large, and a study of the peculiar beauty of each, and the position for which it is best adapted, is one to which we ask the marked attention of the reader. Their appropriate or improper placement will make or mar the beauty of the grounds.

Vines, though in some respects classed with shrubs, have so distinct a beauty of their own that they constitute a separate element of embellishment. Their proper places are so evident, and generally so well understood, that fewer mistakes are made in placing them than any other class of plants. Housekeepers differ widely whether to have or not to have their interlacing foliage on porch and verandas, or embowering their windows. Of their loveliness to the eye in those situations there is no question. Whether their beauty compensates for the occasional inconvenience of the insects they harbor, is to be decided by each lady housekeeper for herself. It is a clear case for toleration and Christian forbearance, if we would retain these most winsome features of cottage decoration. Of vines on ornamental frames we will treat further on, here remarking, that, as usually placed, on garish white frames, in the most conspicuous positions, they are much like graceful and beautiful girls – less lovely when thus thrust forward to attract attention, than when, in more modest positions, their grace and beauty draw one to them.

Flowers – So beautiful and varied are they, that a thousand life-times of study could not learn all their infinite varieties. Henry Coleman, the distinguished agriculturist of Massachusetts, once naively wrote: 'When I hear a man ask, "What's the use of flowers?" I am always tempted to lift his hat and see the length of his ears!' All civilized beings love flowers, and ladies often 'not wisely, but too well'. We will endeavor to show, hereafter, how they may be wisely cherished.

Water – Of water, we can only require that it be pure and clear, and in motion. The scope of this work is too limited to deal much with the capabilities of this lovely element in the hands of the landscape gardener. Only in large and expensive places can artificial ponds or lakes be introduced to advantage as a decorative element. But we protest against all those abominations made with water, called fish-ponds; or indeed any ponds at all where the surrounding earth, or the earth beneath them, is rich enough to cause water-vegetation, or scum, in them. To invite a clear rippling brook to spread itself out into a stagnant pool, is as bad as to inveigle your most entertaining friend into 'a dead-drunk'. It is an outrage on nature and decency. But a brook may be made doubly interesting, sometimes, by obstructing it with stones; by creating cascades; by forcing it to rush and hide in narrow crevices, to emerge foaming with excitement, and, finally, to spread over a shallow bed of bright pebbles, and sparkle leisurely in the sun. Such brooks can be made a perpetual charm. All their beauties may be heightened by art, but not the art of the mill-dam, or fishpond maker. The fish and fevers bred in such places are not of sufficient value to the producer to warrant the outlay.

The needful works of art – houses, walls, fences, and decorative constructions – belong more to the architect than to the landscape gardener, and the employment of only architects of thorough education and culture, is the policy of the citizen who wishes to make a permanently pleasing home, and no foolish expenditures. The building of expensive summer-houses and arbors in ordinary suburban places is rarely necessary. Where grounds are large enough to make them real conveniences, the strong rustic cedar constructions much used of late years (of which admirable examples are to be seen in the New York Central Park), are well adapted for shady places away from the house and the street.

9

# Faults to Avoid: Plan Before Planting

Rigid self-denial, in dispensing with many things that seem desirable, will be found essential to the best effect and enjoyment of those home-adornments which we can afford. Limited as most men are in income; circumscribed as their building lots usually are, and fixed by circumstances quite different from those which would influence a choice for landscape gardening alone, one of the most difficult lessons to learn is, to proportion planting and expenditures to the lot and the income. And not this alone, but to the demands of a refined taste, which is intolerant of excesses and vulgarity even in gardening. To build a larger house than the owner can use or furnish, or to lay out grounds on a more costly scale than his means will enable him to keep in good order, is a waste, and may result in making his place unsightly rather than a beautiful improvement. We doubt the good taste of a man, whose enthusiastic love of company induces him to invite to his house such incongruous numbers that they crowd and jostle each other at table, and must be lodged uncomfortably on floors and in out-buildings. But it is just this kind of over-doing which is the stumbling block of many who are embellishing their homes. The cost of superfluous walks, if they are well made, is apt to suggest an early inquiry into their needfulness, but trees and shrubs are so cheap, and so small, at first, that excessive planting is almost as certain to be indulged in, as excessive eating by one who has long fasted. A dozen varieties of trees, and scores of shrubs, each of which has a special and familiar beauty, call winningly to the planter, 'choose me!' If he good-naturedly yields to every beauty's beckoning, he finds, too late, that in trying to please all he has satisfied none, and perhaps done injustice to all. Crowded together more and more as they grow, each will hide the beauty of the other, and only darken the ground they were intended to adorn. A single native tree, growing alone, or, if the ground be very small, a single full-grown shrub, with room and soil enough to give luxuriant development of all its

beauty, will do more, far more, to beautify one's home, than the finest variety of trees, growing together like an overgrown nursery. Yet, in planting a small lot, where no trees are already grown, those who love variety must be chary of planting even one full-sized tree. Eugene Baumann, of Rahway, N. J., one of the few thoroughly cultivated garden artists in this country, in alluding to the folly of planting large trees at all in small lots, very happily illustrates its absurdity by likening it to the choice of a table for a small drawing-room, the four corners, of which would touch the four walls. Few persons realize the rapidity with which trees grow and time flies, and in planting are pretty sure, after a few years, like the Vicar of Wakefield, to find their sylvan family pictures too big for the room.

Let it, then, be borne in mind that the *smaller the lot, the smaller should be the materials used to adorn it.* For city fronts of from 10 x 20 feet to a few rods in area, the arts of gardening will take an architectural direction, so that cut-stone walks, bordered with bedding plants and low annuals, and well-placed and well-filled vases, will be the only form in which vegetable beauties can be introduced. For places of a rood in extent, (we mean only the space devoted to decorative planting), a lawn will be essential, and there may be introduced many shrubs as well as flowers, but trees sparingly, if at all. Of architectural or constructive decorations, there will be room for considerable expenditure, and more discretion. Only on places having upwards of half an acre devoted to ornamental keeping, ought trees which attain large size to be planted. If, however, there are fine trees already growing on any lot, all the arrangements of walks and plantings should be made to avail of their beauty, and to heighten it.

Kemp's observations on this subject are so pertinent that we shall quote them, premising that *garden* as here used by him, means the pleasure-ground of a place.

Possibly the greatest and most prevalent error of those who lay out gardens for themselves is, *attempting too much*. A mind unaccustomed to generalize, or to take in a number of leading objects at a glance, finds out the different points embraced in landscape gardening one by one, and, unable to decide which of them can most suitably be applied, determines on trying to compass more than can readily be attained. One thing after another is, at different times, observed and liked, in some similar place that is visited, and each is successively wished to be transferred to the observer's own garden, without regard to its fitness for the locality, or its relation to what has previously been done. A neighbor or a friend has a place in which certain features are exquisitely developed, and these are at once sought to be copied. The practice of cutting up a ground into mere fragments is the natural result of such a state of things.

There are several ways in which a place may be frittered away, so as to be wholly deficient in character and beauty. It may be too much broken up in its *general arrangement*, and this is the worst variety of the fault, because least easily mended and most conspicuous. To aim at comprising the principal features proper to the largest gardens, in those of the most limited size, is surely not a worthy species of imitation, and one which can only excite ridicule and end in disappointment …

A place may likewise, and easily, be too much carved up into detached portions, or overshadowed, or reduced in apparent size, by *planting too largely*. Trees and shrubs constitute the greatest ornaments of a garden, but they soon become disagreeable when a place is overrun with them, by contracting the space, and shutting out light, and rendering the grass imperfect and the walks mossy. Nothing could be more damp, and gloomy, and confined, than a small place too much cumbered with plantations. Nor is the consideration of its influences on the health of the occupants at all unimportant; for where sun and wind cannot get free play, a moist and stagnant air, injurious to all animal life, is necessarily occasioned …

In the immediate neighborhood of the house, moreover, it is particularly desirable that trees and large shrubs should not abound. Independently of darkening the windows, they communicate great dampness to the walls, and prevent that action of the wind upon the building which alone can keep it dry, comfortable, and consequently healthy.

Another mode in which the effect of a garden may be marred by too much being aimed at, is *in the formation of numerous flower beds*, or groups of mixed shrubs and flowers on the lawn. This is a very common failing, and one which greatly disfigures a place; especially as, when intended only for flowers, such beds usually remain vacant and naked for several months in the year.

The necessity of avoiding to shade a house with trees, or shrubs against its walls, is doubtless much greater in Great Britain than in our much dryer and hotter climate; still, it is certain that the suggestions of the author just quoted are quite too much disregarded in this country; so much so, that some of our highest medical authorities, of late, attribute much of the consumption so fatal in New England families, to the want of sun, the damp air, and the tree and shrub-embowered and shutter-closed houses peculiar to its villages and farms.

A common error in fitting up a home is the idea, apparently acted upon by the owner, that his own place 'is all the world to him'. Now, a glimpse of a near or distant mountain, river, pond, or lake; of a single beautiful tree, or a church spire, or a neighbor's pretty house and lawn, or a distant field-chequered farm, are all our own if we choose to make them so. As H. W. Beecher pithily puts it: 'Men's eyes make finer pictures, when they know how to use them, than anybody's hands can.' To shut one's place out of view of one or all of these things, by planting it full of little trees and little bushes, to be admired principally because they are 'my' little trees and bushes, is surely a sad weakness; yet how many homes are seen, commanding pictures of great interest or beauty, which have been completely shut out of view by plantations of trees and shrubs, in consequence of the ill-directed zeal of the master or mistress of the house to fill 'our yard' with beautiful things. Fig. 18 (overleaf) is a view out of the narrow sidelight of a friend's bay-window. It scarcely takes in more than an eighth of a rood of his own ground, and yet makes a charming outlook, over an animated river, to distant fields, and homes, and fine trees, of which the engraving gives but a bare suggestion. A single tree, or a group of shrubs planted in the wrong place, would have shut out, completely, this pleasant picture.

It cannot be too strongly impressed on the reader's mind, that most grounds, *and all that are nearly level, can be much better arranged on paper,*

Fig. 18

*where all parts are under the eye at the same moment, than upon the ground, while planting.* Beginning to erect a house before a plan has been made, is not more sure of begetting blunders, than beginning to plant in the same way, and though the blunders of misplanting may not be so costly, they are certain in the end to be quite as unsightly.

We would by no means recommend every man to be the planner of his own grounds, if competent garden artists are to be had, but in the absence of such, and on the supposition that we are addressing men and women studious of culture in the art, who may, by dint of such study, and pondering over their own dear home-plan, do something better for themselves than the common run of such vegetable gardeners as they can find can do for them, we would only endeavor to aid them in the attempt. And we firmly believe that a knowledge of the best arts of gardening will be increased by recommending, to educated men and women, the careful study and maturing of their own plans. The first result of such labor will be to elevate their conceptions of the range of gardening art, to impress them with their own ignorance, and to enable them to better appreciate, and therefore set a higher value on the professional services of educated gardeners. It would be as absurd for the mass of men, engrossed in active business, to devote a large amount of time to the study of the mere rudiments of gardenesque art, simply to enable them to lay out a half acre or acre of land, as it would be for the same business man to pore over an architect's library and pictures to enable him to design his own house – provided skillful planters were as easily found as competent architects. Twenty years ago there was the same dearth of architects of culture as there now is of educated gardeners. The general study of domestic architecture, which Downing's works then aided to make a fashion, produced, at first, an astonishing fermentation and rising of architectural crudities, but it also produced, afterwards, a crop of architects. If we can induce every family who have a home to adorn, to study the art of planning and arranging their own grounds, the seed will be planted that will germinate, in another generation, in a crop of art-gardeners of such high culture, and of such necessity to the educated community, that it will be one of the honored professions of our best collegiates. Now, however, the number of such men, devoted to this profession, is so small, that we have not heard even of more than half a dozen skilled, professional gardeners among our thirty millions of native Americans, and not greatly more than double that number of educated foreigners, who have established a deserved fame among us as men of culture in their art. Even these men, with few exceptions, are little known outside the wealthy circles of the great cities, nor half appreciated where they are known. Until employers are themselves persons of culture, artists, even when employed, are regarded as a kind of dilettanti, whom it is necessary to employ rather to conform to 'the fashion', than for such service as the employer is competent to appreciate, and really enjoy the results of. We know of nothing that will at the same time cultivate a taste for the fascinating art of gardenesque designing, and produce a quick return of pleasure for the time spent, as the study of paper plans for one's own grounds.

Ignorant gardeners, and self-sufficient business men who know nothing about gardening, are apt to indulge in ridicule of this paper gardening, but it is the ridicule only which is ridiculous. Architecture, in execution, becomes a matter of stone, brick, mortar, wood, and iron, but who, except an ignoramus, would expect the skillful architect to devote himself to the handling of these materials, instead of to his books, his pictures, and his drawing-board? Good garden designs necessitate the same kind of thought, and taste, and careful comparison of different plans, and consideration of expense, before commencing to handle the materials, that are to be used to carry out the design. The plan must be complete before commencing work on the foundations, whether for architecture or for decorative gardening. The time to do this can best be given during the days and long winter evenings preceding the season for work; and cannot be in those few lovely days of swelling buds, into which so many kinds of spring work are necessarily crowded. If, however, there is any skillful garden designer within reach, we advise, unhesitatingly, his employment. He will do the planning in one-tenth the time that an amateur can, and probably a great deal better, and his services should be paid for as for those of other professional men of education and culture.

If the reader will be governed by our advice, we shall insist on his having a correct map made of the lot upon which he has built, or proposes to build, and plant; showing accurately the location and plan of the house, and all the outbuildings, and the position of every tree or large shrub already growing. Such trees or shrubs should have the breadth of their tops lightly sketched in. Rock boulders, or ledges, which are not to be removed, should also be distinctly platted. The map should be drawn on a scale that will permit of its being pasted on a drawing-board not larger than two feet by three. The best of drawing-paper should be used. It should be moistened, and put on by some draughtsman familiar with the mode of doing it. If a lot 100 x 300 is to be platted on a scale of one-eighth of an inch to a foot, it will cover 12½ x 37½ inches of paper. Scaled one-twelfth of an inch to a foot, the same lot would cover 8⅓ x 25 inches of paper, which would be the best scale for a lot of that length. For a larger lot it would be advisable to reduce the scale to one-sixteenth of an inch to the foot (or sixteen feet to one inch), and for a lot not more than a hundred feet long, or where not more than one hundred feet need to be planned for planting, a scale of four feet to the inch (¼ of an inch to the foot) may be used. It is best to have the scale fourths, eighths, twelfths, or sixteenths an inch, as these divisions of a foot come on all ordinary measuring-rules. There should be a clear margin of at least two inches of paper outside the lot lines; the outer inch to paste the paper to the board, and the inner inch for a margin, when it becomes necessary to cut the paper from the board. A duplicate should be made of this skeleton map, as first made, to keep safely in the house, and as the plans for planting are matured and carried out from the board, or 'field map', the house map should have such work platted upon it, in duplicate. The map which is pasted to the board may be materially protected from damage by rain, wet grass, or dirt, to which it may be exposed during the planting season, by covering it with ordinary transparent tracing linen.

To facilitate the planning or arrangement of the various things to be planted on different parts of the lot, as well as to make the plan more easy to work from in planting, the map should be divided into one-inch squares by ordinary blue lines, and these subdivided into eighth-inch squares by very faint blue lines. Each side of these inch squares will then represent four, eight, twelve, or sixteen feet, according to the scale chosen. One accustomed to the use of a decimal scale, may have the squares made one and one-fourth inches on each side, and then subdivided into tenths, each one of which will then be an eighth-inch. Paper thus ruled for the use of civil-engineers and architects, may be procured at most large stationers. These squares, when the distances they represent are borne in mind, serve as a substitute for measurements on the map. Plate I, which is on a scale of 32 feet to one inch, (our page being too small to admit any larger scale), illustrates the mode in which a map should be made. It will be seen that the intersections of the square lines with the exterior boundaries of the lot are numbered on one side and lettered on another, from the same point, marked *o*. This is to facilitate measurements and references to the intersections. Before proceeding to lay out walks, or to plant from the plan, it will be necessary to have the fence measured and marked in the same way, 1, 2, 3, 4, etc., on two opposite sides of the lot, and A, B, C on the other sides. These marks may be made distinct on the inside of the fence, in some inconspicuous place where they will not mar it.

Now let us suppose that the house and out-buildings have been correctly platted on the map of the lot, as shown on Plate I, and that the walks, trees, shrubs, and flower-beds have been planned and drawn as shown thereon. The first out-door work to be done is to lay out the walks on the ground in conformity to the plan. The front walk is six feet wide. This will be laid out simply by making its center on the center line of the main hall, extended to the front fence, or by taking for the center, at the street, a point two feet to the right of J, (looking towards the house). This walk is here supposed to be made with a stone coping at the sides, (after the manner shown in the vignette of Chapter IV,) terminating eight feet from the front steps, with low pedestals and vases, and a circular stone or gravel area, as shown on the plate. The plan supposes the lot to have a street on the side as well as in front, and that its surface is elevated from two to four feet above the front street.

The rear walk and carriage-road are combined in a roadway eight feet wide, four feet on each side of station 17, which is 136 feet ($17 \times 8 = 136$) from the front corner. By counting the squares (each four feet), the size and form of the graveled space in front of the carriage-house will be readily ascertained. The curves may be made by little stakes or shingle splinters

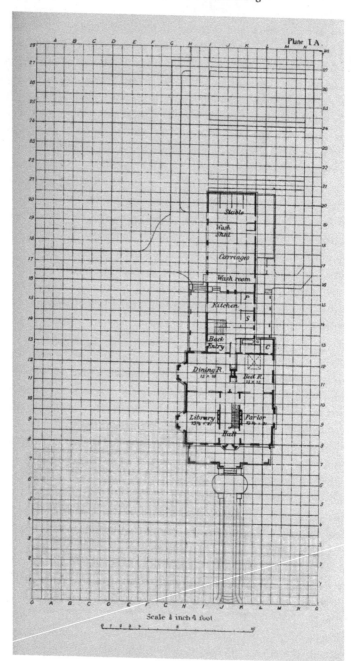

Plate I A.

Stable

Wash
Shed

Carriages

Wash room

Kitchen    P

S

Back
Entry    C

Dining R.    Bed R.
15 x 16    14 x 14

Library    Parlor
15 x 17    12 x 14

Hall

Scale ⅛ inch = 1 foot

stuck until they are satisfactory. The grape walk, which is eight feet between the outside of the trellised posts, is on a right line with the rear part of the house, so that no mistake can be made in its location. The walk at the left is four feet from the trellis, and four feet wide, with a rose or other vine trellis, or a low flower vase, facing its extremity. The walks for the vegetable garden are too simple in their character to need more than mention. They open at three points into the grape walk, by openings or arches under the top slat of the trellis. It will be observed that the carriage-house, stable, and kitchen department of the house are under a continuous roof; a plan that we commend for those gentlemen who keep all things tidy on all parts of their home-grounds, as economical, exceedingly convenient, cleanly, and, in the hands of a good architect, effective in adding to the apparent extent and home-look of the place. But for persons unaccustomed to maintain the same cleanliness around the outbuildings as in the 'front yard', it may not do so well.

The walks being disposed of, let us attend to the planting, and begin with the front. Further on we may describe in detail what trees and shrubs may be especially adapted to the different places here marked; our object now being only to allude to the manner in which the plan, that has been completed on paper, may be worked out on the ground. At $a$, $b$, and $c$ are three pairs of trees, intended to form a short umbrageous approach-avenue to the house. They are all seven feet from the walk; $a\ a$ are two squares, or eight feet from the front; $b\ b$, five squares, or twenty feet; $c\ c$ are eight squares, or thirty-two feet. Flanking these, on the left, is a mass of evergreens, several of which are on the line H, and others on the intersections of squares to the left, as shown by the plan. At the intersection of the lines 2 and A, or sixteen feet from the front, and eight feet from the side fence, is the small tree $f$; at the intersection of 2 and D is a small tree or shrub $e$; and four feet farther right, and four feet nearer the front street, is its companion shrub $e$. The small tree or large shrub $d$, is shown by the squares to be eight feet from the front, and twenty feet from the side street, on the line *1*. The intelligent reader will see how easily the plan for the arrangement of trees and shrubs may be worked out in this manner throughout, and, after a few years' growth and good care of his plantings, ought to realize plainly the superior beauty of a well-considered plan.

# 10

# Walks and Roads

If, as we have insisted, a correct map has been made of the grounds, with all the buildings, and the trees already growing, marked thereon, the next work is to lay out roads or walks upon this map. First, question your wants as to where the street entrances or gates had better be made. This is to be decided principally by the direction of daily travel over them. They should always be in the directions that the family go oftenest, and should be laid out so as to connect most conveniently the street or streets with the entrance doors of the dwelling and outbuildings. *No more walks should be made than are wanted for daily use, either for business or pleasure.* In small grounds, walks made merely for the purpose of having 'pretty walks' meandering among suppositional flower-beds, convey the impression of a desire for show disproportionate to the means of gratifying it. Where there is an acre, or more, of ground devoted to decorative gardening, and it is intended to keep a gardener in constant employ in the care of it, then walks conducting to retired seats, or summer-houses, or made for the purpose of revealing pleasing vistas, or intricacies in the shrubbery, or charming surprises in flowers that may be arranged upon their borders, may add greatly to the beauty of the place. We would not advise having any carriageway to the front entrance of a house, unless the distance is from eighty to one hundred feet between the steps and the street, and on a lot at least one hundred and fifty feet in width. For most residences the front street is near enough for a carriage to approach with visitors and callers, who generally choose fair weather; and the family can go to and from their own vehicles by some of the rear entrances of the house, past which the road from the street to the carriage-house should lead. Where houses are designed so that their main entrance is on the side, then a carriage-road may pass it properly, though the lot should be narrower than the size just mentioned. For lots having such narrow street fronts in proportion to their depth, this is the

best arrangement for the house, as it leaves the finest rooms adjoining each other in the front. See Plates XIII, XXV, and XXVII.

In laying out a carriage-drive avoid sharp turns, and, as far as possible, the segments of circles reversed against each other, as in a geometric letter S. Such parts of circles, though graceful on paper, give the effect of crooked lines, as seen in perspective. A line that will enable the driver to approach the main steps most conveniently is the true line, unless trees or shrubs already growing prevent, in which case the same rule must be followed as nearly as practicable. By the most convenient approach is meant that which a skillful driver would make if he were driving over an unbroken lawn from the entrance-gate to the porch.

Nearly all amateur landscape-gardeners will blunder in their first attempts to lay out roads or walks, by making the curves too decided. The lines most graceful on paper will not appear so in perspective, as we walk along them, and it will not do, therefore, in laying them out on a paper plat, to suppose they will appear the same on the ground. If grounds were to be seen from a balloon the effect would be the same as upon your plan, but as we are all destined to look along the ground, instead of vertically down upon it, it will be seen why curves that look graceful on paper are likely to be too abrupt and crooked in perspective. If the reader will place the paper plan nearly on a level with his eye, and glance along the line of the proposed road or walk, he will be able to judge how his curves will seem as seen when walking towards or upon them; supposing, of course, that the ground to be platted has a tolerably level surface. There are several of the plans which follow whereon the walks will have the appearance, at first sight, of being awkwardly direct, having neither the simplicity of a straight line, nor the grace of Hogarth's line of beauty, but if the hint just given about glancing along the line of the walk with the eye nearly on a level with the paper is followed, they will be found more pleasing.

There are many places where the house is large compared with the size of the lot, on which straight walks are not only admissible, but where to attempt curved walks would be ridiculous. Some of the succeeding plans will illustrate such. The vignette of Chapter IV illustrates an elegant approach of this kind, over which trees have formed a noble arch. Steps and copings of cut stone, with pedestals and vases, may be designed to make such entrances as beautiful architecturally as the means of the proprietor will justify. The mere platting of walks on such places is too simple a matter to require any suggestions here. All foot-walks should approach the entrance steps either at right angles or parallel with them, and in all cases should start at right angles with the line of the entrance gate.

The width of roads and walks must vary according to the extent of the grounds and the character of the house. For a cottage with small grounds, make the walks narrow rather than wide. The apparent size of the ground will be diminished by too ambitious walks. But there are limits of convenience. A broad walk always gives one a sense of freedom and ease, which is wanting when we must keep our eyes down to avoid straying from the narrow way. For small places, therefore, we must compromise between the prettier external effect of narrow walks and the greater convenience of wide ones. Four feet is the least width appropriate for a cottage main walk, and two feet for the rear walks. But for most town or suburban places, from four to six feet for the main walk and three feet for the rear walks, are appropriate widths. It is essential, however, that no shrubbery or flower-beds approach nearer than two feet from them. A walk three feet wide, with two feet of closely-shaven lawn on each side of it, is really just as commodious as a walk six feet wide closely bordered or overhung by rank annuals or gross shrubs. At the foot of the steps it is desirable to have greater width than in other parts of the walk.

The width of carriage-drives should be governed by the same considerations as the walks. Eight feet is the least width, and fourteen feet the greatest, that will be appropriate to the class of places for which this book is designed, and whatever the width elsewhere, it should not be less than twelve feet opposite the main entrance steps, unless it traverses a porte-cochere. The turnway in front of the main entrance should be on a radius of not less than ten feet to the inner line of the road, and more if space permits; but not to exceed a radius of twenty feet, unless the location of trees or the shape of the ground make it specially desirable to turn a larger circuit.

Opportunities to make or lose pleasing effects are always presented where there are trees or shrubs already grown. To conduct walks or roads so as to make them seem to have grown there; to arrange a gateway under branches of trees or between old shrubs, or leading around or between them; to have walks divide so that a tree shall mark their intersection; to weave a turnway smoothly among old tree trunks – all such arts as these are precisely the small things which prove the taste, or lack of it, in the designer.

In making the carriage-road and the walks, there is an immense difference in expense between excessive thoroughness and the 'good enough' style. Digging out from a foot and a half to two feet of the soil the whole width of the road or walk, tile-draining on each side, then filling up with broken stone or scoriae, and finally covering the surface with several inches of pure gravel, and paving the gutters with pebbles, is the thorough style. But on sandy and gravelly soils we have seen excellent walks and roads (for light carriages) made by simply covering the ground with from two to three inches of good gravel or slate. The preparation necessary for this kind of road-making being to excavate below the level of the border, so as to leave a rounded surface with tile of three to four inches diameter, placed in the bottom of trenches on each side, as shown by the accompanying sketch. Four inches thickness of gravel on a road thus prepared will, with proper care, make an excellent road. On clay, roads can be made with no more additional preparation than to provide for a few more inches of gravel.

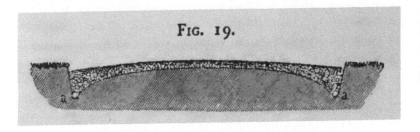

FIG. 19.

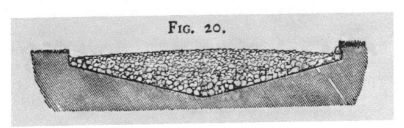

FIG. 20.

Fig. 20 shows a suitable form for such a roadway. Of course the grades of the roads lengthwise must be such as to carry the water in the gutters and drains to proper outlets. We suggest this method of road-making for those sections of the country where stone is costly, and for those improvers who cannot afford to use a large amount of money in road foundations.

The main thing to secure good walks or roads is constant care. Weeds and grass must be kept from encroaching by the use of the hoe and edging-spade; the gravel must be kept in place by the use of the rake and roller. No thoroughness of construction will make such care needless, and by it the least expensive walks and roads may be kept in excellent condition at small cost.

Solid stone flagging, if neatly dressed, is of course preferable for walks to gravel, and will be used where it can be afforded. Where the asphaltum or coal-tar composition, now used with great success for walks in the Central Park, can be put down by some one thoroughly conversant with the mode of doing it well, it will be found a very fine material, but while green it involves much risk to carpets. Where the soil is clay, and good gravel or composition not easily obtained, (as in many parts of the western states), and flagging is too expensive, seasoned white pine board or plank walks may be substituted. These, if carefully laid, (across the line of the walk), and the edges sawed to the requisite curves or straight lines, make very comfortable walks. The main difficulty is to find mechanics who will have skill and patience to put them down in the graceful curved lines that are desired. Inch lumber, daubed on the under side with hot coal-tar to postpone rotting, will answer very well for walks from two to three feet wide. For wider ones two-inch plank is recommended.

Pine walks, if made of good stuff, and tarred as suggested, will last from eight to ten years, and if sufficient care is used in their construction, will be found very satisfactory substitutes for stone or gravel, even for curved lines. For straight walks they are always satisfactory as long as sound. In districts where stone and gravel are scarce and dear, they must long continue in use, and there is no reason why they should not be shaped into graceful forms, since wood is so much more facile to work than stone. Several methods of preserving wood from decay are now attracting great attention, and it is believed that some of them will be effectual to so increase the durability of wood that its use for walks will be far more desirable than heretofore. It is essential in all walks that the sod shall be about an inch above the outer surface of the walk, so that a scythe or rolling mower may do its work unobstructed in passing near or over them.

To lay out the carriage-drive and the walks in conformity to the paper plat that has been made, is a work requiring some patience and skill. There are persons whose love for beautiful effects in landscape-gardening is evident, who are so wanting in what is called a mechanical eye, as to be incompetent to lay out their own grounds, even with a plat before them. If you, kind reader, are one of those, send for the nearest good gardener to do the work for you; or invite some friend or neighbor, who has given evidence of this talent by the making of his own place, to come and help you. He will not be likely to turn away from your appreciation of his taste and skill. If, however, your ground is large enough to admit of much length of walks, the labor of laying them out would more properly devolve upon a professional gardener – if such there be in your neighborhood. It will not, however, be advisable to listen to all the suggestions of improvements that any 'professional gardener' may volunteer for your guidance. Genuine landscape-gardeners are rare everywhere, and bear about the same proportion to good common gardeners that accomplished landscape-painters do to house-painters. The probabilities are that your neighborhood has some gardener competent to plat walks, lay turf, cut your shrubbery-beds, and do your planting, but, ten chances to one, he will lay more stress on the form of some curlecue of a flower-bed than on those beautiful effects of rich foliage and open glades – of shadow and sunlight – that are often produced with the simplest means by Dame Nature or the true landscape-artist. If, therefore, you have a well-matured plan, and the gardener is competent to study it intelligently, let him make suggestions of changes before the work on the ground commences, but thereafter oblige him either to work faithfully to your plan, or else furnish you with a better one, and do not let him bluff you into an entire surrender by his professional sneers at paper plans. Of course these remarks are intended to apply to the common run of illiterate gardeners, who have happened to make a trade of this species of labor, and not to another class who may have chosen the profession from a love for it, and who have intelligence or imagination enough to understand something of the art of arranging their sylvan and floral materials so as to make pictures with them.

Almost every neighborhood has a few gentlemen of superior taste in such matters, whose dictums will, perforce, help to educate the common run of self-sufficient gardeners, and it is hoped that so promising a field of labor will soon attract the attention of Americans of the highest culture, to whom we can turn for professional work in ground designs; who, as Pope describes one,

Consults the genius of the place in all
That tells the waters or to rise or fall;
Or helps the ambitious hill the heavens to scale,
Or scoops in circling theatres the vale:
Calls in the country, catches opening glades,
Joins willing woods, and varies shades from shades;
Now breaks or now directs the intending lines,
Paints as you plant, and, as you work, designs!

# 11

# Arrangement in Planting

Though set rules, in matters of art, are sometimes 'more honored in the breach than in the observance', it is also true that every art has certain general principles, the observance of which will rarely lead to great faults, while their violations may. We therefore hope that the following suggestions or rules, drawn to meet the requirements of small suburban grounds, will be of some use, and serve as a starting-point for that higher culture which educates the intuitive perceptions of the artist to dispense with rules, or rather, perhaps, *to work intuitively by rule*, as an aesthetic instinct.

I. Preserve in one or more places (according to the size and form of the lot) the greatest length of unbroken lawn that the space will admit of.

II. Plant between radiating lines from the house to the outside of the lot, so as to leave open lines of view from the principal windows and entrance porches; also find where, without injuring the views to and from the house, the best vistas may be left from the street into the lot, and from one point to another across the grounds, or to points of interest beyond.

III. Plant the larger trees and shrubs farthest from the centre of the lawn, so that the smaller may be seen to advantage in front of them.

IV. On small lots plant no trees which quickly attain great size, if it is intended to have a variety of shrubs or flowers.

V. In adding to belts or groups of trees or shrubs, plant near the salient points, rather than in bays or openings.

VI. Shrubs which rest upon the lawn should not be planted nearer than from six to ten feet from the front fence, except where intended to form a continuous screen of foliage.

## RULE I

*Preserve in one or more places* (according to the size and form of the lot) *the greatest length of unbroken lawn that the space will admit of.*

To illustrate this rule we ask the reader's attention to some of the plates. Plate No. IV represents in the simplest manner one mode of observing it. It is a lot of fifty feet front, and considerable depth, isolated from the adjoining properties on both sides by a close fence or hedge. On it is a small compact house, thrown back so as to leave about eighty feet depth between it and the street. Each bay-window of the principal rooms has a look-out upon all the beauty that may be created on this small space. To economize ground for the greatest extent of lawn possible on this lot, the main walk to the house is entirely on one side of it and of the line of view out of the bay-windows over the lawn, and leads directly to the main veranda entrance. From the bay-windows to the street, in a right line between them, not a tree, shrub, or flower is to be planted. If the grounds were of greater extent, it would be desirable to have the views out of each of these windows different from the other, so that in going from one room to the other, and looking out upon the lawn, it would exhibit a fresh picture. But to attempt to divide this lawn into two by a middle line of shrubbery would belittle both, and crowd the shrubbery so that nothing could be seen to advantage. The lot is quite too small to attempt a variety of views, and the lawn is made to look as large as possible by placing all trees and shrubbery on the margin; in short, the greatest length and breadth of lawn that the lot will admit of is preserved. Plate VII shows a village lot of the same frontage as the preceding, but on which the house is only twenty-five feet from the street. There can be no good breadth of lawn on this lot, since the house occupies the ground that forms the lawn on Plate No. IV. But a peculiar little vista over narrow strips of lawn skirting the walk is obtained on entering the front gate. This is upwards of one hundred feet in length, and widens out around the flower-bed S, so that in perspective, and contrasted with the length and narrowness of the strips of lawn near the house, it will give the effect of greater distance and width than it has. Such a plan as this requires the most skillful planting and high keeping. Indeed, there is more need of skill to make this narrow strip a pretty work of art than on the larger lots that are planned for this work. Plates XIV and XV show corner lots also of fifty feet front, with houses entirely on one side of the lot, and lawns as long as the depth will admit of, margined by assorted small shrubs and clipped trees. On the former the house is placed against the side street, leaving the lawn on the inside, and a pleasing vista over it to an archway that opens into a long grape arbor. This will make a lengthened perspective of lawn and garden as great as the size of the lot will allow. On Plate XV the house is placed so as to leave the lawn space between it and the side street, and the main garden walk is arranged so that from the back veranda and the library windows it will form a little perspective. The latter plan, it will be seen, is for a city basement-house, while the former has a kitchen on the main floor. Plates Nos V and VI are of lots 60 x 150 feet, where the lawns occupy as great a length as can be spared for decorative purposes. These side lawns are no wider than those of Plates XIV and XV, as the additional ten feet width of lot, on the right, is shut out of view, and devoted to small fruits. This strip in the hands of a garden artist might be made very charming in itself, but where one man would make it so, a thousand would fail. We therefore advise in general riot to plant anything against the walls of the house in such narrow strips as these, unless they have the most sunny exposure. In towns, where lots of this size are built on, other houses are usually so near such improvements, as to darken the ground with their shade. The degree of exposure to the sun and air in these places must govern their use, but in general it is better to have either grass or pavement in them, or a paved walk and bedding plants, that may be renewed from a greenhouse. Plate XIII shows a lot of one hundred and sixty feet front by three hundred feet deep, on which a vista of unbroken lawn, the entire depth of the lot, is obtained from the main entrance. This place is supposed to adjoin lots whose fronts are improved in common, so that each of the principal windows of the house is provided with a distinct foreground for a picture, the middle distance of which will have such character as the neighboring improvements make. Were the ground improved to conform to this plan the effect would be much finer than the rather formal character of the trees in the design would indicate.

Plates X and XI are of lots two hundred feet front by three hundred feet deep. On the former, the rule we are endeavoring to illustrate is sacrificed in a measure to the requirements of an orchard and kitchen-garden; on the latter, the orchard is given up to secure the beauty of a more extended lawn and more elaborate plantation.

On Plate XXVII are some good illustrations of this rule applied to the laying out of what are usually considered awkward forms of lots to improve. It will be seen that the views from the street-corner, at the point A, on the right-hand plan looking towards the house, and in other directions, are long, open, and well varied, in the grouping of trees, shrubs, and flowers. As one walks along to B and C, at each opening between groups of shrubs the views are over the longest stretch of lawn that the size of the lot will admit of; while the views from the main windows of the house, and from the front and rear verandas, are as extended as possible.

Plate XXII, which is designed to illustrate the advantage of joining neighboring improvements, however cheap or simple their character, is an excellent illustration of the beauty and gardenesque effect that may be secured by leaving an unbroken vista of lawn and low flowers from one side of a block to the other, as shown on the line B C, though the block is covered by five inexpensive residences. The vignette of Chapter IV is a view taken from the point A, and gives but two-thirds of the length of view that is seen from either of the side streets. Of course the flowers to be planted in the beds on the lawn in the above line of view, should be only those which grow within a few inches of the ground; otherwise the effect intended would be marred.

Plate XXIX is a good example, on a larger scale, of long and open views.

Plate XXI is an illustration of the rule to which we ask the reader's attention, as an example of triple vistas on a lot only one hundred feet wide; first, that formed by the small shrubs and flowers bordering the main walk, with the terrace steps and the house bounding the view at one end, and a hemlock archway at the other. From the bay-windows of the house the two other divisions of the lawn are designed to show to the best advantage, and over the low clipped parts of the front hedge, at *a a*, made low for this purpose, their beauty can also be seen by passers on the street.

## RULE II

*Plant between radiating lines from the house to the outside of the lot, so as to leave open lines of view from the principal windows and entrance porches; also find where, without injuring the views, to and from the house, the best vistas may be left from the street into the lot, and from one point to another across the grounds, or to points of interest beyond.*

The accompanying plan, adapted from Loudon, gives a good illustration of the observance of the second rule. The plan represents the part of a lot in the rear of the dwelling, all of which is devoted to lawn and decorative planting; the entrance-front being close to the street. The plantation is supposed to be entirely secluded from the street and from contiguous properties by walls. The space covered is about 150 x 300 feet. The dotted lines radiating from the bow-window show the apparently loose, but really well studied distribution of groups of trees and shrubs in radiating lines. On the right, one of these groups forms a screen of shrubbery to divide the lawn from the elaborate flower-garden which forms the distinctive feature of the view from the dining-room window. On smaller lots the first part of the second rule cannot be illustrated with so much effect, but a general conformity to it may be observed in many of our larger plans.

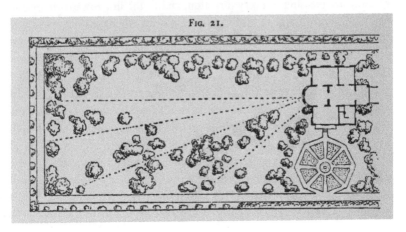

FIG. 21.

Plate II represents a lot one hundred and fifty feet front by two hundred and fifty deep, where the house is placed much nearer the front of the lot, and nearly in the centre. So placed, the longest views over its lawn cannot be obtained from the house in any direction, but from many points in the front street, and within the grounds, the lines of view are as long and unbroken as the size of the lot will admit of; while a partial privacy is given to the space between the bay-windows and the side street, by a close plantation of hedge and shrubbery. Openness, rather than privacy, is the characteristic of this plan, however, and its best views are obtained on entering or passing it. Yet the lawn, as seen from the bay-windows, will be broken by shrubs and trees into a much greater variety of views than a careless examination of the plan would lead one to suppose. From 0, at the intersection of the two streets, the eye ranges between two near groups of shrubbery, which frame the view over the lawn to the bay-windows, and on the right, in front of the back veranda, between slender conical trees, a flowerbed and a pyramid of roses, under the shade of fruit trees in the backyard, to the carriage-house front: a distance equal to the entire length of the lot. From the point marked 2, the view changes; the croquet-ground, and the intervening compact shrubs and flower-beds, and an evergreen group at $g$, come into view. Or the eye rests on the near group of shrubs opposite Fig. 3; or to the left, ranges to the various groups on that side of the grounds. At Fig. 5 the view on the right, of the trees, hedge, and shrubbery, from $g$ to $w$, together with pleasing views in other directions, make this point the one from which the whole place is seen to the best advantage. The views through the archway of trees over the front gateway are pleasing in every direction, and in the line towards $u$, extend nearly the entire length of the lot. This form of lot, when the house is so near the centre, is less adapted to illustrate the rule under consideration than most others, and we have pointed out its peculiarities in this connection to show the effort to conform to the rule under adverse circumstances. The reader will please to observe on this plan a dotted line from $d$ to the left, parallel with the front street. This is forty feet from the front. Within a distance from ten to fifty feet from such fronts is usually the part which should be left unplanted, in order that all the places in the block may, on that line, form a continuous lawn of such park-like character as no one lot could furnish. Most of our plans are designed in this manner to secure the advantages of associate improvements, and 'views from one point to another across the grounds, or to some point of interest beyond the grounds.'

## RULE III

*Plant the larger trees and shrubs farthest from the centre of the lawn, so that the smaller may be seen to advantage in front of them.*

The necessity of observing the third rule, in small places, is so obvious, and it is so easy to follow, if one but knows the character of the trees and shrubs he is using, that few remarks upon it are necessary. The vignette at the head of this chapter is intended as an illustration of the great number and variety of shrubs and small trees which may be exhibited in a single group, in such a manner that each may show its peculiar beauty without concealing any of the others, and at the same time form a harmonious collection. Not less than twenty species of trees and shrubs may be seen at once in such a group, each growing to a perfect development of its best form; while by a different arrangement in planting, the beauties of all the smaller shrubs might be lost to the eye, and their growth marred by the domineering habits of the larger ones. It will be noticed that in this vignette the weeping elm forms the centre of the group. Close to it may be planted some of the large shrubs which flourish in partial shade and under the drip of trees. Outside of these a few of the smallest class of trees, of peculiar and diverse forms, and then the smaller and finer shrubbery arranged to carry out the spirit of the rule. No engraving, however, can do justice to the variety of character in foliage, flowers, forms, and colors, that such a group may be made to exhibit.

## RULE IV

*On small lots plant no trees which quickly attain great size, if it is intended to have a variety of shrubs or flowers.*

The fourth rule is somewhat difficult to illustrate, because of the frequency with which good taste may insist on exceptions to it. Few suburban places are so small that one or two large trees, not far from the house, will not add greatly to their home-look and summer comfort. Trees which overhang the house and form a background, or vernal frame-work for it, are the crowning beauty of a home picture. But, in planting small lots, the need of a few fruit trees, such as cherries and pears, which one cannot well do without, and which, for the safety of the fruit, must be near or behind the house, is a necessity that obliges us to dispense with the grandeur of great trees where their beauty is most effective, and to endeavor to develop another type of beauty for small places, viz.: that of artistic elegance in the treatment of small things. And it is some satisfaction to know that, with the latter, what we attempt may be achieved in a few years, while, if we set about planting to secure the nobler effect of large trees, a life-time will be required to see its consummation. Where any large tree is already growing, the style of planting must conform to its position, size, and character, but where the plantation is on a bare site, the rule is a proper one to follow. In the former case the fine tree is to be considered 'master of the situation', and all things are to be arranged with due regard to it; but in the latter there is an open field for the taste and judgment.

## RULE V

*In adding to belts or groups of trees or shrubs, plant near the salient points, rather than in bays or openings.*

The fifth rule is one which novices in planting are always violating. It is such a temptation to plant a tree or shrub 'where there is most room for it', and 'where it will show handsomely', that the ignorant planter at once selects some clear place on his lawn, or some open bay, for the new comer; quite forgetful that a few such plantings will break the prettiest of lawns into insignificant fragments, and change the sunny projections and shadowy bays of a shrubbery border into a lumpish wall of verdure.

The placement of large and showy bedding plants or annuals and perennials must be made on the same principle. They are to be regarded as shrubs, and the places for them must be determined by their usual size at midsummer.

Low-growing flowers, or brilliant-leaved and bushy plants, may occasionally be relieved to advantage in the shady bays of a shrubbery border, especially if a walk leads near them, but in general, flower-beds (except such as are formed into artistic groups as a special feature of a window-view), should be either near walks or the points of shrubbery projections. Like gay flags on a parade ground, they show to best advantage in the van of the advanced columns.

## RULE VI

*Shrubs which rest upon the lawn should not be planted nearer than from six to ten feet from the front fence, except where intended to form a continuous screen of foliage.*

The sixth rule is one which may not be practicable to follow on very small lots, or where the space is narrow between the house and the street, but there would be a marked improvement in the appearance of most places by its observance. In the first place, the shrubs themselves, which, it must be supposed, are only planted because they are beautiful, will show to much better advantage with this introductory lawn or foreground to spread upon. To crowd against a fence groups of shrubs which will bend gracefully to the lawn on every side if room is given them, is much like the misplacement of elegant robes in a crowd, where they may be injured, but can never be seen to advantage. Such a strip of introductory lawn is to the ground what a broad threshold stone is to the house entrance, giving the place a generous air, and seeming to say that the proprietor is not so stinted for room that he must needs crowd his sylvan company into the street. Yet it must frequently happen that the exigencies of small or peculiarly shaped lots, require a violation of this rule, in order to secure sufficient breadth of lawn within, to present a good appearance from the house. The plans on Plates XXII, XXIII, XXIV, and XXVII, are examples of this necessity. Plates II, XII, XIII, and XVIII, on the other hand, show a general attention to the rule; while in the other plans it is kept in view more or less, as the circumstances of each case seem to require.

There is another matter which can hardly be made the subject of any rules, but yet demands the attention of every planter. Nearly all trees and shrubs are more beautiful on their southerly than on their northerly sides, and some trees which glow with beauty towards the sun are meagre and unsightly towards the north. This fact must therefore be borne in mind in deciding where to plant favorite trees or shrubs, so that their fairest sides may be towards those points from which they will be most seen, and as there are a few varieties and species of trees which are beautiful on all sides – the box and hemlock, for instance – they may be placed in locations where the others will not show to advantage.

# 12

# Relative Beauty of Lawn, Trees, Shrubs, and Flowers

The true lover of nature is so omnivorous in his tastes, that for him to classify her family into different grades of usefulness or beauty, is about as difficult a task as to name which of her vegetable productions is the best food. But though a variety is better than any one, there is, in both cases, strong ground for a decided choice, and we repeat what has already been suggested, that, of all the external decorations of a home, a well kept Lawn is the most essential. Imagine the finest trees environing a dwelling, but everywhere beneath them only bare ground: then picture the same dwelling with a velvet greensward spreading away from it on all sides, without a tree or shrub upon it, and choose which is the most pleasing to the eye. The question of value is not to be considered, but simply which, in connection with the dwelling, will make the most satisfactory impression on the mind. The fine trees are vastly the more valuable, because it requires half a life-time to obtain them, while the lawn may be perfected in two or three years.

The comparative value of trees and shrubs depends much on the extent of the ground and the taste of the occupants. If the lot is small, and the family has a decided appreciation of the varied characteristics of different shrubs, they will have much more pleasure from a fine collection of them than from the few trees which their lot could accommodate. But if the occupants are not particularly appreciative of the varied beauties of smaller vegetation, then a few trees and a good lawn only, will be more appropriate for their home. Larger lots can have both, but the foregoing consideration may govern the preponderance of one or the other. When once the planting fever is awakened, *too many of both are likely to be planted*, and grounds will be stuffed rather than beautified.

One full grown oak, elm, maple, chestnut, beech, or sycamore will cover with its branches nearly a quarter of an acre. Allowing seventy feet square for the spread of each tree (all the above varieties being occasionally much

larger), nine such trees would completely cover an acre. But as we plant for ourselves, instead of for our children, it will be sufficient in most suburban planting to allow for half-grown, rather than full-grown trees. Grounds, however, which are blessed with grand old trees should have them cherished lovingly – they are treasures that money cannot buy – and should be guarded with jealous care against the admission of little evergreens and nursery trees, which new planters are apt to huddle under and around them, to the entire destruction of the broad stretches of lawn which large trees require in order to reveal the changing beauty of their shadows. Where such trees exist, if you would make the most of the ground, lavish your care in enriching the soil over their vast roots, and perfecting the lawn around them, and then arrange for shrubs and flowers away from their mid-day shadows. Even fine old fruit trees, if standing well apart on a lawn, will often give a dignity and a comfortable home-look to a place that is wanting in places which are surrounded only with new plantings.

But it is an unfortunate fact that nine-tenths of all the town and suburban lots built on are bare of trees, and therefore, after the attainment of a fine lawn, the lowly beauties of shrubs and flowers, with all their varied luxuriance of foliage and fragrant bloom, must be the main features of the place, while the trees are also growing in their midst which may eventually over-top and supersede them. If one could imagine Americans to live their married lives, each pair in one home, what a pleasing variety might the changing years bring them. An unbroken lawn around the dwelling should typify the unwritten page in the opening book of earnest life. Young trees planted here and there upon it would suggest looking forward to the time when, under their grand shadows, the declining years of the twain may be spent in dignity and repose. Flowers and shrubs meanwhile repay with grateful beauty all their care, until, overshadowed by the nobler growth, they are removed as cumberers of the ground, and give way to the simplicity that becomes 'a fine old home'.

Most small places can be much more charmingly planted with shrubs alone, than with trees and shrubs mingled. Indeed, it is one of the greatest blunders of inexperienced planters to put in trees where there is only room enough for shrubs. A small yard may be made quite attractive by the artistic management of shrubs and flowers whose size is adapted to the contracted ground, but the same place would be so filled up by the planting of a cherry tree or a horse-chestnut, that no such effect could be produced.

Where the decorative portion of the grounds do not exceed a half-acre, there can be little question of the superior beauty of shrubberies to the very small collection of trees that such narrow limits can accommodate. The greatly increased beauty of shrubs when seen upon a lawn without any shadowing of trees, nor crowded one side or another 'to fill-up', can only be appreciated by those who have seen the elegance of a tastefully arranged place planted with shrubs alone.

The part which annuals and low growing flowers should have in home surroundings may be compared with the lace, linen, and ribbon decorations of a lady's dress – being essential ornaments, and yet to be introduced sparingly. Walks may be bordered, and groups pointed, and bays in the shrubbery brightened by them; or geometrically arranged groups of flower-beds may be introduced in the foreground of important window views, but beware of frequently breaking open stretches of lawn for them. Imagine bits of lace or bows of ribbon stuck promiscuously over the body and skirt of a lady's dress. 'How vulgar!' you exclaim. Put them in their appropriate places and what charming points they make! Let your lawn be your home's velvet robe, and your flowers its not too promiscuous decorations.

Of constructive garden decorations (in which are included pillars and trellises for vines, screens, arbors, summer-houses, seats, rock-work, terraces, vases, fountains, and statuary), and their comparative value, we will merely say that really tasteful and durable ornamentation of that kind is rather expensive, and therefore to be weighed well in the balance with expenditures of the same money for other modes of embellishment before ordering such work.

The following remarks from Kemp's admirable little work on Landscape Gardening express our views so fully that we will give them entire: (This is an English work entitled 'How to lay out a Garden', a work so complete and well condensed, that were it not for the difference in the climate, and in the style of living (and consequently of the plans of dwellings, and their outbuildings and garden connections), which English thoroughness and cheaper labor make practicable, there had been no need of this book):

> A garden may also be overloaded with a variety of things which, though ornamental in themselves, and not at all out of keeping with the house, or the principal elements of the landscape, may yet impart to it an affected or ostentatious character. An undue introduction of sculptured or other figures, vases, seats, and arbors, baskets for plants, and such like objects, will come within the limits of this description. And there is nothing of which people in general are so intolerant in others, as the attempt, when glaringly and injudiciously made, to crowd within a confined space the appropriate adornments of the most ample garden. It is invariably taken as evidence of a desire to appear to be and to possess that which the reality of the case will not warrant, and is visited with the reprobation and contempt commonly awarded to ill-grounded assumption. An unpresuming garden, like a modest individual, may have great defects without challenging criticism, and will even be liked and praised because of its very unobtrusiveness. But where a great deal is attempted, and there is much of pretension, whether in persons or things, scrutiny seems invited, incongruities are magnified, and actual merits are passed by unnoticed, or distorted into something quite ridiculous.

The improver must decide, before he begins to plan for planting, what the size and features of his lot, and his own circumstances, will enable him to accomplish most perfectly.

If there are trees or shrubs already of good size growing on the lot, the first study should be to develop and exhibit all their traits to the best advantage, and to this end a rich soil and a perfected lawn are the most essential.

If the lot is bare of trees, a smooth surface and fine lawn are still ground-works precedent to planting, whether the lot be large or small. If large enough, choose among large trees the principal features of its embellishment; if less than an acre, plant sparingly trees of the first class; if a rood, or but little more, then lawn, shrubs and flowers should be its only verdant furniture.

We class among shrubs many dwarf evergreens, which, because they belong to species which usually attain large size, are included in nursery catalogues under the head of trees. They will be found classified in our Appendix. We also regard as shrubs, in effect, those vigorous growing annuals or perennials like the ricinus, cannas, dahlias, and hollyhocks, which grow too high to be seen over, and which cast shadows on the lawn near them.

# 13
## The Lawn

Whether we look, or whether we listen,
We hear life murmur, or see it glisten;
Every clod feels a stir of might,
    An instinct within it that reaches and towers,
And, groping blindly above it for light.
    Climbs to a soul in grass and flowers.

*Lowell*

On each side shrinks the bowery shade,
Before me spreads an emerald glade;
The sunshine steeps its grass and moss,
That couch my footsteps as I cross.

*Alfred B. Street*

A smooth, closely shaven surface of grass is by far the most essential element of beauty on the grounds of a suburban home. Dwellings, all the rooms of which may be filled with elegant furniture, but with rough uncarpeted floors, are no more incongruous, or in ruder taste, than the shrub and tree and flower-sprinkled yards of most home-grounds, where shrubs and flowers mingle in confusion with tall grass, or ill-defined borders of cultivated ground. Neatness and order are as essential to the pleasing effect of ground furniture as of house furniture. No matter how elegant or appropriate the latter may be, it will never look well in the home of a slattern. And however choice the variety of shrubs and flowers, if they occupy the ground so that there is no pleasant expanse of close-cut grass to relieve them, they cannot make a pretty place. The long grass allowed to grow in town and suburban grounds, after the spring gardening fever is over, neutralizes to a certain degree all attempts of the lady or gentleman of the house to beautify them, though they spend ever so much

in obtaining the best shrubs, trees, or flowers the neighbors or the nurseries can furnish. It is not necessary to have an acre of pleasure ground to secure a charming lawn. Its extent may always be proportioned to the size of the place, and if the selection of flowers and shrubs and their arrangement is properly made, it is surprising how small a lawn will realize some of the most pleasing effects of larger ones. A strip twenty feet wide and a hundred feet long may be rendered, proportionally, as artistic as the landscape vistas of a park.

And it needs but little more to have room to realize by art, and with shadowing trees, the sparkling picture that the poet, Alfred B. Street, thus presents in his 'Forest Walk'.

> A narrow vista, carpeted
> With rich green grass, invites my tread:
> Here showers the light in golden dots,
> There sleeps the shade in ebon spots,
> So blended that the very air
> Seems net-work as I enter there.

To secure a good lawn, a rich soil is as essential as for the kitchen garden. On small grounds the quickest and best way of making a lawn is by turfing. There are few neighborhoods where good turf cannot be obtained in pastures or by roadsides. No better varieties of grass for lawns can be found than those that form the turf of old and closely fed pastures. Blue-grass and white clover are the staple grasses in them, though many other varieties are usually found with these, in smaller proportions.

The ground should be brought to as smooth slopes or levels as possible before laying the turf, as much of the polished beauty of a perfected lawn will depend on this precaution. If the ground has been recently spaded or manured, it should be heavily tramped or rolled before turfing, to guard against uneven settling. A tolerably compact soil makes a closer turf than a light one. Marly clay is probably the best soil for grass, though far less agreeable for gardening operations generally than a sandy loam. After compacting the soil to prevent uneven settling, a few inches on top must be lightly raked to facilitate laying the turf, and the striking of new roots. Before winter begins all newly laid turf should be covered with a few inches of manure. After the ground settles in the spring this should be raked off with a fine-toothed rake, and the lawn then well rolled. The manure will have protected the grass from the injurious effect of sudden freezing and thawing in the winter and early spring, and the rich washings from it gives additional color and vigor to the lawn the whole season. The manure raked from the grass is just what is needed to dig into the beds for flowers and shrubs, or for mulching trees. This fall manuring is essential to newly set turf, and is scarcely less beneficial if repeated every year. Cold soap-suds applied from a sprinkling-pot or garden-hose when rains are abundant, is the finest of summer manure for grass. If applied in dry weather it should be diluted with much additional water. The old rhyme –

Clay on sand manures the land,
Sand on clay is thrown away

is eminently true in relation to the growth of grass. The clay should always be applied late in autumn.

If grounds are so large that turfing is too expensive, the soil should be prepared as recommended above for turfing, and seeded as early in the spring as the ground can be thoroughly prepared and settled. If the surface has been prepared the preceding autumn, then it will be found a good practice to sow the grass seed upon a thin coating of snow which falls frequently early in

March. Seed can be sown more evenly on snow, because better seen, than on the ground.

A variety of opinions prevail concerning the best grasses for seeding. It will be safe to say that for lawns timothy and red clover are totally unsuited, and that the grasses which make the best pastures in the neighborhood, will make the best lawns. The following mixture for one bushel of seed is recommended in Henderson's Manual of Floriculture, viz:

12 quarts Rhode Island Bent Grass.
4 quarts creeping Bent Grass.
10 quarts Red-top.
3 quarts Sweet Vernal Grass.
2 quarts Kentucky Blue Grass.
1 quart White Clover.

We have seen very successful lawns made with equal parts, *by weight*, of Kentucky blue grass, red-top, and white clover seed. The quantity required is about a half bushel to each one hundred feet square.

When rains are frequent, *no lawn can be brought to perfection if cut less often than once a week*, and two weeks is the longest time a lawn should remain uncut, except in periods of total suspension of growth by severe drouth. Where shrubs and flowers are placed properly, there will always be clear space enough to swing a lawn scythe or roll a lawn machine. Only in the most contracted yards should there be nooks and corners, or strips of grass, that an ordinary mower cannot get at easily, and without endangering either the plants or his temper. Places that are so cluttered with flowers, trees, and shrubs that it becomes a vexatious labor for a good mower to get in among them, are certainly not well planted. Good taste, therefore, in arrangement, will have for its first and durable fruits, economy, a product of excellent flavor for all who desire to create beauty around their homes, but who can ill afford to spend much money to effect it, or to waste any in failing to effect it. The advice to plant so as to leave sufficient breadth to swing a scythe wherever there is any lawn at all, is none the less useful, though the admirable little hand-mowing machines take the place of the scythe; for a piece of lawn in a place where a scythe cannot be swung, is not worth maintaining.

Rolling mowers by horse or hand power have been principally employed on large grounds, but the hand machines are now so simplified and cheapened that they are coming into general use on small pleasure grounds, and proprietors may have the pleasure of doing their own mowing without the wearisome bending of the back, incident to the use of the scythe. Whoever spends the early hours of one summer, while the dew spangles the grass, in pushing these grass-cutters over a velvety lawn, breathing the fresh sweetness of the morning air and the perfume of new mown hay, will never rest contented again in the city. It is likely that professional garden laborers will buy these machines and contract cheaply for the periodical mowing of a neighborhood of yards, so that those who cannot or do not desire to do it for themselves may have it done cheaply. The roller is an essential implement in keeping the lawn to a fine surface, and should be thoroughly used as soon as the frost is out of the ground; for it will then be most effective to level the uneven heaving and settling of the earth. After heavy rains it is also useful, not only in preserving a smooth surface, but in breaking down and checking the vertical tendency of grass that is too succulent.

The season after seeding, many persons are discouraged by the luxuriance of the weeds, and the apparent faint-heartedness of the grass. They must keep on mowing and rolling patiently. Most of these forward weeds are of sorts that do not survive having their heads cut off half a dozen times; while good lawn grasses fairly laugh and grow fat with decapitation. Weeds of certain species, however, will persist in thrusting their uninvited heads through the best kept lawns. These are to be dealt with like cancers. A long sharp knife, and busy fingers, are the only cure for them.

# 14

## Artificial Adaptations of Trees

All weave on high a verdant roof
That keeps the very sun aloof,
Making a twilight soft and green,
Within the column-vaulted scene.

*Alfred B. Street*

All modes of growing trees for decorative or business purposes may be considered artificial, but what is here meant by artificial adaptations are those less common forms of culture, by which shrubs and trees are brought by skill, or persistent manipulation, into unusual forms for special purposes. Hedges, screens, verdant arches, arbors, dwarfed trees, and all sorts of topiary work, are examples of such arts. It is sometimes objected to these formally cut trees, that they are unnatural, and therefore inadmissible in good decorative gardening. But houses, fences, and walks are not natural productions, nor are lawns or flower-beds. All our home environments are artificial, and it is absurd to try to make them seem otherwise. The objection arises from a common misunderstanding that all decorative gardening is included in, and subject to the rules of landscape-gardening: an unfortunate error. The word landscape conveys an idea of breadth and extent of view, so that landscape-gardening means gardening on a great scale, in imitation of natural scenery. All the effects that can be produced artificially with small trees, by topiary arts, may seem puerile as parts of a landscape, but in the dimensions of a small lot, where each feature of the place needs to be made as full of interest as possible, no such idea is conveyed. On the contrary, whatever little arts will render single sylvan objects more curious and attractive, or more useful for special purposes, may with propriety be availed of. It is as absurd to apply all the rules of grand landscape-gardening to small places, as to imitate in ordinary suburban dwellings the models of palaces. The only limit to the use of topiary work of the character we are about to treat of is, that whatever is done shall be subsidiary to a general and harmonious plan of embellishment, and *that the forms employed shall have some useful significance.* To shape trees into the forms of animals, or to resemble urns or vases, or into ungraceful forms suggestive of no use or beauty, are farcical freaks of gardening art to be played very rarely and unobtrusively. As one of Walter Scott's famed Scotch Judges, when caught in the act of playing king in a court of buffoons, is made to say that it takes a wise man to know when and where to play the fool, so in such freaks of art as those just named, great prudence is necessary. The safest course is not to worry or coax nature into such caricatures. But hedges, arches, arbors, and bowers of verdure are all useful, and the tribute that nature renders to art in such forms is as proper and sensible as the modes by which her grains and vegetables are improved on farms and in gardens.

## HEDGES AND SCREENS

These are usually made of shrubs or trees which naturally take a dense low growth, and, if for barriers against animals, of those which are thorny. The wild thorns, and other trees clipped by browsing cattle and sheep until they seem condensed into solid masses of leaves and thorns, doubtless suggested the use of hedges, which has become more general in England than in any other country, and there the climate and the high rural tastes of the people continue to produce their greatest variety and perfection. With us they are never likely to be used to so great an extent for fences owing to the cost of maintaining them, but as ornamental and useful screens, and for other decorative purposes, there need be no limit to their variety. For these purposes some of the evergreens are best.

The arbor-vitaes are peculiarly adapted for hedges and screens; especially for those of medium height, which are not intended to turn animals. The species and varieties of arbor-vitae are numerous, but it is doubtful if there is one among them all more valuable for this purpose than the indigenous American species which is found wild on the banks of the Hudson, and other eastern rivers; though it is claimed for the Siberian arbor-vitae, and with truth, that its foliage has a richer shade of green.

There is a material difference in the value of different forms for hedges, and the kind of tree used, the purpose for which the hedge is intended, and the exposure it is to have, must influence the choice of one form rather than another.

Fig. 22 represents a hedge-plant of the arbor-vitae as grown, say the third year after planting. It must now be decided what form the hedge is to have. Fig. 23 is a section of the most common, and, for the arbor-vitae and hemlock, in open exposures, a good form. But it is evident that a hedge of this form gets less sun at the bottom than near the top, and the natural result is to produce the weakest growth at the bottom, and finally that the lowest branches die out. The shaded parts of hemlocks, if contiguous to moisture, do not seem to suffer for want of the direct rays of the sun, but a majority of hedge-plants need a full and even light upon them. It is not merely the direct rays of the sun which are essential, but that constant light from the sky which, with or without the sun, always rests upon the top of a hedge. If the top be broad as in Fig. 24, it receives nearly all the direct light from above, and shades the part below, and if one side of the hedge is towards the north, that side will be deficient in sunlight also. A form where the top is as broad as the bottom is therefore bad. Besides, a flat top with vertical sides is a clumsy form, and even were it not liable to lose its foliage at the bottom, would not be desirable. It is difficult to keep a full and healthy growth at the base of such hedges after the first five years of their growth, though the hemlock and arbor-vitaes are more manageable in this respect than many other hedge-plants. The best form for a hedge is the pyramidal, as in Fig. 25. This has the benefit of an equal distribution of light from all directions on the two sides of the hedge. It is also the simplest form to make and keep in order, and is recommended for evergreen hedges or screens in ordinary exposures. But the thin sharp points at the top, and at the bottom on each side, are much more liable to injury, and thus mar the continuity of the hedge lines, than the rounded form of Fig. 23. This objection may be remedied by cutting off the top so as to leave a thickness of about six inches of level surface there, and the same of vertical surface at the sides, as in the section Fig. 26. And as a graceful concave surface is prettier than a straight one, the sides above may be hollowed slightly, as shown in the same cut. This form tends to give strength and density of foliage to the bottom of the hedge, by exposing it more fully to the light from above. Fig. 27 shows the same principle applied to a tall hedge-screen, such as may be made with the Norway spruce. Very perfect high hedges may be made with this tree in the simple cone form with less labor than the form indicated by Fig. 27 will

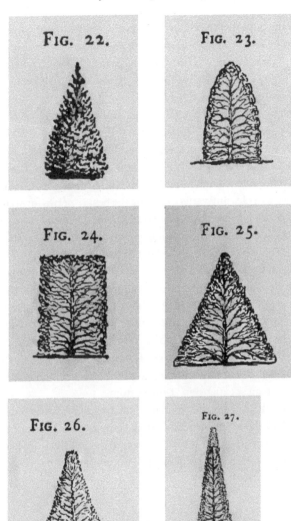

FIG. 22.

FIG. 23.

FIG. 24.

FIG. 25.

FIG. 26.

FIG. 27.

require, but the latter is the best in principle, as well as the most beautiful. The different lights and shadows which fall on contiguous curved surfaces, or different planes, may be studied with good effect in forming hedges. Fig. 28 is a very pretty and practicable form which we suggest for those who are willing to take the trouble to perfect it.

Where one side of a hedge has a northern exposure, or is much shaded by trees, it may be well to vary the form so that that side shall present a broader surface to the vertical light to compensate for the lesser sunlight, as shown by Figs. 29 and 30. The two sides of a hedge are rarely seen at one view, so that its apparent symmetry will not be marred, and this difference of form may be recommended as a pleasing variety – giving the beauty of two forms of hedge in one – as well as for the purpose of equalizing the vigor of the two sides.

Arbor-vitae and hemlock hedges may be made of any height, from three to fifteen feet. Those which are to be kept of the minimum size will require almost as much time to perfect them as the taller ones, as they must be cut back frequently from the start, to force the plants into a dwarf habit, and ought to be grown to the required breadth at the bottom before they are of full height. For a height of three feet, let the hedge be two feet wide at the bottom. As the height is increased the base need not increase proportionally. A hedge six feet high may have a base of three and a half feet, one ten feet high five feet, and so on; remembering to give the side which is to have the least light the greatest expansion at the bottom.

We consider the tree box, where hardy, the best of all evergreen trees for low hedges, and though its growth is slow compared with that of the trees already named, we would use it in preference to anything else for hedges not designed to be more than three feet high. But it may not be hardy enough

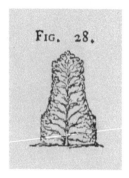

Fig. 28.          Fig. 29.          Fig. 30.

to be reliable in a climate more severe than that of the city of New York, and as it does best in partially shaded places, it is less beautiful in open, dry, and sunny exposures. For such places the arbor-vitae is better.

For topiary screens of great height the hemlock and Norway spruce, both of which bear cutting well, are very beautiful. More care is required in making hemlock, than arbor-vitae hedges, as they are not so tenacious of life, and require a soil of greater moisture.

There should be a small reserve of trees kept in one's own garden for the purpose of filling the gaps the next season following the planting. It is desirable to obtain plants not more than one foot high which have been twice transplanted in the nursery. They may be planted from one to two feet apart, according to the size of the hedge intended. The larger the hedge is to be, the greater the distance that may be allowed between the trees. The hemlock loves a cool, as well as moist soil, and does well in partial shade, though *if the roots be in cool, moist soil*, its greatest luxuriance and beauty is developed in the most sunny exposure; that is to say, it should have its roots in the shade and the top in the sun. Its own boughs trail naturally on the ground to make such a protection for the roots, and in forcing the tree into a hedge form it should be allowed, and even forced, to make the greater part of its growth laterally. For some years after planting, the top growth should be continually cut back, and the side branches allowed full license. At the end of three years the hedge should be pyramidal, and not more than three feet high, and the same width at the bottom. For a hedge from five to eight feet high, a width of four feet is sufficient, and the top should not be allowed to increase faster than six inches a year till the required height is attained. Where a hedge of greater altitude is desired, we would allow the hemlock to attain the full breadth required for the perfected hedge before permitting much increase in height. If, for instance, a screen fifteen feet high is wanted, then the trees that compose the hedgerow should be allowed to grow until they cover five feet in breadth, while the top should be kept back, so that in four years after planting its section will present the form of an equilateral triangle. Thereafter the bottom should be kept nearly the same width, and the top allowed to increase in height at the rate of not more than a foot a year until the required height is attained. The hemlock and arbor-vitae may be trimmed at any time from the middle of June to the first of October. June and September are, however, the best periods. The soil along young hedgerows should be cleanly cultivated as for a row of garden vegetables. The arbor-vitaes grow so naturally into a hedge-form, that little skill is required to shape them. The hemlock and other evergreens require much more attention.

Where it is necessary to have a high screen without delay, we would plant the Norway spruce, and let it grow pretty nearly in a natural way, until it reaches the height needed. The plants need not be nearer than two feet apart, and are apt to grow more evenly when small trees – say from one to two feet high – are planted. Those which grow fastest must be kept back to the same rate of growth as the weakest, or the former will in a few years over-top and kill out the latter. Further than for this purpose, the lower branches should not be cut back unless the top is also cut. A verdant wall of Norway spruce twelve feet high may be grown in six years from the time of planting, and must be allowed three or four feet on each side of the stems for the lateral extension of the lower branches. When the required height is attained, the tops can be kept cut to it, and both sides clipt back to the form of the section of a cone, the base of which is equal to half its height. The screen can thereafter be cut late every June, so as to leave but an inch or two of the last growth, and again in September if a second growth has pushed strongly.

It is seldom desirable to make topiary screens more than ten or twelve feet high, as the trouble and expense of clipping them from a movable scaffold is considerable. Where there is need, and room, for higher screens, the object may be attained less expensively and less formally with groups and belts of pines and firs. But it happens sometimes that a screen of considerable height is required where there is not ground to spare for the growth of trees in a natural way, and in such cases it is practicable to form Norway spruce hedges to any height at which they can be clipped, and without occupying for the base of the hedge more than from six to ten feet in width.

In general, hedges should be within a height that a man on the ground, with the proper instrument, can cut any part of them.

For evergreen hedges of a defensive character, that is to say, which have the strength, or the thorns, to prevent animals from going through them, we know of none that have been proved. What is called the Evergreen thorn, *Craetegus pyracanthus*, is an admirable thorny hedge-tree, but not truly an evergreen. It may, perhaps, rank as a sub-evergreen. The Menzies fir, *Abies menziesii*, seems to be peculiarly fitted for such a hedge, its leaves being sharp and stiff as needles, the growth compact, the foliage dense, and pointing in all directions. It is now a high-priced tree. When it becomes cheap we hope to see it tried for hedges. Like the hemlock and the balsam fir, it does best in a warm, humid soil, and it is possible that in the exposures required for hedges, it may not prove hardy enough to resist both the sun and the cold. The Cephalonia fir, *Picea cephalonica*, though its leaves are less cutting than those of the Menzies fir, are still somewhat formidable and as its growth is vigorous, healthy, and compact, it may prove valuable for large hedges.

There are some dwarf species of white pine which will make exquisite low hedges of a broader and rounder form than is recommended for any of the foregoing trees, but they are not yet furnished at such rates as to make their use practicable, and the common white pine may be clipped into hedge forms.

The American holly, *Ilex opaca*, has stiff glossy leaves armed with spines on their scolloped edges, and will probably make the most formidable of evergreen hedges for this country.

The yews, much employed in England for hedges, are not hardy enough to be used north of Philadelphia.

Among deciduous trees and shrubs the number adapted to hedges is much larger than most persons suppose. Almost the whole family of thorns, natives of this country, as well as of Europe, besides the fragrant hawthorn, are easily made into excellent hedges. Our wild crab-apple tree can be trimmed into a compact form of superlative beauty and fragrance in the blooming season, and sufficiently offensive by its thorns to turn trespassers. The mere capability of any tree or shrub to become a strong, dense, and handsome wall of foliage, if kept down to a hedge form, is not a sufficient recommendation. It is not so much a question of what trees and shrubs *can* be made into hedges, as which of them can be grown for that purpose, and kept in handsome and serviceable shape with the least annual expense and liability to accidents or diseases. Hedges may be made of the honey locust, but the labor of restraining their sprouts and suckers is about as profitable as that of training a Bengal tiger to do the work of an ox. The beautiful osage orange partakes somewhat of the same wild character, but has been subdued with great success, and is likely to prove the most valuable of live fencing in the Middle and Western States. But we see no advantage for merely decorative purposes on suburban grounds in confining a deciduous tree of such erratic luxuriance within monotonous hedge-limits, while evergreen trees of greater beauty, which naturally assume formal contours, can be more easily grown and kept in order for the same purpose.

Hedges, formidable by reason of their thorns, are only required for suburban places, on boundary lines contiguous to alleys or streets, where trespassers are to be guarded against. In such localities there is probably nothing better than the osage orange.

The beautiful English hawthorns, with their variety of many-colored blossoms, will develop their greatest beauty and bloom in other than hedge-forms. The buckthorn so much lauded twenty years ago for a hedge-plant, is one of the poorest and homeliest of all. The Fiery or Evergreen thorn, *Craetegus pyracanthus*, is a variety with very small leaves, almost evergreen, which assumes a hedge-form naturally, is formidable with thorns to resist intrusion, and covered with red berries in autumn. It grows slowly, and will make a charming low hedge. The Japan quince will also form a fine hedge with sufficient patience and labor. Its growth is exceedingly straggling, and the wood so hard to cut that it is expensive to keep in shape, but when grown to the proper size and form, its showy early bloom and glossy leaves, hanging late, make it one of the prettiest. The common privet belongs to a different class. It is a natural hedge-plant, strikes root freely from cuttings, grows quickly, and its wood cuts easily. The leaves appear early and hang late, and though not of the most pleasing color, they form a fine compact wall of verdure. It is, therefore, natural that the privet should long have been a favorite for garden hedges. The wax-leaved privet, *Ligustrum lucidum*, and the California privet, *L. californica*, are shrubs of larger and more glossy foliage, and probably hardy in most parts of the country. The lilacs, bush honeysuckles, syringas, altheas, weigelias, and some wild roses, may all be grown as hedges with pleasing effect where deciduous plants are used. In short, good hedges are much more the result of the patience and persistent care of the gardener than of the natural tendencies of certain shrubs or trees.

## VERDANT ARCHES AND BOWERS

In Chapter VI some allusion was made to the pretty effect of verdant gateway arches. There is no limit to the charming variety of effects that can be produced by training and pruning trees and large shrubs, both evergreen and deciduous, into fanciful forms for gateway and garden arches, verdant pavilions, and bowers.

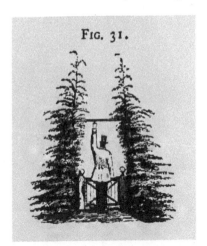

As evergreens are most constantly beautiful for such purposes, we will first call attention to a few forms in which they may be used. The hemlock can be treated as illustrated by Figs 31, 32, and 33 (overleaf), which we here repeat. The first represents two hemlocks which have been planted two feet away from, and on each side of an ordinary gateway.

After five or six years' growth they may be high enough to begin work upon. A crotched stick about two feet shorter than the distance of the trees apart, is stretched from one to another, from six to seven feet from the ground, and fixed there to keep the tops apart up to that point. Above the stick, the tops (supposing that they are tall enough to admit of it) are to be bent towards each other until they join, then twisted together, and tied so that they cannot untwist. To do this so as to form a graceful arch, the trees must be about eleven or twelve feet high. After they are firmly intertwined at the top, which is usually in about two years' growth, the clipping of the sides and tops can be going on to bring the arch to a form like that of Fig. 32, or to any similar design the proprietor may desire. An arch like the latter figure may be brought to considerable perfection in the course of ten years. Fig. 33 shows the probable appearance that a hemlock archway would present in twenty years after planting, supposing the trees were allowed to develop more naturally after their artificial character was well established. Such arches increase in quaint beauty as they grow old, and after the first ten years will need but little care. Fig. 34, as we have already mentioned in Chapter VI, is intended to show another effect, which may be produced with

Fig. 33.

Fig 34.

the same side trees, by joining and twisting together two side branches to form the arch, leaving the main stems to form two spiry sides, and trimming to produce this form. Another mode that, if well executed, would produce a curious effect, is to unite the main stems as in the first mode, but instead of twisting them to grow vertically over the middle of the gate, the twist should be made horizontally, so that the tops would project sideways, as shown farther on for elm-tree arches. This in time would develop into a wide crescent, inverted over the arch, or it might be likened to a pair of huge horns guarding the arch. The variety of novel forms that such trees can be made to assume after ten or twelve years' growth will surprise most persons. The same kind of arches on a smaller scale can be made with the arbor-vitae, but the branches are not so pliable. It may be used to advantage for narrower and lower arches.

For arbors or bowers the hemlock is equally well adapted. We would suggest as the simplest form to begin with, that four hemlocks be planted at the intersection of two walks, say five or six feet apart. By cutting back the side branches to within one foot of the trunk, the growth at the tops will be increased so that in five or six years they may be tall enough to allow the opposite diagonal corners to be twisted together. If the trees are all thrifty, the twist will become fixed in two years. The fragrant and graceful foliage of the hemlock can thus be made to embower retired seats, or make quaint openings for diverging paths. Such arbors or arches can be made much more quickly with carpentry and lovely vines, but the permanent and more unusual structures made with living trees must nevertheless be more interesting.

The hemlock may be used to make artificial pavilions of a still larger kind if trained through a period of ten or fifteen years. Suppose six trees to be planted at the corners of a hexagon ten or twelve feet in diameter. Let them feather naturally to the ground on the outside of the group, and trim to within one or two feet of the trunks on the inside. When twelve feet high, pass a rope around the circle, on a level, two or three feet below their tops, so as to draw them towards the centre of the circle as far as the main stems may be safely bent, which will probably be about three feet inside of the perpendicular. If the circle is twelve feet in diameter, this will still leave six feet uninclosed at the top. The rope is to be left around them until the trees have grown five to six feet higher, when another binding will bring their tops together, and if they are long enough they may be twisted together. Fig. 35 is a section of the stems alone, to illustrate the general form intended. When the six trees are together at the centre they should be made to grow like one, and the branches that grow from the upper sides of the curved stems must be cut back to prevent them from becoming leaders. Fig. 36 shows one development of this mode of training; the sides and top having been trimmed in mosque-dome form, the curve of the living frame of the pavilion being well adapted to produce it. It will require from twelve to fifteen years

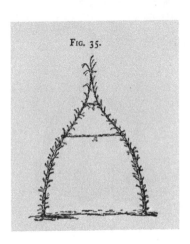

Fig. 35.

to perfect such a pavilion, but the group will be pretty, and interesting at every stage of its growth. In this, as in most other things in life, it is well to remember Shakespeare's lines –

What's won is done; – joy's soul lies in the doing.

A pretty variation of the above plan, for larger verdant pavilions, may be created by simply bending the tree-tops towards the centre in the manner above described, but not close together, leaving a circular opening six feet wide over the centre, in the manner of a dome sky-light.

The fir trees, though fine for lofty screens or hedges, have more rigid wood, and do not bear so much bending; still very beautiful results of a similar kind may be produced with the Norway spruce, which is the best of the firs for this purpose. It bears cutting quite as well as the hemlock. The *Cypressus Lawsoniana* which combines a rapid growth, and the freedom of the hemlock, with arbor-vitae-like foliage, will be an admirable tree for large works of this kind, if it continues to prove hardy.

The pines are mostly disposed to drop their lower limbs as they increase in height, and this peculiarity may be availed of in producing other forms of growth. If, for instance, it is desired to make an evergreen umbrage in which to take tea out of doors in summer, it may be provided by planting

Fig. 36.

four white pines, say twelve feet apart each way, and when they are from eight to ten feet high, cutting their leaders out so as to leave a tier of branches as nearly as possible at the same height on the four trees. The following year see to it that none of these upper branches turn up to make leaders, and if necessary tie them down to a horizontal direction. By attending to this for two years the top tier of shoots will make a horizontal growth, which will meet in a few years over head, and form a table-like top of foliage. But to insure this effect, the tree must be watched for some years to prevent any strong shoots from taking an upward lead, and thus draw the sap away from the horizontal branches. After these have met over head, and form a sufficient shade, the part above may be allowed to grow as it will. The check and change in the growth of the trees by such manipulation, carried on for several years, insures a novel and picturesque form for the group that will be permanent. As the white pine attains great size at maturity, it is not well to attempt such an arbor on quite small grounds.

Deciduous trees being more subject to insects on their foliage, are less desirable than evergreens for these uses, but they spread at the top more rapidly, can be more quickly grown to the required forms, and are covered at certain seasons with beautiful and fragrant blossoms; so that in variety of attractions some of them are unequalled by any evergreens. The latter wear throughout the year the beauty of constant cheerfulness, while the former, with the changing seasons, are alternately barren of graces, or bending with foliage and glowing with blossoms.

Fig. 37.

For archways there are no finer deciduous trees than the English hawthorns, and the double flowering scarlet thorn, *Craetegus coccinnea flore plena*. They can be planted at the sides of footpath gates, in the same manner as recommended for the hemlock, and it will only be necessary to trim them on the inside, so as to keep the opening unincumbered; as the hawthorns bloom best on their extended garland-like branches. But they should be trimmed enough to prevent any decidedly straggling outline, to show that they are intended as artificial adaptations for a purpose. Fig. 37 shows a suitable form for a hawthorn arch.

For bowers, or umbrageous groups surrounded by open sunny ground, the same form suggested for hemlocks and pines is adapted to the hawthorns; viz., planting in a square or circle so that the interior can be used for a cool summer resort for smoking or reading, a place to take tea, or a children's playhouse. A dense canopy of leaves forms the coolest of shades in the hot hours of summer days. To form such a canopy with hawthorns will require about ten years, and may be made by planting six trees in a hexagonal form. All our readers may not remember that if they make a circle of any radius, that radius applied from point to point on the circle will mark the six points of a hexagon. The following varieties of hawthorn are recommended for five of these places, viz.: the common white, *Craetegus oxycantha*, the pink flowered, *C. o. rosea*, the dark red, *C. o. punicea*, the double red, *C. o. punicea flore plena*, the double white, *C. o. multiplex*, and for the sixth the double scarlet thorn, *C. coccinnea flore plena*. These will in time make a bower of exquisite beauty in the time of bloom, and of such full and glossy foliage that it will have great beauty during all the leafy season. After such bowers are well thickened overhead by the annual cutting back of the rankest upright growth, they are interesting objects even in winter, by the masses of snow borne on their flat tops, and the contrast presented between the deep shadows under them, and the brightness of the snow around.

Some gardeners object to the use of the hawthorn in this country, on account of its alleged liability to the attacks of a borer that injures the trunk, and the aphis which attacks the leaves. We shall not advise to refrain from planting it on this account, believing that if planted in deep good soils, and the ground beneath kept clean, it will usually make so vigorous a growth as to repel the attacks of these insects, which usually choose feeble and stunted trees to work in. The hawthorns are all bushy when young, and their development into overarching trees will be somewhat slower than that of the following deciduous trees.

The sassafras is eminently adapted to form a useful bower of the kind above described, as it naturally assumes a parasol-like top, grows rapidly, and dispenses with its bottom limbs quickly. Being disposed to form crooked stems, some care must be used in choosing straight-bodied thrifty nursery trees, and protecting the trunks until they are large enough not to need it. Six thrifty trees will grow into a perfect canopy, of the size suggested, within five years, if their central stems are cut back, and kept to a height of about eight feet. For the next five years all the upright growth at their tops should be annually cut back, so that the trees will not exceed twelve feet in height. Afterwards they may be allowed to grow naturally, but their greatest beauty will not be attained in less than fifteen or twenty years.

Fig. 38 shows the appearance they should make in ten or twelve years after planting.

Next to the sassafras, probably the judas or redbud trees, *Cercis canadensis* and *C. siliquastrum*, form most naturally into this kind of flat-roofed bower. The white-flowered dogwood, *Cornus florida*, is also adapted to the same use. Both spread lower than the sassafras, but do not grow so rapidly when young. The moose-wood or striped-barked maple, on the other hand, attains the height required in a single season, and its green and yellow-striped bark is ornamental. The branches, after the trunk has attained the height of ten or fifteen feet, radiate naturally to form a flat-arched head, and grow much slower than the first vigorous growth of the stem would lead one to suppose. The foliage is large and coarse, but the form of the tree is suited to the purpose under consideration. Its large racemes of winged seeds, of a pinkish

Fig. 38.

color, are very showy in August. The paper mulberry is also a valuable tree for such uses, and attains the required size and density of head in less time than any of the others. The foliage is unusually abundant and of a dark green color.

Perhaps the most beautiful of all small trees for such purposes is the weeping Japan sophora. It is grafted from seven to ten feet high on other stocks, and for many years its growth is slow, but if one will have the patience to wait, a more charming and curious bower can be made with a circle of sophoras than of any tree we know of. An engraving of this variety may be found in the description of the species, Part II, Chapter III.

We have named only a few of the trees which may be made use of for growing these artificial bowers. For very small grounds there are many arboreous shrubs which may be used to produce similar effects on the inside, and appear as naturally grown groups on the outside.

Single apple trees sometimes form great bowers with their own branches alone. There is a beautiful specimen of this kind in the grounds of W. S. Little, Esq., of Rochester, N. Y. It is an old tree of the twenty-ounce pippin variety. At the height of seven or eight feet its branches spread horizontally, and finally bend to the ground on all sides, enclosing in deep shadow a circular space forty feet wide; an arched opening is made on one side. A sketch of this tree is given in the engraving at the end of this chapter.

Elms may be used with good effect for arches of a larger growth than those already suggested. The adjoining sketch, Fig. 39, will illustrate one mode of procedure, where there is room for large trees. Two common weeping elms

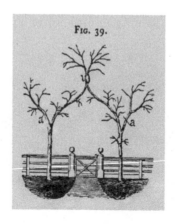

Fig. 39.

are to be chosen, each having two diverging branches at the height of six to eight feet from the ground, and to be so planted that the extension of these branches will be parallel with the fence. For a foot-walk gateway, plant them about two feet back from the fence-line, and the same distance, or less, from the walk. After the trees have grown so that the branches towards the gate are long enough to be connected, as shown in Fig. 39, and upwards of half an inch in diameter, they may be brought together and twisted round and round each other vertically, and tied together so that they cannot untwist; or they may be grafted together as shown on the sketch at *l*. The twist will, however, be the strongest and simplest mode. The branches that proceed from the twisted ones below the union, must be kept cut back to within two or three feet, so as to encourage the strongest growth in the part above the twist. The next spring, if these united branches have done well, the outer branches of both trees may be cut off at *a, a*, and grafted with scions of the Scamston elm. If the grafts take, and the growth and trimming of all parts are properly attended to, the lower growth forming the gateway arch should be all Scamston elm, crowned over the centre with the loftier common elm, presenting an appearance in the course of ten years something like the accompanying engraving.

FIG. 40.

The Scamston elm grows with great vigor in a horizontal and downward direction only, and its long annual shoots, and dark glossy leaves overlap each other so closely that an arch cut in one side has the appearance of being cut through a mound of solid verdure. Their tops are flatly rounded, like unfinished hay-stacks, and the common elm emerging from the centre (as shown in the engraving), and bending its long arms over the former with a freer growth, might, we think, present a combination of grotesque grace less formal in expression than our illustration.

A broad flat-topped arch of a similar character may be made by grafting all four of the branches with the Scamston elm at *a, a,* Fig. 39, and the points opposite. This may be perfected more quickly.

For an archway over a carriage entrance two common elms may be planted by the sides of the gateway, and when their side branches are long enough, may be twisted round and round each other, and tied together, and the other parts of the tree trimmed to develop the best growth of the branches depended on to form the arch. Fig. 41 illustrates the appearance of the trees without their leaves a year or two after the twist has been made.

FIG. 41.

# 15

# Plans of Residences and Grounds

Before proceeding to examine the plans, the reader is requested to observe the symbols used, as shown on the preceding page.

We desire also to offer a few preliminary explanations. First, every intelligent reader knows that no two building lots are often exactly alike in any respect. Not only in size and form, but in elevation, in shape of surface, in the exposure of the front to the north, east, south, or west, or intermediate points; in the presence and location of growing trees, large or small; in the nature of the improvements to the right or left, in front or rear; in the aspect of the surrounding country or city; in the connections with adjacent streets or roads; in the prospective changes that time is likely to bring which will affect their improvement for good or ill; all these things are external conditions as similar in the main as the colors of the kaleidoscope, and as invariably different from each other in their combinations. Not only these external conditions, but an equally numerous throng of circumstantial conditions connected with the tastes, the means, the number, and the business of the occupants, tend to render the diversities of our homes and home-grounds still more innumerable. It is, therefore, improbable that any one of the plans here presented for the reader's study will precisely suit any one's wants, but that their careful examination and comparison will be of service in planning houses and laying out lots of a somewhat similar character, we earnestly hope. We furnish them as a good musical professor does his instrumental studies, not to be used as show-pieces, but to be studied as steps and *points-d'appuis* for one's own culture.

In naming the selection of trees and shrubs for many of the smaller places, we have endeavored to be as careful in their selection as if each place were an actual one, and our own; leaning, however, in most cases, to that style of planting which will have the best permanent effect, rather than to an immediate but ephemeral display, and fully conscious that a skillful gardener may name many other and quite different selections for the same places,

that will be equally adapted to them, and that in carrying out such plans on the ground, the insufficiency of designs on so small a scale to present all the finishing small features that make up the beauty of a complete place, will be very evident. The choice of trees and shrubs for locations otherwise similar, must be influenced by a consideration of the climate. Many which do well near the sea-coast are not hardy on more elevated ground in the same latitude; while others are healthy in the high lands that prove sickly in more southern and alluvial valleys. A selection for a lot near New York should not be altogether the same as for Saratoga or St Pauls, Richmond or Louisville, and for the Gulf States (except in the most elevated regions) it would be totally unsuited. Southward from the latitude of New York, each degree (except so far as the influence of latitude is counteracted by that of altitude) will enable the planter to grow some tree or shrub not safe to plant, under ordinary conditions, any further north. As the latitude and climate of New York city represent the average requirements of a greater population than any other, in this country, our selection for the places described in this chapter are generally suited to such a climate, and in planting, the reader must be directed by his own study as to what substitutions are necessary in latitudes north or south of it.

We have remarked in a preceding chapter on the impracticability of furnishing plans for grounds of uneven surfaces, or for those which have trees growing on them, without an accurate survey of all these features.

The plans which follow, therefore, pre-suppose bare sites, and rather level ones; but the study of arrangement on these will be found to embrace most of the questions that interest those who are forming or expecting to form suburban homes.

## PLATE I – B

*Plan for a Compact House and Stable on a Corner Lot 128 x 220 feet.*

Reference has been made to this plate in Chapter IX for the purpose of illustrating a mode of planning the grounds on paper, and working from the paper plan. The lot has an area of less than two-thirds of an acre. The main house is thirty-six feet square, with a kitchen-wing twenty-two feet wide, carried back under a continuous roof to form the carriage-house, wash-shed, and stable – in all sixty-four feet in length. We believe that it is rarely that so many of the requirements of a pleasant house are brought within so small an area. Doubtless most lady-housekeepers will rebel against the thought of having the carriage-house and stable in such close proximity to the dwelling. It is the only plan in this work thus arranged, but in our north-border States we believe it to be a wise arrangement; not only vastly more economical in construction, and convenient for the family and their servants, but also, in the hands of a good architect, capable of adding greatly to the attractiveness of the house by giving it an air of extent and domesticity that so many of the box-like suburban houses of the day are totally wanting in. We do not believe there is any more need of being annoyed by flies or smells from a stable than from a kitchen, and if the latter can be kept so that it is a pleasant room to have within ten feet of living-rooms, where doors open directly from one to another, we know no reason why the stable may not be within fifty feet, where there are no direct connections, and four or five intervening partitions. One only needs to see how pleasantly it looks and works in the keeping of a neat family, to be surprised that this system has not long ago been adopted at the north. It is not only a great economy in the first cost of the house and stable, but an equal economy of lot-room. Here is a lot of but little more than half an acre, with the apparent ground-room for a mansion; with a lawn two hundred and twenty feet in length, a large variety of trees and shrubbery, an abundance of summer fruits, and a sufficient kitchen-garden for the use of one family, and yet nothing is crowded. This economy of space is in part attributable to the compact unity of the dwelling and domestic offices.

Let us now examine the ground-plan. The street in front is supposed to be two feet and a half below the ground-level on that front, and to have a wall with a stone coping level with the grass; the side-street rising so that where the carriage-road enters it, the two are on the same level. The coping of the front wall is carried around and continued up the sides of the main entrance-walk in a style similar to, but not quite so costly, as that illustrated in the vignette of Chapter IV. This walk is six feet wide. Street trees, if any are planted in front, should be placed so that the middle of the space between them is on the line of the middle of the walk continued, and should be the same distance apart as the trees of the short avenue on each side of the walk; that is, twenty feet. Supposing the street trees are elms, we would plant at *a, a,* weeping Scotch elms, *Ulmus montana pendula*; at *b, b,* weeping beeches; at *c, c,* cut-leaved weeping birches. The evergreen screens on the right and left are to be composed principally of hemlocks. That on the right is intended to make an impervious screen so that the yard behind it on that side cannot be seen from the street. The flower-beds on the parlor side of the lot are designed to be the especial charge of the lady-florist of the house, and these evergreen screens will give a partial privacy to that section of the lot. The screens also act as boundaries of the avenue, making the entrance-walk a distinct and isolated feature – a shadowy arbor of the overarching foliage of deciduous trees, with a background on each side of evergreen verdure. The depth of shadow in passing through such an approach will serve to bring into bright relief the unshadowed front of the house, and the open expanse of sunny lawn around it. The evergreen trees that are within fifteen feet of the deciduous trees which form the avenue should not be allowed to make their full natural growth upwards, but be topped irregularly so that the latter may not be obstructed in their natural expansion. The avenue trees are to be considered the rightful owners of all the space they can grow to fill, and the evergreens only tenants at will so far as they occupy places which the branches of the deciduous trees will eventually overgrow. But for many years both may grow unharmful to the other.

In the back part of the lot let us take an inventory of the utilitarian features of the plan, and then of their connection with the decorative effect. The grape-walk, it will be seen, is on a right line with the length of the side veranda. A double arch marks the entrance to this and the dwarf pear walk. Arch openings in the grape-trellis give access to the walks of the kitchen-garden for the family, while for work and for servants' use, another walk leads from the wash-room and the back veranda. The vegetable garden is thus entirely out of sight from the house, and from every part of the grounds, and yet has a sufficiently open exposure, and the most convenient proximity to the kitchen. The long grape-walk trellis will have a good exposure, to whatever point of the compass its length tends. The same may be said of the dwarf pear border. There are six standard pear trees, four cherry, two peach, and one apple tree marked on the plan. Other peach trees may be planted in between the cherries and pears if the owner will be sure to cut them out as soon as the cherry and pear trees need all the room. Few persons are aware how much healthier and more productive fruit trees are which are allowed to grow low, and with unlimited expansion from the beginning. Therefore we warn against planting permanent trees too thickly, and against leaving short-lived trees, like the peach, too long in the way of the permanencies. There are, however, some dry clay soils where the peach tree does not quickly become decrepit – as it is pretty sure to do in a light sand or rich loam – and there it may be well to allow it the necessary room for mature growth, independent of the growth of other trees. It will be seen that the borders of the lot offer ample room for the growth of small fruits for one family. Strawberries may be grown in cultivated strips under the standard pear trees.

From the dining-room window which opens upon the veranda, pleasing vistas down the grape-walks and the pear-walks will be seen through the vine-covered parts of the veranda, and the arches that mark the entrances to those walks. The height of the veranda floor will conceal one-third of the gravel space in front of the carriage-house from the eye of a person sitting in the dining-room, so that the vines that should wreath the end-opening of the veranda and the arches beyond, and their interior perspective, will be the principal objects in view. Between the row of dwarf pears and the side-street the arrangement of fruit trees is such that, seen from the front, the open lawn space surrounded by them will have quite as elegant an air as any other portion of the ground. The large fir tree at the end of the row of pear trees, and the arbor-vitae hedge between it and the arch, are intended to shut from view the tilled ground under the pear trees, and, together with the large pine tree nearer the house and its subjacent evergreen shrubs, to give a cheerful winter tone to this most used portion of the 'backyard'.

On the front portion of the lot, the trees indicated by letters on the plan are intended to be the following – the list being made for a climate like that near the city of New York.

At *d*, the dwarf white-pine, *P. strobus compacta*; at *e, e*, a pair of Japan weeping sophoras; at *f*, Parson's American arbor-vitae, *Thuja occidentalis compacta*; at *g, g*, the American and European Judas trees; at *h*, the *Kolreuteria paniculata*; at *i*, the golden arbor-vitae; at *j*, the Indian catalpa; at *k*, the erect yew, *Taxus erecta*; at *l*, the golden yew, *Taxus aurea*; at *m* and *n*, *Weigelas amabilis* and *rosea*; at *o*, the new weeping juniper, *J. oblonga pendula*; *p* and *g*, the weeping silver-fir and the weeping Norway spruce; *r, r, y*, and *z, z*, an irregular belt of Siberian and other arbor-vitaes; *s, s*, weeping arbor-vitaes, *Thuja pendula*; at *t*, Sargent's hemlock; at *u*, a cherry tree (this in lieu of the cherry tree near the carriage-road gate, where, if the soil is congenial, we would plant a pair of white-pines, one on each side of the gate-way, and not far from the posts). Under and between the trees *h*, and *g, g*, we would have a mass of rhododendrons; or, if cheaper and more rapid growing materials for a group are preferred, the space may be filled with the variegated-leaved and wax-leaved privets and low-spreading spireas; at *v, w*, and *x*, in the next group, may be planted a choice of deutzias, honeysuckles, syringas, lilacs, and snow-balls – one of each. Around the firs at *p* and *q*, while they are small, a group of rhododendrons may be planted. The single small shrubs (or trees) opposite the front corner of the house, may be single well-grown bushes of *Deutzia gracilis*; or the double flowering-plum, *Prunus sinensis*; or the purple-leaved berberry; or, if dwarf evergreens are preferred, the Irish and Swedish junipers, the Japan podocarpus, the tree-box (for clipping), the golden arbor-vitae, the golden yew, or the erect yew, *Taxus erecta*, may all be rivals for these places. With constant care to keep them to their most slender form, those beautiful novelties, the weeping Norway spruce and silver firs, *Abies excelsa inverta* and *Picea pectinata pendula*, might grace this place better than anything else, though they may in time grow to great height.

In the four inner angles of the two bay-windows, unless the exposure is to the south or southwest, we would plant rhododendrons of medium size, and fill the corner-beds with the same, graded down to the smallest varieties at the points. In the middle, between the bay-windows, two feet from the house, plant the *Cephalotaxus fortunii mascula*, and beyond it, to complete the group, three flowering deciduous shrubs graded in height as follows: Six feet from the house the double-flowered pink deutzia; two feet further out the *Deutzia gracilis*, and two feet from that, on the point, the *Daphne creorum*. While these shrubs are small, use the ground between them for annuals and bulbous flowers.

The group under the pine tree, and between it and the rear veranda steps, may be composed of two varieties of the tree-box near the steps – the common and the gold-edged leaved – Sargent's hemlock near the corner of the road, and the variegated-leaved privet, the purple berberry, the variegated-leaved elder, and some kalmias to complete the bed. It is essential that there should be a sufficient mass of evergreen verdure around the pine to shut the carriage-yard out of view from the front.

The border near the right-hand fence, in front, is a hemlock, or an arbor-vitae screen; with single specimens standing in front of it, of any of the choice varieties of common deciduous flowering shrubs. The plan fails to show the continuity of the evergreen screen along that side of the lot, and consequently some of the deciduous shrubs are too near the fence. The hedge back of the large flower-bed should also occupy double the width shown on the plan. The isolated, very small shrub-marks, represent slender junipers, or single brilliant-leaved plants.

The few flower-beds that are shown on the lawn-side of the house can probably be filled by most ladies quite as tastefully as we could suggest. The continuous bed opposite the large window of the parlor will demand much skill in arrangement, if filled with annuals and perennials. But as these are likely to be changed every year, and as skill in such matters is the result of experience alone, it is needless to specify any one list of varieties, or order of arrangement for them. In case the occupants of the place prefer not to take care of a great bed of annuals, the entire bed may be devoted to the culture of roses, and if these also involve too great an annual outlay of time and money, the ground may be left in lawn alone, and the border broken by a few fine shrubs upon it.

The location of the parlor on this plan, with its principal window looking out on the shortest and most unsatisfactory view of the place, may be open to criticism. But it must be borne in mind that, on small lots, all the sides of a dwelling cannot have park-like exposures, and the room that is least used, and least looked out of, is the one that should have the least interesting exposure. Parlors are principally used by day as reception rooms for casual callers, and in the evenings for sociable gatherings. In neither case are the guests, or the family, in the habit of paying much attention to out-of-door views. The furniture of a parlor is likely to be scrutinized more than that of other rooms, but the outlooks from it are of less importance than from those rooms which the family and their intimate friends frequent.

## PLATE II

*A Corner Lot having one hundred and fifty feet front on one street, and two hundred and fifty feet on another.*

The figures at the bottom, and the letters on the side of the plate, represent spaces of ten feet each. The house is commodious, and its form the most simple and compact. The fronts (veranda lines) are sixty feet from the two streets respectively. A carriage-house of suitable size occupies the rear corner of the lot, with a stable-yard behind it, and a passage-way for a cart around it. A straight walk to the front door, and a straight road to the carriage-house, are the most appropriate ways to each; while the side-entrance walk, being prolonged to form the walks to the kitchen, the garden, and the stable, is laid down in a curved form to make it most convenient for these purposes. A covered trellis or arbor forms a continuation of the back veranda, and a dry passage from the back hall to the out-buildings. This is designed for grape vines. The kitchen-garden occupies a space about 45 x 90 feet, including the walks. The side fence or wall of the garden, if the exposure is to the east, south, or southwest, may be covered with grapes; if to the north, with currants or raspberries. The main square of the kitchen-garden is drawn as if covered with small fruits. It may be so used, or filled with vegetables alone. A row of fine cherry trees are set forty feet from the side fence, starting ten feet from the carriage road, and twenty feet apart, and a sixth at the same distance from the first, on the line towards t. The plan indicates the locations for five pear trees, two peach trees, quinces, raspberries, etc. A greater number may be planted in these spaces, but not without eventual injury to the appearance of the grounds. Peach trees are short-lived, and usually scrawny and ill-favored after the first five years of their growth. We would place them reluctantly in any part of grounds that may be seen in connection with other parts which are occupied by lawn-trees and flowers under high keeping. But a place for a few trees having been indicated, it may be as well to put out four or five there as two. They will soon crowd each other too closely, but they pay for themselves quickly, and die early. There is no question of the great superiority of peaches grown to ripeness on one's own trees, over the half-ripe beauties of the markets, and if the proprietor, to have their fruit, is willing to guard their health, he must also be willing to bear with their mature ugliness.

We will now describe the plan with reference to those things which are planted for their decorative effect alone; premising, however, that walks, arbors, and fruit trees, are quite as much a part of the embellishments of the ground as evergreens or flowering shrubs, and are all placed with reference to their effect in connection with the latter.

The plan supposes a slight downward slope of the ground from the house to the outside street boundaries; the floor of the house being about four feet above the lawn adjoining it, and the latter unbroken by terraces or architectural forms of any kind. It is intended as a plain example of conformity to good taste in arrangement, rather than of any great art in gardening, and combines as much length of open lawn, with as great a variety of trees, shrubs, and flowers as the size will admit of, without making it an expensive place to keep.

The front walk is six feet wide. The gate posts are set back five feet from the street line. On a line with the posts, and from two to five feet from them, a pair of trees are to be planted to form an arch over the gate. If large trees like elms or pines are used, let them be planted at the greater distance; if small trees like the sassafras, the nettle tree, or the red-bud or Judas tree (*cercis*) are employed, two feet from the posts will be enough. If a more artificial form of verdant arch is desired, the proprietor can choose some of the trees and forms recommended in Chapter XIV. The American weeping elm or the Scotch elm, arch a gateway quickly and nobly, but will eventually be so large as to shade the whole of that part of the yard. A pair of sassafras trees, planted within two or three feet of the walk, would make one of the richest natural canopies over the gate, but perhaps too much like a parasol, and not enclosing the way sufficiently on the sides, but by planting beneath them, in the inner curve of the fence, the tree-box, which does well in partial shade, and surrounding the trunks on the other sides with some low-growing shrubs that also do not suffer by shade, the arch may be made complete with a variety of surroundings. Just beyond, say fifteen feet from the gate, are two Irish junipers. The lawn between these and the steps is unbroken save by six beds for very low flowers, as shown on and near the dotted line ending at *d*, and between it and the veranda. The line *d* is intended to designate a strip upon and near which nothing should be planted; so that a continuous open lawn-view may be had across this place to the places on the left of it, and from them back to the street on the right at *d*. The group above Figs 11 and 12 may be composed of dwarf evergreens as follows: on the right, the dwarf white pine, *P. strobus compacta*; on the left, six feet from it, the golden arbor-vitae; in the middle above them, four feet from each, the yew, *Taxus erecta*, the foliage of which is very dark, and above, close to it, the golden yew, with leaves and twigs, as its name imports, prettily tinged with a golden hue; next above, as shown by the speck on the plan, a plant of the dwarf fir, *Abies gregoriana* or the *Andromeda floribunda*, either of which is exceedingly dwarf. These would in time make a charming small evergreen group, but the dwarf trees which compose it grow slowly, so that it is necessary to keep the ground cultivated between the trees, and filled with bulbs, annuals, or perennials, until the evergreens are large enough to meet. Fig. 42 is a sketch made in the home-grounds of Mr. S. B. Parsons, at Flushing, L. I., showing an actual group somewhat similar to the one just suggested, composed of but four trees or shrubs, and three species. The low one in front is the *Andromeda floribunda*, the next the golden arbor-vitae, and the two behind it the Irish yew, *Taxus baccata*. An engraving can scarcely suggest the beautiful contrasts of colors and surfaces that these present. On either side of the veranda, and about twelve feet in a diagonal line from its corners, two large trees are indicated. The choice of these may safely be left to the reader. They should be of hardy, healthy, thrifty sorts. Horse-chestnuts, maples, and elms are usually the most beautiful rivals for such places. Of horse-chestnuts we would recommend the common white for one side, and for the other side the double white flowering, which blooms several weeks later than the common sorts, and forms a taller tree in proportion to its breadth. The red-flowering horse-chestnuts are lower and rounder-headed trees, of slower growth, and would not pair so well with either of the sorts named, but would be very appropriate if used on both sides. Of a totally different character from any of these named, is the cut-leaved weeping birch, of rapid growth, elegant at all seasons, and also adapted to these positions.

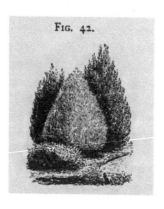

Fig. 42.

Opposite *g*, ten feet from the fence, is a Norway spruce, or, if the location and latitude are not too cold for it, the Nordmanns fir, *Picea nordmaniana*, which, in rich soils, has foliage of unusual beauty. Back of it towards the fence, fill in with hemlocks, arbor-vitaes, and yews, which grow to the ground and make an impenetrable mass of evergreen foliage. The side gateway is intended to be covered with a hemlock-arch of some of the forms suggested in Chapter XIV, which should connect with a continuous hedge, broken at *m*, *n*, by one or two pines, and varied from the pines to the carriage-way gate with a belt of many kinds of shrubs. At *c*, five feet from the fence, plant the *Kolreuteria paniculata*, and at *b*, near the fence, a bed of low-growing spireas. The group between 2 and 4 may be composed of bush honeysuckles or of shrubby evergreens. The small shrub nearly over 2 may be an *Abies gregoriana*, or a golden yew. The group in the left-hand corner may be composed of good old shrubs like lilacs, the purple berberry, weigelas, deutzias, and the purple-leaved filbert, and for the two trees we would suggest the common catalpa for the place ten feet from the fence, and the *Magnolia machrophylla* for the one nearer the house. On the left, on the line of the middle of the front veranda, and twenty feet from the left side of the lot, a single specimen of the Bhotan pine, *P. excelsa*, or the two weeping firs, *Abies inverta* and *Picea pectinata pendula*; just behind them some of the yews of the podocarpus or cephalotaxus tribe; back of these, along the fence, a dense mass of hemlocks, with now and then some light-colored or variegated-leaved small plants or shrubs on the border in front of them. The group beyond, projecting towards the house, is supposed to be composed of a variety of the best arbor-vitaes broken in color by some of the dark yews, – the little out-lying member of the group to be the Irish juniper.

It is impracticable to trace through all the details. The reader must observe that the very small shrubs which are indicated in isolated positions on the lawn are intended for very compact evergreen or other shrubs, which take up but little room and are pleasing objects at all seasons of the year. At the four outer corners of the two bays may be planted, in pairs, specimens of the Irish and Swedish junipers, or some of the slender yews. At the corner of the open space in front of the carriage-house is a horseblock, to be shaded by a white pine. Nearly in front of the side entrance to the house is a rosary, for which may be substituted with good effect a Bhotan pine, with a cut-leaved weeping birch close behind it, if the proprietor does not wish to make and keep up the rose-bed with the expense and care which it annually requires.

If the birch just named has been selected for the tree near the corners of the front veranda, it need not be repeated.

These grounds, with no other plantings than are indicated, would doubtless look bare for some years. The places which the trees and shrubs are ultimately to cover, must be filled, in the intervening time, with annuals and bedding-plants which will make the best substitutes for them. We would decidedly advise not to plant trees or large shrubs any nearer together than they ought to be when full grown, on the tempting plea that when they crowd each other some of them may be removed. Nine persons out of ten will not have the nerve to remove the surplusage so soon as it ought to be done, and when they do see the unsightly result of a crowded plantation, there will be one good excuse for not doing it, viz.: that trees which have grown up together have mis-shaped each other, so that when one is cut away those that remain show one-sided, and naked in parts. It is better to have patience while little trees slowly rise to the size we would have them, and, while watching and waiting on them, let the ground they are eventually to cover be made bright with ephemeral flowers and shrubs. When the trees approach maturity they will have developed beauties that crowded trees never show.

## PLATE III

*Crowded and Open Grounds Compared, on a Cottage Lot of fifty feet front.*

Here we have two lots 50 x 200 feet each. The plan and position for a small cottage-house, and the walks, are the same on both. The plan on the right is intended to show the common mode of cluttering the yard so full of good things that, like an overloaded table, it lessens the appetite it is intended to gratify. Let us picture Mr and Mrs A, master and mistress of the house, unskillful but enthusiastic, engaged in their first plantings. The lot is a bare one. Fruit trees are the first necessities; places are therefore found for four cherry, and five pear trees, without trespassing much on the 'front yard', which is sacred, in true American homes, to floral and sylvan embellishments. It is to fill this ground that our proprietors are now to make choice of trees and shrubs. Mr A and wife are agreed that evergreens are indispensable, and that the balsam fir and the Norway spruce are the prettiest of evergreens – for 'everybody plants them'. Accordingly a couple of Norway spruces flank the gate at a little distance inside, and a pair of balsam firs (prettiest of trees as they emerge, fragrant, from the nurserymen's bundles) are placed conspicuously not far from the house-steps, on each side the main-walk. Mrs A suggests that the weeping-willow is the most graceful of all trees. Who can gainsay that? Mr A does not, and in go two willows in the two front corners of the yard. Then there's the mountain ash with a 'form as perfect as a top, and such showy clusters of red fruit', suggests Mrs A, 'and everybody plants them'. Of course this tree is planted, one on each side of the yard, midway between the walk and sides of the lot, in that open space above the willows. Then the walk is bordered from the gate towards the house with rose-bushes of all sorts, while lilacs, honeysuckles, spireas, syringas, and whatever else is known to be beautiful and easily obtained, are crowded along the side fences. Mrs A insists that a space shall be left on both sides of the main-walk for her flowers. Accordingly the beds are formed as shown on the plan, and planted with all the fine flowering bulbs and annuals that she can get plants or seeds of. There is still wanting a feature that some neighboring place has, viz.: one or more fanciful trellises – masterpieces of delicate carpentry, brilliant with white paint – upon which to train pillar roses. 'There's just the place for them,' says Mrs A, 'just in the middle of the yard, on each side,' and there they are placed.

We need not follow their planting further. The plan (on the right) shows how the place will be filled in two or three years. Each latest planting is put in the most convenient open space, and every spring brings some new candidate for a place. At the end of eight or ten years let us look in upon the ground and see the result. There should be a home-picture, with its encircling foreground, its open middle distance, its vine-clad cottage centre, smiling like a speaking portrait well framed. What will it be, if it has been planted and kept in this mode, still so common in suburban places? A mass of agglomerated and tangled verdure. Pass along the street, and the lovely foliage of the two willows marks the spot, but beneath their overshadowing foliage the evergreens and other trees have a feeble existence, and their spindling forms as they essay, with prim pertness, to stretch above the crowding shrubs and tangled grass around them to maintain their individuality, are met by a wet blanket of the willow's shade in summer, and her damp old clothes in the autumn. Straggling rose-bushes and overgrown shrubs elbow each other over the walk, and quarrel for space with the grass and old annuals that try in vain to get their share of room and light. As some English reviewer says of the bedrooms of little gothic cottages – 'somewhere around among the gables' – may be observed of all the pretty things that have with so much care been planted on this place – they are to be found somewhere among the bushes, and behind all, as if the one great object of planting were to hide it out of sight, is a cottage.

Happily such modes of planting are becoming rarer, but they are still quite too common.

Now we do not mean to convey the idea that this little piece of ground might be made into a little park by judicious planting, or that all of what has been crowded into it might have been put in differently without crowding it. It is a small lot on which it is not possible to have a great variety of trees and shrubs without cluttering it, and losing all appearance of a lawn. Our plan on the left of the same plate is not designed to show the most artistic way of treating this small yard, but to show the most simple way of not overdoing by mis-planting. The fruit trees are introduced in about the same places as in the other plan, but in front of them no overshadowing trees are planted. At the sides, other yards are supposed to connect with this lot, and openings are left in the border shrubbery to avail of whatever pleasant lookouts may thus be obtained. All the middle portion of the yard is unbroken by shrubbery, which is arranged in groups near the corners, and around the house. The entrance gateway should be embellished with a verdant arch of hemlock; the front corners of the lot may be marked by carefully grown specimens of arbor-vitaes or slender junipers; the small trees standing alone, about seven feet from the front, should be choice specimens, either evergreen or deciduous, similar in form, and as dissimilar as possible in color and foliage. Among evergreens we would name for these places the two weeping firs – *Abies inverta pendula* and *Picea pectinata pendula* – as the most appropriate of all; or, for one side the yew *Taxus stricta* or *erecta*, and on the other the yew *Taxas aurea*; or the weeping arbor-vitae for one side, and the weeping juniper for the other; or with dwarfs, of the dwarf pine *P. strobus compacta* on one side, and the mugho pine on the other. With deciduous arboreous shrubs or small trees, the variety to choose from is very great. We will suggest for one side the weeping Japan sophora, grafted not more than seven feet high, and for the other the double scarlet hawthorn, *C. coccinnea flore plena*, cut to resemble the sophora in outline; or for one side the Indian catalpa (see Fig. 129), and for the other a sassafras or a white dogwood, *Cornus florida*, kept clipped down at the top so that it shall not exceed eight feet in height or breadth of top. In selecting some deciduous miniature trees for these places we would choose those that have low, parasol forms, and clean, tree-like, but very short stems. The common orange quince tree, if planted in a deep moist soil, grown thriftily, and treated with the same attention that we would bestow on a valuable exotic, is one of the most beautiful of very low spreading-topped shrubby trees, and well adapted to the places under consideration. The kilmarnock willow, though it has neither the beauty of blossom, leaf, or fruit, that distinguish a well-grown quince tree, is certainly a sort of model of formal grace and symmetry, and might be used on one side and balanced on the other with a low-grown ever-flowering weeping cherry, *Cerasus semperfloreus*. Or luxuriantly grown single bushes of the common fragrant syringa, tartarian bush honeysuckle, rose weigela, or lilac *rothmagensis*, will be appropriate for the same place.

The plan in general is too simple to require explanation, and is introduced to call attention to the superior beauty of simplicity, compared with complexity of planting, on small places.

## PLATE IV, A AND B

*Designs for a Lawn on a Lot of fifty feet front with considerable depth.*

This design has already been alluded to in Chapter XI, on Arrangement in Planting, in illustrating the application of Rule I to small places. The lot has a front of fifty feet, and an indefinite extension in the rear. The plan is designed to show the pretty space of lawn that can be kept on a quite small lot, provided the latter has depth enough, by placing the house well back. The lot is supposed to be between side properties which it is impracticable to connect with, and therefore isolated by close fences and border shrubbery from them. The distance from the street to the bay-windows is eighty feet. The compact house plan is adapted to the position by having its entrance on the side, so that the best window-views possible under the circumstances will be secured from the bays of the two principal rooms. The walk, as we have previously observed, is made near one side, to leave all the central portion of the lot in open lawn. It is not possible to keep this openness of expression, and at the same time have large trees on the lot. They must be dispensed with; and in stocking the borders to make a rich environment of verdure for the lawn, the choice must be exclusively among small trees and shrubs. Let us begin at the gate. Here we would set out to have a hemlock arch; though the trees as shown on the plan erroneously symbolize deciduous trees. At the opposite front corner we would plant the two slender weeping firs, *Abies excelsa inverta* and *Picea p. pendula*. But as their growth is slow compared with that of many fine deciduous shrubs, a mass of the latter may be planted near the firs, to fill that corner with foliage until the latter are from twelve to twenty years old, when the weeping firs will be large enough to fill it beautifully without support. The border on the left should be made up of evergreen shrubs or trees, as varied in foliage as possible, and of those sorts which do not exceed six or seven feet in height and breadth. The isolated small trees or shrubs which stand out from this border are designed to be of deciduous sorts, the most charming for their forms, foliage, or flowers; the largest of which should not, within ten years, exceed ten feet in breadth. These, and the dwarf shrubs which flank them, can be selected from the lists to be found in the Appendix. As some of those which are in time the most interesting are of exceedingly slow growth, bedding plants and annuals which will preserve the same form for the groups by their proportioned sizes may be substituted. But there is no question of the superior beauty, in the end, of the place which is largely composed of trees and shrubs that make it charming in winter and early spring as well as in summer. The quick and brilliant effects that may be produced with bedding-plants can, however, be combined somewhat with more permanent plantings, if the planter will be watchful not to let his vigorous but ephemeral summer-plants smother the slower growing dwarfs. The latter will not long survive being thus deprived of sun and air in summer, and then left bare in the bleak winter, while their summer companions which lorded over them have been carefully removed to the cellar or the greenhouse. A pine tree is shown on the left near the house. This is exceptionally large. It is intended for a white pine, which grows rapidly in breadth as well as height, and might soon cover half the width of the lot with its branches. But it is readily 'drawn up', as foresters say, – that is, it is easily reconciled to the loss of its lower limbs, and sends its vigor to the upper ones; so that it naturally becomes an over-arching tree. In time it will over-top, and form an evergreen frame for that side of the house, while the lawn under it will be unbroken. The small round shrubs near the outside corners of the bay-windows may be, one, a golden arbor-vitae, and the other the golden yew, both rather dwarf evergreens, of pleasing form, and warm-toned verdure. Between the bay-windows, and near the house, is a suitable place for an elegant rose-pillar or trellis, and a bed of roses. Directly in front of it, and sixteen feet from the house, is a good position for a fine vase, or a basket in a bed of flowers, as shown on the plan. The pair of trees nearly in the middle of the front, near the street, we would have the weeping Japan sophora, on a line with the middle of the house, and not more than four feet apart. The main walk is represented on the plan by two modes of planting; the one, marked A, characterized by an alternation of shrubs and bedding-plants on the right, and beds of flowers on the left; the other, marked B, by a symmetric disposition of three groups of trees crossing and arching over the walk, and a belt of shrubs against the fence.

For the first, or shrub and flower-border plan, the following selection of shrubs is recommended on the fence-border. All the way from the street, to opposite the house, we would plant the Irish and English ivy close to the bottom of the fence, and would endeavor to make it cover the latter completely. Supposing the fence not to be more than four or five feet high, these ivies can generally be made to effect this, and although the growth near the top may often be winter-killed, the plants, if taken care of, will finally make a rich wall of verdure. If there is no probability of eventually joining, by openings on that side, with neighbors' improvements, it will be a great addition to the beauty of this border to have the fence a well-made stone wall, upon which the ivy is always most beautiful. From the hemlock arch to a point twenty feet from the fence, plant with tree-box, mahonias, and rhododendrons, set two and a half feet from the fence; then a concave bed ten feet long is devoted to bulbous flowering-plants and annuals; the next ten feet to be occupied by the pink and the red-flowered tree honeysuckles six feet apart, with the fragrant jasmine between them; the next ten feet in flowers as before; the next to be occupied by the *Deutzia crenata alba* and the *Deutzia crenata rubra flore plena*, six feet apart, with the *Deutzia gracilis* between them; the next, flowers, and the last group of shrubs to be the *Lilac rothmagensis* and the *Weigela rosea* six feet apart, with the *Spirea calosa alba* between and the golden yew, *Taxus aurea*, beyond; closing the planting on that side. On the veranda-posts five different vines may be trained; on the fence in front of them nothing better can be done than to cover it with Irish ivy, or such low-growing annual vines, on cords or wires, as will make the best wall of leaves and flowers during the summer, and which can be readily cleared away before winter. Beyond the veranda, on the left, is a place for a group of shrubs of anything that the lady of the house fancies.

The evergreen at the end of the narrow walk around the veranda should be some tall and handsome tree. If the soil is sandy, the white-pine kept well trimmed will make a fine mass of evergreen verdure the most quickly. In a climate not more rigorous than that of Philadelphia, the Lawson cypress, *C. lawsoniana*, is a good tree for the place; further north, the pyramidal spruce, *Abies excelsa pyramidata*, a slender, vigorous, and peculiar variety of the Norway spruce, will answer well, and so will a Bartlett or Seckel pear tree, or any good cherry tree. The evergreen, however, makes the best background setting for the house. By planting an evergreen on each side the walk, at that point, an arch may eventually be cut under them to form a vista from the veranda into the garden. This purpose may be most quickly effected with white-pines or hemlocks.

The embellishment of the walk-border by the other mode, as shown on the plan B, may be done as follows: the border of ivy along the fence or wall, and the principal shrubs for twenty feet next the front, may be the same as on the first plan, but all the flower-beds are to be omitted. Twenty-three feet from the street, and two feet from the walk on the right, plant an American Judas tree, *Cercis canadensis*; four feet further, on the same side, the European Judas tree, *Cercis siliquastrum*; opposite to them, on the left side of the walk, a clean stemmed white-flowering dogwood, *Cornus florida*. Sixteen feet from the upper Judas tree, plant a pair of sassafras trees four feet apart in the same relative positions as the Judas trees in the first group; opposite to them, on the left of the walk, the Scamston weeping-elm, grafted eight feet high on a common elm stock. The next group, sixteen feet further on, is made with a pair of *Kolreuteria paniculata* on the right, and a narrow group of low choice shrubs on the left of the walk. Very dwarf evergreens, or deciduous shrubs, may be planted to the left of each of these groups, as indicated on the plan, or those places may be filled with single plants of rich and abundant foliage, like the more robust geraniums, the *Colleus verschafelti*, cannas, little circles of salvias, etc., etc.

It is intended that the groups of low-growing trees which border this walk shall form flat arches over head, not more than eight feet over the walk, and the trees must be reared and pruned to effect this object. The Judas trees and the dogwood naturally spread quite low. The study with them will be, how to draw them up so that they will not be in the way overhead. The sassafras, though a flat-topped tree, sometimes gets too high before beginning to spread. If it keeps a strong centre-stem it should be topped at eight feet high to hasten its spreading. The *Kolreuterias* are rather too large for their place, but are low-spreading trees of great delicacy of foliage and warmth of color, and even if they finally extend their branches far towards the bay-windows, the view under them will be the more pleasing.

## PLATES V AND VI

*Designs for Village Lots 60 x 150 feet: one an In-Lot, and the other a Corner Lot.*

These designs are very simple and inexpensive in their character, and have been partially described in Chapter XI. The house-plan is the same in both; not compact, but rather stretched along the side of the lot farthest from the street so as to leave a fair space on the other side, upon which the best rooms and the verandas (which may be considered the pleasantest summer rooms of a house) are located. The house-fronts are each forty feet from the main street. Both ground-plans are supposed to open into other yards adjoining, on a line from ten to twenty-five feet from the street; on that line they are, therefore, left unplanted with anything that will obstruct views across the lawn. On Plate V the walks are made in right lines; while, on Plate VI, the entrance being at the corner, convenience dictates curved lines as the most desirable. If, on the latter, the gateway were in the same place as in the former, the straight-line walk would be preferable, as there would be no object in making it otherwise.

**Plate V** – The front gate is to be arched over in some of the modes suggested in Chapter XIV, and on the left a dense screen to the corner is to be made with evergreen shrubs or shrubby trees. Twenty feet from the front, and five feet from the left side, a tree of medium size is represented. It may be any one of the following: a *Magnolia machrophylla*, catalpa, double white or red-flowering horse-chestnut, bird cherry (*Prunus padus*), a cut-leaved weeping birch, purple-beech, *Kolreuteria*, *Virgilia*, red-twigged linden, grape-leaved linden, scarlet maple, purple-leaved maple, *Salisburia* or ginkgo tree (if cut back at the top), or a sassafras. Any handsome tree will do which branches low, but still high enough to allow a person to walk under its branches after it has been planted five or six years, and which does not quickly become a great tree. Five feet from the fence, facing the main entrance steps, we would plant the pendulous Norway spruce, *Abies excelsa inverta*; along the fence towards the front, a dense mass of low-growing evergreens; along the fence on the other side of the spruce (opposite the bay-window), a hemlock hedge, merging as it recedes from the front to the grape-trellis into a belt of evergreens. The groups of shrubs indicated in many places against the house, must be of the best species, which grow from two to seven feet in height, and ought to embrace in each group one or more shrubs with fragrant flowers, so that there shall be no summer month when the windows will not be perfumed from them. It is becoming a fashion to decry the planting of shrubs in contact with dwelling houses. This fashion is a part of an extreme reaction that possesses the public mind against the old and unhealthy mode of embowering houses so completely under trees, and packing yards so densely with shrubs, that many homes were made dark and damp enough to induce consumption and other diseases, and physicians have been obliged to protest against their injurious effects on the health of the inmates. But low-growing shrubs planted against the basement-walls of suburban houses, and rising only a few feet higher than the first floor, are not open to any such objections. A house that is nested in shrubs which seem to spring out of its nooks and corners with something of the freedom that characterizes similar vegetation springing naturally along stone walls and fences, seems to express the mutual recognition and dependence of nature and art; the shrubs loving the warmth of the house-walls, and the house glad to be made more charming in the setting of their verdure and blossoms. Many pleasing shrubs will do well where their roots can feel the warmth that foundation-walls retain in winter, which will not flourish in open exposed ground. Some will do well in shady nooks and northern exposures which cannot be grown in sunny projections; others need all the sun of the latter exposures, and are grateful in addition for all the reflected heat from the house-walls. The foundations (provided of course that they are of a deep and substantial character) thus become protecting walls that offer to the skillful planter many studies in the selection and arrangement of small shrubs. No well-constructed house will be dampened, or have the sunlight excluded from its windows, by such shrubs as we would recommend for planting in the groups indicated against the houses in Plates V and VI. Small as they are, each one of these little places for shrubs are studies. Whether to plant a single robust shrub in each place, which will spread to fill it, or to form a collection of lilliputian shrubs around some taller one, is for the planter to decide. We cannot here indicate, in detail, the plantings for all these places. It will be observed that the right-hand front corner of the lot is filled with shrubs, supposed to be but a part of a group, the other part of which is on the lot of the adjoining neighbor. This may be composed of large shrubs, such as altheas, deutzias, lilacs, etc., for the interior, and weigelas, bush honeysuckles, Gordon's currants, berberries, and low spireas of graceful growth for the outside. The tree ten feet from the right-hand corner should be one of the smallest class. The weeping Japan sophora grafted not more than six feet high, the ever-flowering weeping cherry, the new weeping thorn, the double scarlet thorn (*Coccinnea flore plena*) will make pretty trees for such a place. If something to produce a quick, luxuriant growth is preferred, the Judas tree, *Cercis canadensis*, or the Scamston weeping-elm, grafted on another stock seven or eight feet high, will do; though the latter will eventually become a wide-spreading tree too large for the place.

The isolated small tree, or large shrub, about seven feet from the fence near the middle of the front, may be an *Andromeda arborea*, or the Indian catalpa (the hardiness of which is not fully tested north of Philadelphia), the purple-fringe (grown low as a tree), the tree honeysuckle, *Lonicera grandiflora*, grown low on a single stem, the *Weigela amabilis*, also in tree-form; Josikia or chionanthus-leaved lilac, the dwarf weeping cherry (a very slow grower), the *Chionanthus virginica* (a little tender north of Philadelphia), the rose acacia grown over an iron frame, or any out-arching, low, small tree, weeping or otherwise, the foliage of which is pleasing throughout the season. Or, if a single evergreen is preferred, any one of the following will do: the dwarf white-pine, *P. strobus compacta*, the golden yew, *Taxus aurea*, the weeping silver-fir, *Picea pectinata pendula*, the golden arbor-vitae, or the weeping arbor-vitae. None of these will grow to greater size than the place requires, but they grow slowly. A pretty effect may be produced here by planting the erect yew, *Taxus erecta*, where the centre of the tree is indicated on the plan, with a golden arbor-vitae in front and a golden yew behind it. The erect yew is taller than the others, and very dark, so that if the three are planted not more than one or two feet apart, they will grow into a beautiful compact mass made up of three quite distinct tones of foliage. Or another pretty substitute for the one small tree, as shown on the plan, may be made by using the excessively slender Irish juniper for a centre 1, and grouping close around it the golden arbor-vitae 2, the *Podocarpus* (or *Taxus*) *japonica* 3, the dwarf silver-fir, *Picea compacta*, 6, the pigmy spruce, *Abies excelsa pygmaea*, 4, the dwarf hemlock, *Abies canadensis parsoni*, 5, and the creeping euonymus,

*Japonicus radicans marginatus*. This will in time make an irregular pyramid composed of an interesting variety of foliage and color, and easily protected in winter, if the plants are of doubtful hardiness or vigor.

The vase and flower-beds in front of the bay-window need no explanation. All the flower-beds shown on this plan, except the one opposite the back-porch, should be filled only with flowering-plants of the lowest growth: the bed excepted, and the place behind it, shown as shrubbery, may be occupied by taller plants, which are showy in leaves or flowers, but we think the effect will be more constantly pleasing if the latter is filled with evergreen shrubs from two to seven feet in height, mostly rhododendrons.

At the front end of the bed of roses, on the right, we would plant the Nordmans fir, *Picea Nordmaniana*, an evergreen tree of superior foliage, and believed hardy in most parts of the country. It eventually becomes a large tree, but will bear trimming when it begins to encroach too much upon the lawn.

The hemlock screen represented opposite the bath-room window should be thrown back to the end of the wash-room if the owner prefers to have that strip of ground in lawn, rather than under culture. We ask the reader to excuse us for having placed it where it is, for the space between the house and the currant-bushes allows of a pretty strip of lawn six feet wide, from which narrow beds may be cut adjoining the foundation-walls, for beds of low or slender annuals, which will not sprawl too far away from the house. The space will certainly be more profitable to the eye in this way than it can be in fruits and vegetables.

**Plate VI** – This plan is so similar to the preceding, and both are of so simple a character, that the intelligent reader will learn by an examination of the plate what manner of planting is intended. This plate differs principally from Plate V in having four pine trees of conspicuous size on the street margin of the lot. This presupposes a well-drained sandy soil, for without a congenial soil the pines will not develop great beauty. Supposing this condition to be satisfied, evergreens may be made a specialty of this place, and used as follows: Close by the left-hand gate-post (entering from the street), plant a bunch of the common border-box; a foot from it, and midway between the walk and side fence, a plant of the broad-leaved tree-box; a foot further, on the same mid-line, a plant of the gold or silver striped-leaved tree-box; then fill in with hemlocks a foot apart, and a foot from the fence, as far as the group is designated. Four feet from the same gatepost, and two feet from the walk, plant a *Podocarpus japonica*; eight feet from the gate, and three from the walk, the *Cephalotaxus fortunii mascula*; four feet beyond, and four feet from the walk, the golden arbor-vitae. Between the right-hand gate-post and the pine tree, fill next to the gate with the common English ivy, to trail on the ground and form a bush; next, midway between the fence and walk, and four feet from the post, the golden yew (*Taxus baccata aurea*); next, same distance from the walk, Sargent's hemlock (*A. canadensis inverta*); and between the pine and the fence, fill in with mahonias (*aquifolium and japonicum*). The pine here alluded to, to be the common white pine. The dwarf trees shown on the plan, twenty feet from the gate, are the *Abies gregoriana* on one side the walk, and on the other the *Picea hudsonica*, or the *Picea pectinata compacta*. These, and the gateway groups, form an entrance through evergreens alone. In climates more severe than that of New York city, substitute the *Pinus strobus compacta* for the *Cephalotaxus fortunii mascula*. The pine tree in the right-hand corner may be an Austrian, taking care to select one of short dense growth. Between it and the corner fill in with a mass of assorted rhododendrons, or with such shrubs as bush honeysuckles, deutzias of the smaller sorts, the common syringa, purple berberry, variegated elder, etc. The single tree in the middle of the front may be the weeping Japan sophora, the Judas tree (*Cercis canadensis*), or a neatly grown specimen of the white-flowering dogwood (*Cornus florida*). The two small trees marked on the plan 10 feet in front of each front corner of the house should be the two slender weeping firs, the *Abies excelsa inverta* and the *Picea pectinata pendula*, which will in time form a graceful flanking for the bay-window, and point the two groups of fragrant-blossomed deciduous shrubs shown on each side of it. The shrubbery shown between the walk and the main side veranda and its column vines should be entirely composed of bedding plants of rich foliage and successive bloom, which can be cleared away late in autumn. The remainder of the plan is so like that for Plate V, that no further designation of trees and shrubs need be made. A planter who is familiar with the dimensions and qualities of trees and shrubs may make a different choice, perhaps improve on those here named, and give another character to the place. The gateway entrance, for instance, may be bordered by low-growing umbelliferous trees like the Judas tree, the weeping sophora, the Scamston elm, the sassafras, or the *Kolreuteria paniculata*, of which any two would soon grow to form a natural arch. The use of any of these trees will not prevent the planting, under them, of those small evergreens like the ivy, the box-wood, and some others which flourish in partial shade. Or, some of the trees mentioned in Chapter XIV for artificial arches, may be employed in the same place instead of the groups of low evergreen shrubs, or the trees just named. The pine trees which are shown on the plan (if, as before remarked, the soil is congenial to them), in connection with the other evergreens, in the course of ten years would give an evergreen character to the outer limits of the lot without trespassing too much on the lawn space, and although a repetition of the same species of tree is not usually desirable on a small lot, the white pine unites so many more qualities which suit it for the places indicated, than any other evergreen, that we would make its use a specialty of the plan. The exquisite Bhotan pine is still of doubtful longevity with us; that is to say, it occasionally dies out after eight or ten years of healthy growth, just when its fountain-like tufts of drooping foliage have become so conspicuously beautiful as to endear it greatly to the owner. The same may be said of the long-leaved Pyrenean pine. Neither the Austrian or the Scotch pines drop their lower limbs with so little injury to their symmetry as the white pine, nor have either of them so fine a texture of foliage or wood when seen near by. On small lots, ground-room cannot well be afforded for that extension of the branches of evergreens upon a lawn, which constitutes one of their greatest beauties where there is space enough around to allow them to be seen to advantage. Therefore trees which develop their beauty overhead, and permit the lawn to be used and seen under their boughs, are more desirable.

## PLATE VII

*A long, narrow House, with Front near the Street, on an In-Lot sixty feet wide, and of considerable depth.*

We have here an inside lot of sixty-feet front, occupied to the depth of one hundred and thirty feet by the house, the walks and the ground embellishments. The kitchen-garden is back of the grape trellis, which should be of an ornamental character. The house is stretched out to correspond with the form of the lot, which is supposed to have no desirable ground connections with the adjoining lots, yet not so disagreeably surrounded as to make it necessary to shut out by trees and shrubs the out-look over the fences from the side-windows of the bay. The style of planting here shown is such as would suit only a person or family of decided taste for flowers, and the choicest selections of small shrubs. In the rear left-hand corner is room enough for two cherry trees, under which the lawn forms a sufficient drying-yard, and a convenient currant-border utilizes a space next the fence. Besides the cherries, no large trees are to be planted except hemlocks (marked H), which are gracefully shrubby in their early growth, and can be so easily kept within proper bounds by pruning, that they are introduced to form an evergreen flanking for the rear of the house, and background for the narrow strips of lawn on either side of it. In time they will overarch the walk, and under their dark shadows the glimpse of the bit of lawn beyond, with its bright flowers, will be brought into pretty relief. Our engraver has been somewhat unfortunate in the extreme rigidity of outline given to all the trees and shrubs shown on this plan, yet precision and formality are peculiarities which the narrow limits of the lot render necessary, and the completeness with which this specialty is carried out will constitute its merit. Nearly all the shrub and tree embellishment is with small evergreens, flowers of annuals, and bedding plants. Flowers are always relieved with good effect when seen against a background of evergreens. It will be observed that the close side-fences are, much of their length, uncovered by shrubbery. They must, therefore, be very neatly, even elegantly made, if the proprietor can afford it. They then become a suitable backing for the flowers that may be made to form a sloping bank of bloom against them. By finishing the inside of the fence *en espalier*, it may be covered all over with delicate summer vines whose roots, growing under it, will interfere little with planting and transplanting seeds, roots, and bulbs in front of them. In naming the trees intended for this plan, it must not be supposed that other selections equally good, or better, may not be made by a good gardener. The following is suggested as one of many that will be appropriate to the place:

A, A. Two hemlocks planted two feet from the fence and from the walk to form an arch over the gate when large enough, as shown in Chapter XIV.

B. Parson's dwarf hemlock two feet from the walk and six feet from the fence.

C, C, C, C. Irish junipers two feet from the walk.

D. Space between juniper and corner post on the right may be filled with mahonias, English ivy, and azalias that love shade.

E (next to the fence). Dwarf weeping juniper, *J. oblonga pendula*.

E (in the centre of front group). The pendulous Norway spruce, *Abies excelsa inverta*, the central stem of which must be kept erect by tying to a stake until it is from six to eight feet high.

F, F. One, the dwarf Norway spruce, *Abies gregoriana*, and the other the dwarf silver-fir, *Picea pectinata compacta*.

G (in the front group). Golden arbor-vitae.

G (opposite bow-window of living-room). A bed of assorted geraniums.

G (opposite dining-room). A single plant of *Colleus verschafelti*.

H, H, H. Hemlocks; for the left-hand front corner use Sargent's hemlock, *Abies canadensis inverta*; its main stem to be kept tied to a stake until it has a firm growth six feet high.

I, I, I (on the left side of walk). Dwarf-box for clipping.

I (on right side of walk). The weeping arbor-vitae and the dwarf weeping juniper, *J. oblonga pendula*.

J. *Podocarpus japonica*, if protected in winter.

K. Parson's arbor-vitae, *Thuja occidentalis compacta*, two feet from the fence. Between K and L plant a golden arbor-vitae.

L. The pendulous silver-fir, *Picea pectinata pendula*, four feet from the fence. Directly back of it, midway between it and the fence, the erect yew, *Taxus erecta*, whose deep green foliage will contrast well with the golden arbor-vitaes near it, and as its hardiness in all localities is not so well proved as that of the other trees near it, its placement back of them, and near to the fence, will serve to insure its safety from cold.

M. Irish and Swedish junipers near the fence.

N. The dwarf white-pine, *P. strobus compacta*, four feet from the fence; and behind, on each side, small rhododendrons. Four feet above the pine, near the fence, plant a common hemlock, and when it is large enough to form a background for the dwarf pine – say from eight to ten feet high – keep it well clipped back to prevent it from spreading over the dwarfs, and taking up too much of the lawn.

O, O. Round beds for verbenas or other creeping flowers of constant brilliancy.

P. Bed for favorite fragrant annuals or low shrubs.

Q (by the side of the kitchen). Bed for flowering-vines to train on the house, or, if the exposure be southerly, or southeasterly, some good variety of grape-vine. Whichever side of the rear part of the house has the proper exposure to ripen grapes well, cannot be more pleasingly covered than with neatly kept grape-vines; which should not be fastened directly to the house, but on horizontal slats from six inches to a foot from the house, and these should be so strongly put up that they may be used instead of a ladder to stand upon to trim the vines and gather the fruit.

R. Rhododendrons.

S. Bed of cannas, or assorted smaller plants with brilliant leaves of various colors.

T, U, V, X, Z. A bed of rhododendrons.

W, W, W. May be common deciduous shrubs of any favorite full-foliaged sort.

Y. Rhododendrons and azaleas.

Opposite the corner of the veranda where fuschias are indicated, the space should be filled between the Irish juniper and the fence with the golden arbor-vitae, and the *Podocarpus japonica*, planted side by side.

The foregoing list for planting is made on the assumption that the owner is, or desires to be, an amateur in the choicest varieties of small evergreens, as well as in flowers, and willing to watch with patience their slow development; for there is no doubt that with deciduous shrubs a showy growth of considerable beauty can be secured in much less time. Yet the type of embellishment made with such a collection of evergreens as have been named for this place, is so much rarer, and has so greatly the advantage in its autumn, winter, and spring beauty, that we would have little hesitation, in adopting it.

For the benefit, however, of those who wish a quicker display of verdure in return for their expense and labor in planting, we subjoin an essentially different list of trees and shrubs for the same plan, viz.:

A, A. Two Scamston elms (planted two feet from fence and walk) grafted on straight stocks eight feet from the ground, to form a tabular topped arch over the gateway, by interweaving the side branches which are nearest to each other. These grow so rapidly that all the space within ten feet from the centre of the gate will in six years be deeply shaded by them, so that only those plants which are known to flourish in deep shade should be planted near the gate. Among these the English ivy may occupy the same place in the corner as before.

B. May be the *Cephalotaxus fortunii mascula*, or purple magnolia.

C, C (nearest the gate). *Daphne cneorum*. C, C (near the veranda). Should be Irish juniper as in the first plan, and the space marked fuschias to be filled as before recommended; C on left-hand front of lot to be an Irish or Swedish juniper.

D. Box-wood, spurge laurel, hypericum, purple magnolia, or rhododendrons.

E (middle group). *Andromeda arborea*, or, south of Philadelphia, the Indian catalpa, *C. himalayensis*.

F, F. *Spirea reevesii flore plena* and *Spirea fortunii alba*.

G (of same group). *Spirea Van Houtti*. In the spaces between G and F the *Deutzia gracilis* and the *Andromeda floribunda* may be planted within two feet of the stem of the *Andromeda arborea*.

H (in left-hand corner). Two deutzias, the white and red, *D. crenata alba* and *D. crenata rubra flore plena*, planted side by side. The other Hs to be hemlocks as in the other plan.

I, I, I, I. Tree-box on left of walk, Siberian arbor-vitae on the right.

J. *Deutzia gracilis*.

K. Purple berberry two feet from fence. Above it, the same distance from the fence, the variegated-leaved althea.

L. Common red Tartarian honeysuckle, four feet from fence. Behind it, next to the fence, the spurge laurel, *Daphne laureola*.

M. Two Swedish junipers one foot from fence.

N. *Weigela rosea* three feet from fence. Close to fence, on each side of it, the English ivy.

O. Beds for creeping flowers as in previous plan.

P. Bed for annuals or low shrubs.

Q. Same as in former list.

R. A bed of salvias, to fill in between the hemlocks.

S. Cannas, or some lower bedding annuals.

T. The lilac, *Rothmagensis rubra*.

U. Gordon's flowering currant.

V. Two dwarf rhododendrons, *roseum elegans* and *album candidissima*, and behind them towards the grape trellis and next the fence, the taller rhododendrons, *grandiflorum* and *album elegans*. These will fill as near to the trellis as anything should be planted.

X. Rhododendrons, *grandiflorum* and *candidissima* planted together.

Shrubs shown at the house-corners should be selected from those whose branches droop toward the ground, well covered with foliage, and whose flowers are fragrant; such as the common syringa, bush honeysuckles, jasmines, wild roses, purple magnolia, etc., etc.; the beauty and abundance of the foliage throughout the season being of more importance than the blossoms. But there are shrubs which combine nearly every merit of foliage, bloom, and fragrance, and these are often the common sorts best known.

It is not practicable to name in detail everything which may be planted on a lot of this size, and the two lists just given will form a ground-work into which may be interwoven a great variety of quite small shrubs without breaking the arrangement intended.

In whatever way this place is planted, the area in lawn is so narrow that it can only be made to look well by the nicest keeping.

## PLATE VIII

*A simple Plan for a Corner Lot one hundred by one hundred and seventy feet, with Stable and Carriage-house accommodations.*

By referring to Plates IX and XII, and comparing them with the one now under consideration, it will be seen that there is a similarity in the forms and sizes of the lots and the house-plans. A comparison of their differences will be interesting. Plates VIII and IX represent corner lots 100 x 170 feet, having stable and carriage-house accommodations, while Plate XII is an in-lot 100 x 160 feet, without those luxuries, but with convenience for keeping a cow. Plan VIII is designed to illustrate the utmost simplicity of style, requiring the minimum of trouble and expense in its maintenance. In both plans the nearest part of the house stands thirty feet from the side street, and eighty-two feet from the street upon which the bay-windows look out. On this plan the short straight walk from the side street to the veranda is the only one that requires to be carefully made, and is but twenty-seven feet in length from the street to the steps; while on Plate IX there is an entrance from both streets, connected by a curving walk with the main house entrance, and other walks to the kitchen entrances and carriage-house. This difference in the walks is suggestive of the greater embellishment of the latter plan in all other respects, and, with its vases, flower-beds, and more numerous groups of shrubbery, indicates the necessity for the constant services of a gardener. Plan VIII, on the other hand, with its plain lawn, and groups of trees which require but little care, and its few plain flower-beds, may easily be taken care of by any industrious proprietor, before and after the hours devoted to town business – especially if the wife will assume the care of the flowers – and if the lawn is in high condition, and the trees are kept growing luxuriantly, the simplicity of the planting will not result in any lack of that air of elegance which most persons desire to have their places express; for it is not so much costliness and elaborateness that challenges the admiration of cultivated people as the unconscious grace with which a plain dress may be worn, so as to appear elegant notwithstanding its simplicity. It will be observed that there is no vegetable garden on either plan, but a good number of cherry, pear, and other fruit trees, as well as an abundance of grapes, currants, raspberries, and strawberries are provided for. Yet in the neighborhood of the carriage-house, the ground in cultivation under the trees may serve to produce a small quantity of those low vegetables which take but little room, and are wanted in small quantities only.

Supposing the walks to be laid out as shown on the plan, the first things to be planted are the fruit trees. Three cherry trees – say the mayduke, black tartarian, and late-duke; seven pear trees (not dwarfs) – say one Madeleine, one Dearborn's seedling, one Bloodgood, two Seckels, and two Bartletts; two peach trees, the George the Fourth or Haine's early, and Crawford's early, and a few orange-quinces near the stable, are all the fruit trees there is room for. The sides of the carriage-house and stable will afford the best of places for the growth of grapes; the vines, however, should not be fastened directly to the wall, but on a trellis six inches or a foot from it, to allow a circulation of air through the foliage. Besides these, a few vines may be grown to advantage on a trellis back of the kitchen, and on a circular trellis around the gravelled space in front of the carriage-house, and also on the back fence, marked raspberry border, if preferred. Currant bushes and raspberries do well in partially shaded situations, while grape vines need the most sunny exposure. The places for one or the other must therefore be chosen with reference to the light and shade adjacent to buildings, fences, and trees. (The carriage turn-way is represented a little broader than it need be. There should be ten feet space between it and the back fence to make room for the trellis for grapes).

The fruit trees being disposed of, let us turn to the lawn-ground. The front gate recedes from the street four feet, forming a bay from the sidewalk. On the left, as one enters, the view is all open across the lawn. On the right of the gate, along the fence, there is a heavy mass of shrubbery, to be composed of lilacs, honeysuckles, weigelas, or any of the thrifty common shrubs which do not grow bare of leaves at the bottom. Or, if an evergreen screen is preferred to these blossoming shrubs, the border may be planted irregularly with the American and Siberian arbor-vitaes. On the left, next to the fence, and close against it, we would plant English ivy, tree-box, periwinkle, or myrtle for the first ten feet, and hardy dwarf arbor-vitaes, hemlocks, and yews on the next ten feet. On the right of the walk, and two feet from it, is a straight bed for annual and bulbous flowers, which is backed by a bed of shrubbery running parallel with the walk, designed to shut from view the kitchen drying-yard, under the cherry and pear trees. This screen should be composed entirely of evergreens which can be kept within seven feet in height. In the front, next to the flower-bed, may be a collection, in a row, of the finest very small dwarfs, of as many species as the owner desires to procure, backed by a dense mass of arbor-vitaes and hardy yews intermingled. The row of dwarf evergreens should in time occupy the space which is marked as a bed for annuals, while the former are too small to fill it. The masses of shrubs shown against the house may be of common sorts which are favorites with the proprietor or his family, and that do not exceed seven feet in height. On the left of the walk the flower-beds 1, 2, and 3 may be filled, each, with one species of low flowers not exceeding nine inches in height, so as to make brilliant contrasts of colors. Beds 4 and 6 may be filled with bulbous flowers in the spring, and later, with geraniums, lantanas, or salvias. Bed 5 admits of some skill in arrangement. In its centre, next to the house, we would try the Japanese striped maize; next to it a half circle of salvias; outside of these a half circle of mountain-of-snow geranium; next, a circle of *Colleus verschafelti*, and, next the grassy margin, the Mrs Pollock geranium. Another season the same bed might be splendid with cannas alone, as follows: for the centre, one plant of the blood-red canna, *C. sanguinea chatei*, six feet high; one foot from it, three plants of the *C. sellowi*, four to five feet high; next, a circle of the *C. flaccida*, three feet, and for the outer circle the *C. compacta elegantissima*, two feet high, alternated with the *C. augustifolia nana pallida*. If the occupant of the house does not wish to obtain plants from the greenhouse to stock these beds, they may be cheaply and prettily filled by annuals graded in size in the same manner as above indicated for a bed of cannas. The circular border of cultivated ground between the dining-room bay-window and the hemlock border may also be filled with annuals, graded from those that grow only a few inches high next the grass, to an outer circle made with flowering plants from four to six feet high. Bed 7 is intended for an assortment of geraniums. At 8 is a good place for the pendulous silver-fir, and at 9 for Sargent's hemlock, *Abies canadensis inverta*, trained to a straight stick, and kept small by pruning.

On a line with the side-walls of the house, and twenty feet in front, two sycamore maples are designated. We do not intend to recommend this variety as any better or more beautiful than the sugar, red-bud, or Norway maples, or than the horse-chestnut, but it represents a type of trees with formal outlines, and rich masses of foliage, which are appropriate for such places; unless the style of the house is picturesque; in which case elms, birches, and other loose growing trees would be more appropriate. The centre group of evergreens is mostly composed of common and well-known sorts, the points being representations of the arbor-vitae family, and the centre of the taller hemlocks. Lawson's cypress is still a rare tree, and its hardiness is doubtful north of Philadelphia. Where it may not be safely used, a full-foliaged specimen of the Norway spruce may be substituted. South of New York, near the sea-coast, we would also substitute the *Glypto-strobus sinensis pendula* for the arbor-vitae *plicata*. While these trees are small they will appear insignificant in so large a bed, but we advise no one to trust himself to plant trees more thickly than they should eventually grow, on the plea that when they crowd each other a part may be removed; for however sound the theory, it is rarely carried out in practice. Besides, no trees are so beautiful as those which have an unchecked expansion from the beginning, and this is especially the case with evergreens, some of which never recover from the malformations produced by being crowded during the first ten or fifteen years of their growth. Therefore, let the open spaces between the permanent trees, in the beds which are outlined for cultivation, be filled during their minority with showy annuals or bedding plants; taking care not to plant so near to the young trees as to smother or weaken them by the luxuriant growth of the former.

The evergreen group on the right is intended to be made up entirely of firs – hemlocks, Norway and black spruces – mixed indiscriminately, to show as a mass, and not as single specimens. If the proprietor has a desire for rarities in this family, they can be substituted.

The group on the left, as its symbols show, is intended to be entirely of pines. In the centre, plant a white pine and a Bhotan pine side by side and close together, the former on the south side of the latter. Fifteen feet back of them put in an Austrian pine; towards the front the cembran pine; to the extreme right, the dwarf white pine, *P. strobus compacta*, and in the spaces between fill with the varieties of the mugho or mountain pine, or with rhododendrons.

The deciduous group lightly outlined near the right-hand corner explains itself. If thriftily grown, the trees there marked should make a beautiful group in summer, and a brilliant one in autumn.

The pair of trees near the left-hand corner we would have the *Kolreuteria paniculata*.

The hemlock border on the left, opposite the dining-room bay-window, is intended to form a close screen, to grow naturally till the trees occupy from seven to ten feet in width from the fence, when they are to be kept within bounds by pruning. They should be planted about two feet apart.

## PLATE IX

*Plan for a Corner Lot 100 x 170 feet, planted in a more elaborate style than the preceding plan.*

In describing the preceding plate, allusion was made to the greater expensiveness of this plan. Premising, therefore, that it is intended for a person who loves his trees and plants, and who can afford to keep a gardener in constant employ, we will briefly describe those features of the place which need explanation.

The front entrance of the place (the one at the bottom of the page on the plate) is designed to have an elm tree arch over it, similar to that shown by Fig. 40 in Chapter XIV. The group A, on the right near the gate, may be entirely composed of rhododendrons.

The group E is composed of a pair of weeping silver-firs (nearest the gate), the mugho pine on the left, and the dwarf white pine, *P. compacta*, farthest from the gate.

Group B, on the right, will shade the walk with the low and broadly spreading top of the *Kolreuteria paniculata* at its point, behind which may be another group of rhododendrons, and close to the fence a compact border of hemlocks, which must be allowed to spread well upon the ground, and mingle their boughs with the rhododendrons, but not to exceed eight or ten feet in height.

The group C, with a sugar maple (in the place of which a pair of *Magnolia machrophyllas*, planted close together, might be substituted with good effect) in front of it, is to be composed of a circle of choice dwarf evergreens on the side next the house, backed by a hemlock border along the fence, as described for the preceding group.

From the following list a choice of dwarf evergreen trees or shrubs can be made: *Pinus strobus compacta, Pinus strobus pumila, Pinus sylvestris pumila, Pinus mughus, Picea pectinata compacta, Picea pectinata pendula, Picea hudsonica, Abies nigra pumila, Abies nigra pendula, Abies excelsa gregoriana, Abies excelsa inverta, Abies e. conica, Abies canadensis inverta, Abies canadensis parsoni, Andromeda floribunda,* tree-box, *Buxus arborea, Hypericum kalmianum* and *H. prolificum,* the kalmias, the creeping junipers *Juniperus repens, Juniperus repanda densa, J. suecica, J. suecica nana, J. hibernica, J. oblonga pendula, J. spaeroides, Thuja aurea, Thuja occidentalis compacta, Taxus baccata aurea, Taxus erecta, Taxus baccata elegantissima, Cephalotaxtis fortunii mascula, Taxus* or *Podocarpus japonica,* the rhododendrons, and the mahonias. For the sizes and characteristics of all these, we must refer the reader to the descriptions of evergreen trees in Part II. By selecting the smallest evergreens for the front of the group, and placing the larger ones behind, even a small bed like this will accommodate a large number of specimens. The side towards the veranda is laid out in a formal circle for convenience in first laying it out, but as the planting progresses, and as it becomes desirable to add one small thing after another to the group, this, as well as some of the other groups, may be enlarged in the manner shown by the dotted lines; or, it can be laid out in that manner at first, if the list of small choice evergreens to be purchased is large enough to fill it. Most of the finer dwarf evergreens are rare and costly compared with common sorts, so that the lists must be made with prudence, in order that these, together with other more indispensable purchases from the nurseries, shall not amount to so large a sum as to surprise and discourage the planter. Where the resources of the proprietor will not permit him to procure at once everything that can be advantageously used on the place, it is best to plant, the first season, all the larger (which are usually the commoner and cheaper) trees and shrubs, keeping the beds filled with showy annuals, while acquiring, year by year, choice additional collections of permanencies. But it is quite essential to the formation of tasteful grounds that all the large permanent trees and shrubs be placed properly in the beginning, so that whatever is afterwards added will be of such subsidiary character as will group with and around the former.

The group D, from the gate to the pear tree, should be composed of a mass of low evergreen trees or shrubs planted about six feet from the walk, and from the foot-walk gate to the carriage gate with a hedge of Siberia arbor-vitae planted two feet from the fence. Between this hedge and the pear tree, at the intersection of the walks, there will be room enough for the following: mugho pine (*P. mughus*), the dwarf white pine (*P. s. compacta*) the *Cephalotaxus fortunii mascula*, the conical yew (*Taxus erecta*), the golden yew (*Taxus aurea*), the golden arbor-vitae (*Thuja aurea*), Sargent's hemlock (*Abies canadensis inverta*), and the weeping juniper (*J. oblonga pendula*). By alternating the dark and light colored foliage of these evergreen shrubs, placing the dark ones farther from the walk than the light ones, they will form an interesting border, and in time a dense screen.

Fifteen feet from the end of the veranda towards the front street, and twelve feet from the walk, a pine tree is indicated. This may be either the common white pine, or the more beautiful Bhotan pine, if one is willing to risk the permanence of the latter; – unless the soil of the locality is such that neither of these pines will develop its beauty – in which case we would substitute either Nordmanns fir (*Picea nordmaniana*), or some deciduous tree which branches low. This tree is placed for the purpose of breaking the view from the street to the veranda, so that persons sitting in the latter will have a partial privacy from the street passers. If the soil is deeply fertile, and not too dry, the *Magnolia soulangeana* may be substituted for the pine, in climates not more severe than that of New York city; while further north the double white-flowering horse-chestnut, allowed to branch low, is admirably adapted to the position. The white birch, in front of the centre line of the house, should be the cut-leaved weeping variety, which is too beautiful and appropriate to the place to allow anything else to be substituted for it. The tree in front of the other corner of the house, in the climate just mentioned, may be the *Magnolia machrophylla*; in the northern States, any one of the following: the red-flowering, or double white-flowering horse-chestnut, purple-leaved beech, grape-leaved linden, the sugar, red-bud, Norway or sycamore maple (especially the gold-leaved variety of the latter), the oak-leaved mountain ash, or the tulip tree. While the tree is young a group of shrubs may be planted on an irregular line with the side of the house, so that the tree will form its centre, as shown on the plan. The position of two magnolias on the left may be determined by reference to the scale. In a region too cold, or a soil too thin or dry for the magnolias, we would substitute a group of three beeches – the weeping beech in the centre, the cut-leaved nearest the house, and the purple-leaved nearest the street. It will be observed that this side of the lot connects quite openly with the adjoining lot – having few trees or shrubs on the margin. If there is no division fence, or only a light and nearly invisible one, and that lot is pleasingly improved, the views across it from the parlor and dining-room windows will exhibit a generous expansion of lawn which it is desirable to secure; and it will probably include in the view from them some embellishments which this place has not. If, however, there is anything unsightly in the neighbor lot, or any unfriendly disposition on the part of its owner that induces him to ignore the advantage of mutual views over each other's lawns, and to fence or plant to prevent it, that side may then be filled with masses of shrubbery in a manner similar to that shown on the left of Plate IV.

The group G, at the left, may be planted from the street to the pine with the strong growing old shrubs – lilacs, weigelas, honeysuckles, syringas, deutzias, etc., etc. Under, or rather near, the white or Austrian pine (the former pine if the soil is sandy, the latter if it is clayey), plant almost any of the yews, the Sargent hemlock, the *Hypericum kalmianum* and *H. prolificum*, the tree-box variety *angustifolia*, and the variegated-leaved elder, all of which flourish in the shade of other trees. At the upper extreme of the group plant the pendulous Norway spruce, *Abies excelsa inverta*; eight feet behind it the common Norway spruce, and between this and the pine the Chinese cypress, *Glypto-strobus sinensis pendula*, and some of the evergreen shrubs just named.

The belt of hemlocks against the fence, opposite the dining-room bay-window, is to be terminated at the front by a slender weeping silver-fir, *Picea pectinata pendula*. The trees at the two corners of the dining-room bay are intended for Irish junipers, or the weeping juniper, *J. oblonga pendula*. Other trees and shrubs are designated on the plan, and need no explanation.

There are many small flower-beds on the plan, and one quite large rose-bed in the middle of the front at F. The latter is to have an elegant rose-pillar, or a substantial trellis in the centre, with groups of roses of varieties graded to diminish in size to the points. Or, if preferred, this may be a group of evergreens with the slender weeping silver-fir for a centre, and lower trees and dwarfs around it, so as to form the same figure of a cross. This will, in time, be more beautiful throughout the greater part of the year than the rose-bed, but the latter can be made far more brilliant in summer. Yet the rude, briary appearance of rose-bushes, after the leaves fall, is a serious objection to them when compared with the cheerful elegance of a well-formed evergreen group at all seasons of the year. The other flower-beds are small, and of the simplest forms. Beds 1, 1, 1, 1 should be filled in spring with bulbous flowers, and later with verbenas, portulaccas, *Phlox drummondi*, escholtzias, or similar low plants. Beds 2, 2 may have three geraniums in each, the largest variety in the middle. Beds 3 and 5, in the wall-corners, should have some little evergreen vines, say English or Irish ivies, planted in the extreme corner, with heliotrope and mignonette around them. Bed 4 may be planted as suggested in the description of Plate VIII. Beds 6, 6, 6, 6 may be filled with four varieties of cannas of about equal height; 7, 7, and 9 with low bulbs in spring, and later with gladiolii in the centre and petunias or other flowers of similarly brilliant and abundant bloom, around them. Bed 8 to have a mountain-of-snow geranium, or a *Wigandia caracasana* in the centre, and three robust plants of *Colleus verschafelti* on the points; 10 is a mass of cannas; 11 may be a bed of hollyhocks, with a tall sort in the centre, and low varieties around it. We have merely suggested the flowers for the various beds as a starting-point for persons unfamiliar with flowers. Most intelligent ladies, as well as gardeners, are more familiar with flower culture than with any other gardening art, and will be able to vary the beds from year to year, and to improve on the selections here given. They will also learn by experiment, better than they can be told, the best materials to use in embellishing with flowers and wreathing leaves, the vases near the entrance steps.

## PLATE X

*A Simple Plan for Planting an Interior Lot two hundred feet front and three hundred feet deep.*

This plan represents a large mansion on an in-lot two hundred feet front by three hundred feet deep. Plate XI is the same house and lot treated more elaborately. The same differences, carried out on a larger scale, may be observed between these two plans of grounds, as between those of Plates VIII and IX; the one here described having a less extent of drive, walks, and ornamental plantations than the plan shown by Plate XI. All the surroundings are supposed to be the same, and the different modes of laying out the grounds are meant to represent simply the different tastes or means of occupants. Here the proprietor is supposed to desire grounds of the most simple character, which will be at the same time suitable to the mansion and the lot. The entrance road, turnway, and drive to the stable are the most direct and simple that can be made, and they constitute also the only entrance walks to the house. Ninety feet of the rear of the lot is devoted to utilities, viz.: to carriage-house conveniences, to a kitchen-garden, and an orchard; the ground in the latter being also devoted to culture for small fruits and vegetables until the fruit trees are large enough to shadow the whole ground. The front two hundred and ten feet is all devoted to the house and its ground embellishments. The drive is ten feet in width; the circle around which it turns is thirty feet in diameter. An avenue of three elm trees on each side of the entrance-drive are its only decorations, though the street-trees in a line with them will give it the appearance of an avenue of eight instead of six trees. In the centre of the circle a pine tree is designated – to be a white pine if the soil is sandy, otherwise an Austrian. These trees are chosen because they are of rapid and healthy growth, and cast their lower branches as they grow large, so that the lawn beneath them, while it is deeply shadowed, is not destroyed, and the view under the branches is unobstructed. This will be rather an objection than a merit with those persons who desire the main entrance to be quite secluded and concealed from view. We would recommend for them that the circle be planted with a group of firs, whose branches rest upon the ground during all stages of their growth, and would eventually cover the whole circle with an impenetrable mass of foliage. A single Norway spruce planted in the centre will do this. So, probably, would a Nordmanns fir, *Picea nordmaniana*. While these trees are small, the borders of the circle (supposing it to be desirable to shut out the view of the approach road from the porch) may be planted, four feet from the road, with quick growing deciduous shrubs, such as bush honeysuckles, lilacs, weigelas, deutzias, etc., which can be removed when the centre tree begins to crowd them. Or, with one of the same large evergreens in the centre, a gardenesque border may be formed around the circle with single specimens of rare dwarf evergreens, planted four feet from the road. Doubtless the noblest feature of such a turn circle is a single great spreading tree like a mature white oak or American chestnut, and if the proprietor appreciates the pleasures of hope, and desires the greatest simplicity of effect, he had better plant the latter. We have seen specimens of the American chestnut of colossal size, which men now living remember as sprouts.

A lot so large as this must needs have a ground-plan of the planting made on a large scale, and as it is extremely difficult to carry out any system of planting for such a place from a verbal description, we shall not attempt to describe in detail all the materials that form the plantation, but make merely a rough inventory of its properties. Though it is an in-lot, and in the main designed without connection with adjoining lots, from which it is shown to be separated by high fences or walls and shrubbery to within sixty or seventy feet of the street, yet on this front space we have left openings on each side for connections with adjoining grounds. Back of this, each side of the lot is bounded by screens of evergreens. On the right of the drive to the carriage-house is a cold grape-house. The house-front is supposed to be to the east, so that this grapery has a southern exposure. It may seem to have no border for the roots of the grape vines, if it is supposed that the road in its front has been made by excavating all the good soil and substituting broken stone and gravel only. But we would not have this done. For a road-bed, or for a grape border, the drainage must be equally deep and effective. That being secured we would make the road-bed of the best grape soil, and pave over it with stone, after the 'Belgian' and 'Medina' pavement manner, at least as far as the length of the grape house; using no more sand or gravel than is necessary to bed or fill in between the stone. Of course this bed will rise and fall by the freezing and thawing of the soil beneath, but this will do no harm. The rich soil of the pavement-bed will also start vegetation between the stones, but on so narrow a road, in constant use, the extra labor required to keep the surface clean is inconsiderable. On the other hand the pavement acts as a cooling mulch in summer and the contrary in winter – it equalizes both the temperature and moisture of the roots, and by the reflection of heat from its surface, adds to the heating power of the sun's rays in maturing the grapes within. Were the road-bed not made suitable feeding ground for the roots of the vines within, such a position for a grapery would of course be impracticable; but when thus prepared it becomes the most advantageous for the production of good grapes, as well as convenient of access. Beyond the cold grape-house the fence is made use of for training hardy grape vines. On the left is a bed designed for growing Delaware grapes on stakes, at first, with the intention of making them eventually into self-sustaining low trees. On and near the garden-walk from the back veranda are also trellises and an arbor for hardy grapes. A row of seven cherry trees planted one hundred feet from the back line of the lot forms a sort of dividing line between the decorative and the utilitarian parts of the lot. The orchard-rows back of it, when the trees are well-grown, will, however, add much to the pleasant character of the vistas from the front street, and need not be out of harmony with the groupings on the lawn in front of them. While the trees are small, and the ground cultivated in garden crops, it may be desirable to have a grape-trellis or an arbor-vitae hedge-screen midway between the rows of cherry and pear trees, or a bed of tall and massy annuals, but after ten years the effect will be better if there is no division between the lawn and the orchard.

## PLATE XI

*A Plan for a First Class Suburban Home on a Lot two hundred feet front and three hundred feet deep.*

This plan differs from the country residence of a retired citizen in this, that it is a home which does not include orchards, pastures, and meadows, but is devoted to the development of sylvan beauty rather than pecuniary utilities, or farm conveniences. It is a suitable home for a family of cultivated people, with ample means, and rural tastes.

The orchard which takes an important place in the preceding plan is here omitted, to make a more extensive lawn and a fine pleasure-walk. The entrance-drive is more expensive than in the preceding plan, and a side entrance walk is added. In dispensing with an orchard we have endeavored to introduce in other places enough fruit trees to supply the family with those kinds of fruit which it is most indispensable to have on one's own place. It will be seen that there are four cherry trees on the north (right) side of the house; four pear trees along the border leading to the carriage-house, three more on the left-hand border of the kitchen-garden, and four peach trees. Some of the groups in other parts of the grounds may now and then include a fruit tree. Apple and pear trees, Siberian crabs and quinces, which harmonize well with some of the purely ornamental trees, may be introduced in sufficient numbers in this way to furnish a good supply of summer fruits. The north fence back of the evergreen-screen is a continuous trellis for hardy grapes. Grape trellises also occupy the ends of two divisions of the kitchen-garden back of the house. If a grape-house is added, it may occupy either the place indicated on the preceding plan, or be built with its back to the walk on the left of the garden, and facing the left. In this case a few of the trees there would be omitted, and a slight change made in the arrangement beyond. Raspberries can be grown in abundance on the border next the back fence, strawberries under the growing fruit trees, and currants on the walks where designated. The kitchen-garden is certainly small for so fine a place, being but 60 x 80 feet, including the central-walks, but this space, if well used for those things only which can be better grown than bought, will produce a greater amount of vegetables than many persons suppose; and in addition to this space permanently dedicated to such things, room will be found for many years on the borders and among the young trees of a plantation to grow many vegetables which are by no means unsightly. In fact, such plants as beets, carrots, parsnips, cabbages, and sea-kale, all of which have foliage of great beauty and are of low growth, can occasionally be grown to advantage, to cover ground which needs cultivation, in places where they will fill in with as good effect as flowering annuals. A good gardener can also grow strawberries with profit in young shrubbery plantations, where their presence will not be noticed.

Let us now suppose ourselves in the street on the sidewalk at A. From that corner the house and grounds will be seen to good advantage, but the finest lines of view on the latter will be obtained further to the right. At the point B, the whole length of the lawn to the evergreen boundaries and shrubby groups of the croquet and archery ground is an unbroken expanse, margined on the left by varied groups of trees with clear stems, whose shadows fleck, but do not interrupt the view; behind these, masses of large flowering shrubs form continuous bays and projections of foliage that rest upon the lawn; while on the right, in the distance, glimpses of the pleasure-walk, now open, now lost to sight behind verdant arches and projecting groups, and nearer, the long vine-covered front of the veranda, and the light colors of many flower-beds in dark bays or on open lawn – altogether, will give from this point of view an impression of beauty and extent not often realized on less than an acre and a half. Nor will the view be less pleasing from the main entrance at C, for from this point the trees and the shrubbery on the left are seen to better advantage, and the evergreen groups, summer-house, and flower-beds of the far corner come into view. From D and E the views are shorter, but take in a variety of groups and single trees which will be more or less interesting according to the choice of materials in planting, and the luxuriance with which they are grown. Glimpses may also be seen from these points of the long lawn and the flowerbeds on the south side of the house. At F, over the gateway, we would have a hemlock arch like some of those shown in Chapter XIV. Standing under this arch, narrow openings between shrubs and trees give a glimpse directly in front, margined by low beds of flowers, of the fruit trees and vines that border the drive down to the carriage-house front; which should, of course, be designed to form a pleasing centre of this vista. The views will also be pleasing in every direction as one walks along towards the house. On the line G, H, between thirty and forty feet from the street, an open line of lawn is maintained with a view to reciprocity of vistas with the smaller front grounds of adjoining neighbors.

As remarked of the preceding plan, this design embraces too much for verbal description, and should be planted after a well-considered working plan. But there is one small feature to which we would call attention, viz.: the triangular piece between the entrance-road and turn-ways. This is marked to be planted with fir trees, to grow into a dense mass, in order to counteract as far as possible, by its shadows and the depth of its verdure, the bare exposure of the surrounding roads. The centre tree should be the Norway spruce, and the others surrounding it, hemlocks.

A careful examination of the plan will, we trust, supersede the necessity of any further description.


## PLATE XII

*An Inside Lot one hundred feet front, and one hundred and sixty feet deep.*

Reference was made to this plate in descriptions of Plates VIII and IX, the house-plan and the lot, in form and size, being nearly the same; this plan being an in-lot with no carriage-house and stable, and the others being corner lots with these conveniences. The lot here represented is supposed to have an alley on the rear end, and to front on the south side of an east and west street. This gives the bay-window front of the house a northern exposure. A great advantage, in the outlook from the windows, results from this exposure, viz.: that one sees the sunny-side of all the shrubbery in the front grounds, and thus has the satisfaction of finding his verdant pets always in a smiling humor. The house is sixty feet from the front street, and about the same depth in the rear end of the lot is devoted to the kitchen-garden, fruits, and cow, wood and coal-house; this part being separated from the part devoted to lawn by a grape-trellis and border. Near the street the neighbors' lots are supposed to offer satisfactory openings where indicated by the upper dotted lines on each side. The groups of shrubbery are placed so as to illustrate many of the suggestions of the rules given in Chapter XI. No long vista of lawn is possible, but the groups and single specimens of shrubs or dwarf trees, with a few bedding-plants and flower-beds, if properly chosen, and planted in conformity with the plan, and well grown, will hardly fail to make a yard of superior attractiveness; especially pleasing as seen from the bay-windows; the arrangement having been made with reference to the effect from them.

**Description** – Let us begin at the front-entrance gate, from which a walk four feet wide leads straight to the veranda entrance, and a walk three feet in width to the kitchen entrance. On each side the front gate arbor-vitae trees (the Siberian) are designated, with low masses of evergreen shrubs between them and the fence. An opening to a straight walk like this is especially appropriate for a verdant arch, and if the proprietor has the patience to grow one, the substitution of the hemlock for the arbor-vitae is recommended. For an arch, the trees should not be planted more than two feet away from the walk.

The only large trees on this plan are a pair of maples, about twelve feet, diagonally, from the corners of the veranda and main house respectively; a white or Austrian pine on the right border, four cherry trees in the right-side yard, and the pear trees in the kitchen-garden department. The maples may be the purple-leaved, and the golden-leaved varieties of the sycamore maple. A hemlock screen or hedge bounds the croquet ground on the south; at the corner are a few Norway spruces; next, in front, a group of arbor-vitaes; then a continuous hedge of the same for twenty feet, terminated by a group of arbor-vitaes and yews chosen to exhibit contrasts of color.

The group on the left, between the upper dotted lines, is to be composed of a variety of strong growing common shrubs, with a Lawson's cypress or a Nordmanns fir, or the Chinese cypress, *Glypto-strobus sinensis*, where the symbol of the arbor-vitae is shown. Towards the street from that tree we would put in evergreen shrubs only.

The lilac group in front may embrace all the finest varieties of that family – the common white and Charles the Tenth varieties near the centre; the chionanthus-leaved next towards the house; the Chinese red, *Rothamagensis rubra*, next; the Persian white, *Persica alba*, next; the dwarf, *Syringa nana*, at the point; and the Chinese purple and white for the two wings of the group. Near the fence we would plant a few common bush honeysuckles, as the dust from the street has a less injurious effect on their foliage than on that of the lilacs.

The central front group, to the right of the lilac group, may be: a purple fringe tree nine feet from the fence, and in succession from it, towards the house, the pink-flowering honeysuckle, *Lonicera grandiflora*, five feet from the fringe tree; the *Deutzia crenata rubra*, four feet further; and at the point, the *Deutzia gracilis*, four feet from the latter. The shrub on the right may be Gordon's flowering currant.

The single small trees on each side the entrance, twelve feet from the front, and fifteen feet from the middle of the walk, may be, one the weeping silver-fir, and the other the weeping Norway spruce, grown as slenderly as possible. The shrubs towards the fence, under and next to the fir tree on the right, may be hardy varieties of dwarf evergreens or a bed of mahonias.

The group in the right-hand corner may have at its point towards the house a bed for cannas, or other showy-leaved plants; next to it the Chinese purple magnolia; back of that the *Magnolia soulangeana*, grown low, or a weeping Japan sophora, and between it and the front, a bed of rhododendrons, or two or three mugho pines; the projecting shrub on the left to be the dwarf white pine, *P. strobus compacta*.

The side border, under and near to the large pine, we would have a bed of rhododendrons; next to these, towards the street, the evergreen shrub, *Cephalotaxus fortunii mascula*, and for the point in front of it, the golden yew. Along the fence, above the pine, the border may be composed of the finest collection of hardy evergreen shrubs that the proprietor can afford; or, if they are too expensive, or too long in developing their beauties, the border may be made almost as satisfactory with common deciduous shrubs. The groups in front of the veranda, between the cherry trees, and those against the house, may be composed of shrubs which are family favorites, or with annual and perennial flowering plants of graded sizes. The flower-beds adjacent to the main walk are for low-growing plants only. The two small bushes behind the flower-beds nearest the gate are to be, one the golden arbor-vitae, and the other the golden yew, and in the rear of the next flowerbed on the right, an Irish juniper is intended. Between the bay-windows a weeping juniper, *J. oblonga pendula*, or the weeping Norway spruce, *Abies e. inverta*, may be planted, or the bed may be occupied as described for Plate VIII. The beds directly in front of the bay-windows can be different each year, with such plants as some of the medium-sized cannas, the *Wigandia caracasana*, the *Nicoteana atropurpurea grandiflora*, and the Japanese maize for the centre plant, and round, bushy-headed plants, like the geraniums and the *Colleus verschafelti*, for the projecting parts of the beds.

Since the engraving has been completed, we perceive that the kitchen department of this lot – that back of the grape-trellis – might be more advantageously planned, but as we cannot now correct it, the reader's ingenuity must be exercised to improve it.

## PLATE XIII

*A Plan of the Grounds for a Commodious House with a side-entrance porch, on an Inside Lot having a front of one hundred and sixty feet on the street, and a depth of three hundred and eight feet.*

The front of the main veranda of the house is seventy feet from the street; the distance from the porch-front to the side of the lot is sixty-five feet, and the space between the house and the right-hand side of the lot is forty feet. This is a very desirable form of lot. It allows of a long reach of lawn on the entrance-side, and sufficient openness on all sides to be in keeping with so large a house; while there is ample room for stable and carriage-house conveniences, fruit trees, and a vegetable garden.

This is the first plan that shows a residence with its carriage-porch and main entrance on the side – an arrangement that economizes space to great advantage on narrow lots, and enables the architect to have more liberty in the arrangement and exposure of the principal rooms, and to make more pleasing views from their windows over the grounds. It will be seen that the turn-way of the carriage-road is partly back of the house, around a circular grass plat twenty feet in diameter, in the centre of which is a pine tree. The drive turns close to the back veranda, where a platform-step is provided for easy ingress and egress from carriages. This is likely to be the carriage-porch of the family when unaccompanied by friends. Beyond the turn, the road is straight along the trellised boundary of the kitchen-garden, and widens with abundant space in front of the carriage-house. Near the rear of the lot are a few cherry and peach trees; back of the drying-yard and kitchen are others. A row of pear trees on the left of the main drive are enough to furnish a summer and autumn supply of this delicious fruit; while in other portions of the grounds, apples and crab-apple trees may be introduced as parts of groups. Of the small fruits the garden plan shows an ample provision. (We cannot commend this house plan as particularly adapted to the lot. The plan for the grounds grew up around the house as a thing already fixed. The latter is designed to meet the wants of a man of 'bookish' tastes, as well as wealth, who needs a fine library-room separate from the family room).

The purely decorative portion of the place may be in part described as follows: beginning at the carriage-entrance. This starts from the middle of the opening between two street trees, and is flanked on either side simply by a pair of trees of any fine variety of elms or maples, chestnuts, horse-chestnuts, oaks or beeches, to be planted ten feet from the fence, and the same distance from the drive. While they are young the ground for a radius of six feet around them should be kept in cultivation, and planted on its outer margin with such deciduous shrubs as flowering-currants, purple berberries, variegated-leaved elder, privet, glossy-leaved viburnum, common bush honeysuckles, or whatever else will grow in partial shade, not exceeding six or seven feet in height, and with branches bending to the grass. When the trees are ten or fifteen years planted, all these must be removed. Or the groups of shrubbery around these trees may be composed entirely of rhododendrons if the proprietor can afford it. The group to the left, adjoining the neighbor-lot, is intended as a continuation of the group around the left-hand gateway tree, and may be composed of similar shrubs of larger growth. The two small pine trees farther up on the left, marked 1, are to be the mugho and dwarf white pines – the latter towards the house. The group of shrubs (2) between these and the carriage-way, and near the latter, should be choice small hardy evergreens – say, for the centre, the weeping juniper, *J. oblonga pendula*, or the erect yew, *Taxus erecta*; each side of this, on a line parallel with the road, and three feet from the centre, the golden arbor-vitae, and the golden yew; at the ends, and three feet from the latter, plant the dwarf silver-fir, *Picea pectinata compacta*, and the dwarf spruce, *Abies gregoriana*. Outside the line of these, and midway of the spaces between them, plant the pygmy spruce, the dwarf black spruce, the dwarf Swedish juniper, the juniper *repanda densa*, the trailing juniper *repens*, and the *Daphne cneorum*. The first pair of fir trees on the left, next the fence (3), may be, one the Norway, and the other the oriental spruce. The border along the fence is to be of hemlocks; the next pair of firs (4) may be the cephalonian fir, nearest the fence, and the Nordmanns fir ten feet in advance of it. The pine tree (5) opposite the bay-window of the room marked S, is improperly placed there. It should be fifteen feet further towards the front of the lot; and is intended for the Bhotan pine. The two small trees on the left (6), opposite the turn-circle, are a pair of Judas trees. The group of four trees next the fence (7) may be a pair of sassafras in the middle; a weeping Japan sophora nearest the house, and the white-flowering dogwood farthest from the house. An undergrowth nearest to the fence may be made with the red-twigged dogwood, *Cornus alba*, the flowering-currants, and the variegated-leaved elder; and the border continued to the rear corner with common and well-known shrubs. No. 8 is for a *Kolreuteria paniculata*, connected by overarching shrubs with the side-border; 9 is a weeping beech; 10, 10, masses of hemlocks; the tree in the far corner an Austrian pine; 11 a white pine, and behind it an Austrian pine; and hemlocks and white pines fill the border towards the carriage-house.

On the right of the lawn the fruit trees are sufficiently symbolized. At 12, a purple beech; at 13, a group of the choicest shrubs increasing in size as they recede from the house. For the point nearest the carriage-road the *Andromeda floribunda* is well suited; eighteen inches behind it the *Deutzia gracilis*; the same distance from that, two plants side by side and one foot apart from the *Rhododendron roseum elegans*; then pairs of plants of rhododendrons in the following order, *R. album candidissima*, *R. grandiflorum gloriosum*; and beyond them, for the end of the bed, Sargent's hemlock, or the pendulous Norway spruce, *A. e. inverta*; or, the weeping silver-fir, *Picea p. pendula*. The group at the turn of the carriage-road, and on a line with the pear trees, may be composed of any good common shrubs of large size, being careful to place those which grow bare at the bottom in the rear of those whose foliage bends gracefully to the ground. The bed adjoining the rear veranda is for the choice small pet-flowers of the lady of the house, whatever they may be.

On the front, the large tree to the right of the carriage-road, nearest the house, is intended for the cut-leaved weeping birch, or a pair of them planted but a few feet apart. At 14 may be a single plant of the old red tartarian honeysuckle, grown in rich ground and allowed to spread upon the lawn. At 15, on the end towards the house, a Japan weeping sophora grafted not more than seven feet high; in the middle, on the side towards the street, the *Andromeda arborea*; and on either side of that the *Deutzias crenata alba*, and *Crenata rubra*. At 16, towards the house, the broad-leaved strawberry tree *Enonymus latifolius*; on the left of the group the *Weigela rosea*; four feet to the right of it the *Weigela amabalis*; four feet to the right again, the *Weigela arborea grandiflora*, and at the right end of the group, the great-leaved snow-ball, *Viburnum machrophyllum*; and between these and the strawberry tree, the dwarf snow-ball, *Viburnum anglicum*. At 17 plant the great-leaved magnolia, *M. machrophyllum*. At 18 we would make a flat pine tree arch over the gateway, as suggested in Chapter XIV. At 19 is a bed of shrubs that should be always in high condition, as it is conspicuous from every point of view. We will suggest for its point nearest the house the *Spirea callosa alba*; then the *Deutzia gracilis*; next, two feet from the former, the *Spirea reevesi flore plena*; next (in the middle line of the bed), the *Spirea callosa fortunii*, with a *Daphne cneorum* on each side of it to cover its nakedness near the ground, and for the end of the bed nearest the entrance-gate, the Chinese red, or the Chinese purple magnolia. Or this bed may be filled with evergreen shrubs or shrubby trees alone, as follows: for the point nearest the house, the *Daphne cneorum*; near, and behind it, the *Andromeda floribunda*; next, two feet from the former, a pair of rhododendrons, *Roseum elegans* and *Album candidissima*; next, in the middle, a single rhododendron, *gloriosum*, with a rhododendron, *everestianum*, on each side of it; next, in the centre line of the bed, the *Cephalotaxus fortunii mascula*; and for the end of the bed next the street the golden yew, or the golden arbor-vitae. No. 20 is the weeping juniper, *Oblonga pendula*; 21 is a grand rose-bed; 22, a belt of common shrubs; 23, an Irish juniper; 24, a Swedish juniper; 25, Siberian arbor-vitaes, continued as a high hedge around to 26, where it is terminated by a Nordmanns fir. In the centre of the semicircle which this hedge is intended to describe, and on a line with the centre of the dining-room, is to be an elegant vase for flowers; and four circular beds for low brilliant flowers are intended to make the view from the bay-window more pleasing. The very small shrubs at the corners of that bay-window represent Irish junipers.

The flower-beds in this plan need not be described in detail. Quite a number of vases are marked on the plan, but they are not essential to the good effect of the planting, though pleasing additions if well chosen and well filled.

Fig. 43 is a view of the house on this plan, taken from a point on the street line fifty or sixty feet to the left of this lot, looking across a portion of the neighbor-lot, and its light division fence. The architect having kindly furnished a sketch of the house without any reference to the grounds, we have endeavored to sketch the sylvan features as shown on the ground-plan,

Fig. 41.

from the same point of view, but it is quite impossible in small engravings to do justice to the pleasing effects of such plantations. Photographic views occasionally give exquisite effects of parts of embellished grounds, but even these fail to convey a correct impression of the accessories of the central point of view. It is quite certain that a place planted (and well kept) in the manner indicated by this plate and description, will be far prettier than any picture of it that can be engraved.

## PLATES XIV AND XV

*Two Methods of Planting a small Corner Lot.*

In these two plates we desire to illustrate two modes of treating a village corner lot of fifty feet front, where the small depth of the lot, or other circumstances, requires the house to be placed quite near the front street. The house plans resemble each other in form, though it will be seen that the one on Plate XIV is set but five steps above the level of the ground, and has its kitchen and dining-room on the main floor, while the plan on Plate XV is a city basement house, with kitchen and dining-room under the bedroom and parlor, the main floor being raised ten steps above the street. The two ground plans (by which we mean plans of the grounds) differ essentially in this, that the first has one side-wall of the house directly on the street, so as to throw its narrow strip of lawn, and embellishments, on the inside of the lot, away from the side-street; while on Plate XV the entire length of the house on that side is supposed to be a party-wall, as if it were part of a block, or one of a pair of houses.

**Ground Plan of Plate XIV** – The veranda front is but eight feet from the street. Unless the approach-steps are of a character less plain than those shown on the plan, little can be done to decorate this narrow space. The veranda can be covered with vines, and a strip three feet wide in front of it may be devoted to choice flowers, but we would advise to have nothing there but the vines and the lawn. On each side the steps we would plant either the tree-box, the golden yew, the golden arbor-vitae, or the arborescent English ivy. If the front were to the north or east, and the soil a moist, friable loam, a very elegant sylvan arch might be made in time by planting six hemlock trees; two in the corners just described, and four inside the gate – two on each side, and but a foot apart, as shown by the dots at *a, a*. Two of these could be made to grow into an arch over the gate, and the others to form two arches at right angles to the first, on each side of the walk. This would only be practicable, however, in case the town authorities will allow the trees nearest the gate to develop into the street, but with four feet additional width in front of the veranda, it would be feasible without such privilege. In the left corner of the front, a Siberian arbor-vitae screen is intended. The veranda on the left is intended to be partially inclosed between the posts with lattice-work, and covered with vines – there being just room enough between the veranda-foundation and the street line for the protection of their roots.

Let us now turn to the narrow lawn-strip on the right; a space but twenty feet wide and seventy feet deep to the arch-entrance of the grape-arbor and kitchen-garden on a line with the rear of the house. Midway of this strip the bay-window projects. The two objects to be kept in view in laying out this bit of a lawn are, first, to make the most pleasing out-look from the bay-window, and, second, the most pleasing in-look from the street. It is assumed that there is no desirable connection to be made with the lot on the right, so that a fence necessarily bounds the view on that side. We must suppose also that there is no house built, or likely to be built, up to that line, otherwise it would not be sensible to place the house on the street-side of the lot, but rather in the manner shown by Plate XV.

The close fence, back to opposite the bay-window, should be covered with English ivy if it can be made to grow there. Unless the exposure is due south, there ought to be little difficulty in getting the ivy to cover the fence if the owner will take the trouble to have it thatched over with straw on the approach of winter, and the base well mulched. A fence in such a place, if of wood, must be a neat piece of work, and well painted. Ivy will not creep up painted wood. We would therefore make a kind of trellis from post to post on the inside of the fence, and put down small sticks with the bark on, by the side of the ivy roots. These should be inside the trellis-bars, and reach nearly to the top of the fence, and be fastened there. The plants will readily climb these sticks and soon hide them from sight. In a few seasons, if they have been safely preserved through the first winter, the branching arms of the ivy will extend over the bars of the trellis, and by their radiating growth soon weave a self-sustaining wall of verdure. By the time the barky sticks decay, the ivy will have no need of their support. This ivy-wall being the right flank of our little lawn, it is essential that it be well planted. (The first winter or two, these sticks may be turned down along the fence with the ivy upon them for greater ease in protecting the latter).

At the street front of this lawn are two Siberian arbor-vitaes *b*, *b*, shown on the plan of a size they are likely to attain in about five years after planting. Doubtless at first these alone will leave the front too open, but in ten years they will be all this part of the place will require.

To return to the lawn: *c* is the weeping juniper, *J. oblonga pendula*; *d*, an Irish juniper; *e*, a pendulous Norway spruce, *Abies e. inverta*; *f* a golden arbor-vitae; *g*, the weeping silver-fir, *Picea pectinata pendula*; on one side of the latter may be planted the dwarf silver-fir, *Picea pectinata compacta*, and on the other the *Picea hudsonica*. The dotted circle projecting into the lawn in front of the arbor-vitae is for any showy bulbous or bedding-plants which will not spread much beyond the limits of the bed. At *h*, plant Parson's American arbor-vitae, *Thuja occidentalis compacta*; at *i*, another pendulous Norway spruce; in front of it a vase; at *j*, *k*, and *l*, three bushy rhododendrons; or, the golden yew, *Taxus aurea*, the erect yew, *Taxus erecta*, and the juniper, *Repanda densa*. At *m*, Sargent's hemlock, *Abies canadensis inverta*; *n*, *Andromeda floribunda* and *Daphne cneorum*. At *o* and *v*, plant a pair of *Deutzia gracilis*, or showy bedding plants, or fine conservatory plants in boxes, buried; plants of gorgeous foliage to be preferred: back of *o*, the weeping arbor-vitae; at *p*, the purple-leaved berberry; *q*, *Weigela amabilis*;

*r, r, r, r,* Irish or Swedish junipers. Near the arch entering the garden, two Bartlett pear trees may be substituted for them, but in this case the grape vines on the trellis will be rendered barren as soon as the trees grow to shade them. As the pear trees will probably furnish the most valuable crop and form a not inappropriate feature, there will be no impropriety in using them. The plants for the side of the house will depend somewhat on its exposure. The following list will do for any but a north exposure. From *c*, back to the bay-window, a selection of the finest low-growing monthly roses, alternated with *Salvia fulgens* or *splendens*, or with any of a thousand beautiful annuals or perennials of low compact growth. At the inner angle of the bay-window a group of five rhododendrons; *R. grandiflorum* in the corner, and four of the best dwarf sorts around it, will be appropriate. If the exposure of this wall is to the north, we would cover it with the superb native of our woods, the Virginia creeper or American ivy. At *s*, the old bush honeysuckle, *Lonicera tartarica*. Under the middle window of the bay make a narrow bed for mignonette and helictrope. At *t*, the *Deutzia crenata alba* and *crenata rubra flore plena* planted side by side so as to intermingle their growth; at *u*, the lilac *S. rothmagensis*; at *w*, the variegated-leaved tree-box; at *x*, *Spireas reevesi flore plena* and *callosa*, together; at *y*, the *Weigela rosea*. This completes a selection for this lawn-border. Different selections as good or better may doubtless be made by persons versed in such matters. While the evergreens recommended for the right-hand border are small, tall gay-blossomed plants may be used to fill the bed. If the occupant desires a quick and showy return for his planting, the evergreen shrubs which we have named for this fence-border may be too slow in their growth to suit, and the fine varieties of lilacs, honeysuckles, weigelas, deutzias, spireas, syringas, and snow-balls may be substituted.

The veranda that opens from the dining-room has some flowers at its base, vines on its posts, a lilac-bush at *z* on the right of the steps, and a compact hedge of Siberian arbor-vitaes on the left to screen the kitchen-yard from observation. The trees near the gate may in time be made to overarch it. The grape-trellis should finish with an arch over this entrance to the garden. The tree *r*, in the garden, is an Irish juniper, which is so slender that its shade is not likely to injure the grape vines.

We have considered these grounds too small to introduce any trees, not even fruit trees, but of small fruits the garden may have a good supply.

**Plate XV** – There being no bedroom projection on the side of the house, the lawn is seven feet wider than on the preceding design. The house being a city basement plan, with a high porch, the entrance is designed with more architectural completeness. The street margin of the lot is supposed to stand twenty-one inches above the level of the sidewalk, with a stone wall all around, the coping of which is to have its upper side level with the lawn next to it, and to be surmounted by a low iron fence. The front porch (designed for iron) is approached by three stone steps on the street line, landing on a stone platform 4 x 6. The side walls of the steps to the porch form vase pedestals. The walk to the basement is fourteen inches below the level of the lawn, and seven inches above the street sidewalk. At the angles of the basement area wall, the copings are squared for the reception of vases. The rear walk, from the side street, rises by two steps on the street line, so that it will be below the level of the lawn for ten or fifteen feet from the gate. The ground should rise about one foot from the fence to the house.

For the benefit of readers not very familiar with the study of house-plans, some explanation may be necessary to an understanding of the back-stair arrangement on this plan, which will be found quite simple and convenient. The dining-room being in the basement, broad stairs lead down to it from the main hall. Servants may come up these stairs from the basement, and go into the second story by the back stairs from the passage (which also opens into the library-room) without entering the hall or the living-rooms of the main floor. If it is considered essential to have a direct communication between the bedroom and the basement, a private stairway may be made from the closet, under the back stairway.

The library is to have a glazed door (glazed low) to enter the side veranda. Through this a pretty perspective down the garden-walk will be seen. More space being devoted to lawn in the rear of this house than on the preceding plan, three cherry trees are introduced there.

The best frontage for this place would be to the north, giving the open side of the house an eastern exposure. A front to the east or the south would not be objectionable, as the side lawn and lookout from the house would still be sunny, but if the house were to front to the west, then the open side would be to the north – an uncheerful exposure, that ought to be avoided where possible.

The verdant embellishment for the ground may be as follows: first, four vases filled with flowers, two by the side of the main steps, and two on the area coping. The former should be the more elegant forms. At *a*, is an Irish juniper (which should be set a foot or two farther from the walk); at *b*, a group consisting of a *Lilac rothamagensis* in the middle, and the double white and double pink-flowering deutzias on each side of it; or of the *Weigela amabalis* in the centre, with the common tartarian bush honeysuckle on one side, and the pink-flowering deutzia on the other. These are expected to expand freely over the fence and sidewalk. At *c*, Sargent's hemlock; at *d*, a weeping Norway spruce (*inverta*); at *e*, a dwarf white pine (*compacta*); at *f*, the erect yew, *Taxus erecta*; *g, g*, Parson's arbor-vitae and the golden yew; at *h*, the weeping silver-fir, *Picea p. pendula*; at *i*, the Japan podocarpus, in the climate of Cincinnati, and the golden arbor-vitae farther north. At *j*, another weeping Norway spruce; at *k*, the *Cephalotaxus fortunii mascula* nearest the street, and the weeping arbor-vitae on the side towards the house. At *l*, Nordmanns fir, *Picea nordmaniana*; from *l* to *o*, a screen of Sargent's hemlock; *m*, weeping juniper, *J. oblonga pendula*; *n*, Siberian arbor-vitae; *o*, the pendulous red-cedar, *J. virginiana pendula*; *p*, the weeping silver-fir; *q*, the weeping Norway spruce, *Abies e. inverta*. A hemlock screen to be continued along the street line from *q* across the walk, so that the two trees nearest the gate may in time form an arch over it. At *r*, near the front of the house, may be the dwarf Hudson's Bay fir, *Picea hudsonica*, or the low dwarf silver-fir, *Picea pectinata compacta*, or the slender Irish juniper. The shrubs near the house-wall may be low-growing roses, or rhododendrons alternated with the scarlet salvia among them. In the inner angles of the bay-window, if of brick, we would have the English ivy, or the Virginia creeper; if of wood, then some rhododendron of medium height, and around them at *y* and *z*, compact masses of the smallest sorts; or one side may be more quickly filled with a single pink deutzia, and the other with a tartarian bush honeysuckle. The shrubs at the corner of the rear veranda may be the Chinese sub-evergreen honeysuckle on the post; a Swedish juniper next to it; and the erect yew, the golden yew, and the golden arbor-vitae around the juniper.

The materials for the flower-beds *s, t, u, v, w, x*, need not be specified in detail.

The border back of the rear walk represents currant bushes. It might better be a grape-trellis.

## PLATE XVI

*A large Mansion on an In-Lot of two hundred feet front by three hundred and forty feet deep.*

This house is, in size, much above the average of suburban homes, and the area of the lot is sufficient to harmonize with the mansion-character of the house. The arrangement of the driveway is quite simple. The house being placed nearly in the middle of the width of the lot, and the stable, vegetable-garden, and orchard, occupying the rear third of the length of it, there is not an extent of lawn in proportion to the depth of the lot; the ground design being in this respect inferior to that of Plate XI, where a lot forty feet shorter has a lawn much longer. The difference is mainly in the greater extent of the orchard, the vegetable-garden and the stable yard on the plan now under consideration; and the different positions of the mansion and the stable on the respective lots. The design of Plate XI is for a front to the east; the house is therefore placed near the north side of the lot, the exposures of the principal rooms are to the east, south, and west, and the views out of them are made longer and nobler by thus crowding the house and all its utilitarian appendages towards that side. The present plan is suited to a lot having a frontage to the south, and the plan calls for an equally good exposure for the rooms on both sides of the house. The liberal space allowed for orchard, vegetable-garden and stable-yard necessarily deprives the ground of the fine air that longer and broader stretches of unbroken lawn produce, but each of the principal rooms having exposures differing essentially from the others, the variety of views must atone for their want of extent. (The vignette at the head of Chapter VI is from a drawing of this house, kindly famished by the architect, R. W. Bunnell, Esq., of Bridgeport, Conn., but the grounds as there shown are not intended to illustrate this plan).

The carriage-entrances to this place are shown nearer to the corners than they should be. On so broad a front there should be twenty feet instead of ten, between the drive at the entrances and the nearest part of the adjacent lots. Premising this alteration to be made in the plan, the only change in the planting would be that the trees B, C, and I, J, shall be planted nearer together, and more nearly at right-angles, than parallel, with the front of the lot. The capital letters on the plan are used to designate the larger class of trees of a permanent character, and the small letters, the shrubs and very small trees.

Though this is an in-lot, and generally margined by high fences and close plantations, one opening on each side has been left to give views across neighbor-lots which are supposed to warrant it. If the reader will follow on the plan we will select trees and shrubs as follows: on the left of the left-hand gate as we enter may be a weeping willow, midway between the drive and the adjoining lot line, and ten feet from the front. The margin, b, b, is to be planted with a dense mass of fine common shrubs, or left more open, accordingly as the neighbor-lot at that point is pleasing or the reverse. B, is a golden willow; and C, a weeping birch. All these trees grow with great rapidity. D, may be a weeping beech; E, a group of three sassafras trees; F (nearest the house), the *Kolreuteria paniculata*; F (nearest the street), the purple-leaved sycamore maple; G (northwest of the bed-room), the golden-leaved sycamore maple; H (though it is not so marked), we would prefer to make a pair of pines, the Austrian and the white, the former in the rear of the latter. The pine tree directly west of the bedroom may be either the white, Austrian, Bhotan, or Pyrenean, the two latter being the most interesting, but of uncertain longevity. Beginning at the right-hand front entrance, J, K, may be Scotch weeping elms, and I, the Scamston elm. The shrubbery at and near the entrance is for effect during the first ten years after planting, and to be removed when the elms shadow that entrance sufficiently. At L, plant a *Kolreuteria paniculata*; at M, the paulonia; at N and O, weeping birches; at P, the *Magnolia machrophylla*; at Q, Nordmanns fir; at R, a *Magnolia tripetata*; at S, the weeping beech; at T, a white or Austrian pine; at U, a hemlock screen; at V, group of Norway spruces. The fruit trees on the plan may be known by their symbols.

Of shrubbery and shrubby trees the middle group (unlettered) near the front is the most important, as it is visible from almost every point of view in and near the grounds. Measured on the curved line of its centre, it is fifty feet in length, and may be made an artistic miniature arboretum of choice things, either evergreens or deciduous; but should be all one or the other, on its upper outline; though the under-shrubs may be deciduous and evergreen mingled. In either case its arrangement should be planned, and its materials selected by a skillful gardener. It is impracticable, in the limits of this work, to present the working details for such groups on a scale that can be readily followed; we therefore merely suggest that the centre should be made with something that will not exceed twenty feet in height at maturity, and the group should diminish in height at the sides, so that the points may be occupied by interesting dwarfs that may be overlooked by persons passing on the sidewalk.

The shrubberies at *a*, and *b*, *b*, *b*, *b*, *d*, and *e*, are simply masses of the good old syringas, lilacs, honeysuckles, snow-balls, currants, altheas, and the newer weigelas, deutzias, spireas, and other shrubs, which may be arranged in a hundred different ways to give the foliage and forms of each a good setting.

The small tree at *c*, may be the American red-bud or Judas tree, *Cercis canadensis*; at *f Magnolia conspicua*; at *g*, *Magnolia machrophylla*; at *h*, a mass of hemlocks; at *i*, a pair of weeping Japan sophoras, and behind them the white-flowering dogwood, the broad-leaved euonymus, and the variegated-leaved elder; at *j*, a Norway spruce in front of a hemlock hedge; at *k* (near the front veranda), a dwarf white pine in the centre, the Hudson's Bay fir on one side, and the dwarf silver-fir, *Picea pectinata compacta*, on the other. While these are small, fill in between them with low compact rhododendrons. At *l* and *m*, Austrian pines headed back from time to time to force a dense growth; at *n, n, n*, a belt of hemlocks and arbor-vitaes; *o*, Sargent's hemlock; *p*, the weeping juniper, *J. oblonga pendula*, or the Indian catalpa. The shrubbery adjoining the house on the east side may be composed largely of rhododendrons; on the west side, of shrubs and bedding-plants that flourish in great light and heat.

The rose-bed adjoining the front middle group may be omitted without detriment to the plan, and a smaller rose-bed made in the triangle formed by the intersecting branches of the carriage-road, where a vase is marked, for which a rose-post may be substituted. Besides the climbing roses to be planted one on each side of the post, there will be room in this triangle for three compact rosebushes.

The flower-beds and vases shown on the plan need no explanation to the intelligent reader.

We desire to call the reader's attention to the fact that this house-plan, and the size and form of the lot, are precisely the same as in Plate XVII, following, but the lots have different exposures, the houses are placed quite differently on them, and the ground designs are totally changed to suit the circumstances. A comparison of the two is a good study.

## PLATE XVII

*A large Mansion occupying one end of a Block, with streets on three sides, and an alley on the fourth.*

Having already called the reader's attention to the identity of this house-plan with that of Plate XVI, and to the fact that the lots are of the same size and form, but otherwise differently circumstanced, we will briefly sketch the peculiarities of this design. The lot is 200 x 340 feet. It is supposed to be desirable that the house should front on the street that occupies the long side of the lot. The house and stable conveniences occupy so much room, that if the house were thrown back to introduce a carriage-road to the front steps, it would be crowded close to the alley, and even then the drive would be so short as to belittle the noble character of the house and lot. The mansion is, therefore, placed so far towards the front that its entrance porch is but forty feet from the street; a carriage-road to the front is dispensed with, and a broad straight foot-walk alone conducts to the front steps. The private carriage-entrance is by a straight road from the side street to the steps of the back veranda, and the coach-yard, and the family can get into their vehicles there, or in front, at their option. For visitors, a landing on the sidewalk is quite convenient enough to the front door for all ordinary occasions.

It will be seen at a glance that the distribution and arrangement of the useful and the decorative parts of this plan are unusually convenient and beautiful, and that a place carried out in conformity to it would produce a more elegant effect, with the same materials and expense, than the plan of Plate XVI. This difference is not to be attributed to the greater street exposure of this plan, or to the different position of the house on the lot, which the surrounding streets necessitate, but is principally the result of a more happy distribution of the several parts. It would be difficult to plan with greater economy in the use of space. But the form and exposure of the lot on the plate alluded to, will permit of modifications in the arrangement of its parts that for some persons might prove improvements.

To offset the greater length of carriage-road which the lot as planned on Plate XVI exhibits, this plan calls for a much greater length of foot-walks. In vegetable garden and orchard ground, the two plans are nearly equal. This one, however, lacks a stable-yard, that is shown in the former; which may be provided, if needed, by placing the carriage-house directly in the rear of the residence, and enclosing a space between the former and the vegetable-garden. If this were done, however, it would be necessary to cut off a view of the coach-yard from the main hall looking through the back veranda.

A peculiar arrangement of shrubbery will be observed in front of the house. The latter being close to the street, it is desirable to cover it from too close and continuous observation of the passerby, as far as can be done without belittling the main entrance way, or crowding shrubbery close to the veranda. The walk opening, on the street line, is sixteen feet wide – the gate being in a bay. For this distance the entire front of the house, as well as charming vistas of the lawns on each side, are in full view, and the impression of the place obtained here would be the finest. But passing either way, beyond this opening, along the sidewalk, the lower part of the house is entirely concealed by the two diverging masses of shrubbery, *a, a,* which, while they thus act as a partial screen of the veranda and lower windows, open out so as to leave a fine expanse in front of the house in lawn, vases, and flowers. Two horse-chestnut trees at the points of these groups will make an appropriate flanking for the front entrance.

Though this plan may not be impracticable whatever the point of the compass its front faces, yet the most beautiful interior effects – that is, as seen from the house, and within the grounds – will be realized by a frontage to the north; while the best effect as seen from the streets will be produced by a frontage to the south – either a north or south front being better for this plan than one to the east or west.

The following is one selection of trees and shrubs for the place – the capital letters indicating the large trees, and the small letters the inferior trees and shrubbery. A and B are the purple-leaved and the golden-leaved sycamore maples; C, the weeping willow; D, the weeping beech; E and F, the common and the cut-leaved weeping birches; G, the ginkgo or Salisburia tree; H, the purple-leaved beech; I, the *Kolreuteria paniculata*; J, J, the red-flowering, and the double white-flowering horse-chestnuts; K, K, a pair of pines in each place – the Bhotan (*excelsa*) and white pine in one, and the Bhotan and Austrian in the other – to be planted six feet apart, the Bhotan on the north side in both cases; L, white pine; M, Austrian pine; on the right of N, the weeping Norway spruce, and on the left, the Cembran pine, or (south of New York and near the sea) the cypress, *Glypto-strobus sinensis*; O, the white or the Austrian pine, as the soil may be better for one or the other; P, a mass and belt of hemlocks; Q, a weeping Scotch elm; R, the grape-leaved linden; S, nearest the intersection of the walks, the sugar maple, and to the right of it the purple-leaved sycamore maple; T and V a mass of Austrian pines, with an undergrowth of hemlocks; U, catalpa; W, a pair of weeping Norway spruces, with hemlocks behind them; X, the weeping silver-fir backed by hemlocks and flanked with a group of rhododendrons; Y, a pair of pines, the white and the Pyrenean, six feet apart; Z, the Austrian and the Bhotan pines, the same distance apart.

Of the shrubbery we can indicate only the general character of the groups, and name specimens only when standing singly, or a few in a group. The masses *a*, *a*, may be shrubs of fine common sorts, the taller in the centre line of the group, and the margins filled in with rhododendrons; or may be composed entirely of evergreens, such as the arbor-vitaes, yews, dwarf firs, junipers, and pines, with rhododendrons and azalias among them. The deciduous shrubs, however, would make a fine border in much less time, and at less expense than the latter. At *b*, a *Weigela amabilis* in the centre, and on each side the weigelas *rosea* and *hortensia nivea*; at *c*, the two deutzias *crenata alba* and *crenata rubra flore plena*; at *d, d, d, d, d*, masses of common shrubs, not allowed to exceed seven feet in height, forced to make a dense mass at the bottom, and planted to form an irregular outline next to the lawn; at *e*, the oblong weeping juniper, *J. oblonga pendula*; *f* a pair of weeping Japan sophoras grafted nine feet high, and planted ten feet apart; *g*, the Chinese white magnolia; *h*, a mass of rhododendrons and purple magnolias; *i, i*, hemlock gateway arches – the hemlocks to form a dense screen for ten or fifteen feet on each side of the arch; *j*, the Hudson's Bay fir; *k*, the *Magnolia machrophylla*; *l* (adjoining the house), a mass of evergreens of dwarf character, including rhododendrons, kalmias, and azalias; *m* and *n*, hemlock screens; *o*, a mass of rhododendrons. The small group under the corners of the drawing-room bay-windows may be composed of the English or Irish ivys in the corners, and low varieties of rhododendrons; or, of brilliant bedding-plants alone.

This place is large enough to make a conservatory a desirable feature. If wanted in connection with the house, by using the room marked P as a library-room, the room L (if that side of the house has an east exposure) would be an admirable place for it. If a distinct structure is preferred, a good place would be on a line with the carriage-road, and ten feet from it, in the corner of the orchard nearest the house.

The large flower-bed near L is intended for large bedding plants. The great rose-bed at the intersection of the walks on the right would require to be filled with uncommon skill to make it pleasing throughout the summer season, though it may be superbly beautiful in June, and interesting under ordinary treatment, with partial bloom, until frosts. In winter and early spring, however, it can hardly be otherwise than unsightly. A group for that place, of more continuous beauty, which will cost less labor in its maintenance, may be composed of the following evergreens: for the centre the weeping Norway spruce (*inverta*); around it the following, the positions for which must be determined by a study of their characters: the Sargent hemlock, Parson's dwarf hemlock, variegated-leaved tree-box, golden and weeping arbor-vitaes, the erect yew (*erecta*), the golden yew, the *Cephalotaxus fortunii mascula*, the *Podocarpus japonica*, the creeping juniper (*repens*), the juniper *repanda densa*, the juniper *oblonga pendula*, the juniper *spaeroides*, the Hudson's Bay fir *hudsonica*, and the dwarf firs, *Picea pectinata compacta* and *Abies gregoriana*.

The group of large flower-beds opposite the library window, with a vase in the centre, should be filled with rather low flowers, and made as continuously brilliant as possible. Forming the foreground of a fine stretch of lawn beyond them, the view as seen from the main window of this room may be made quite elegant and park-like in its effect.

## PLATE XVIII

*Plan for a Residence of Medium Size, with Stable and Carriage-house, Orchard, and Vegetable-garden, on a Corner-Lot 200 x 300 feet.*

Here we have a house of moderate size on a lot which gives ample space around it, and which is provided with length of carriage-road disproportioned to the size of the house. It is suited to the use of a small family, who entertain much company, and keep horses and carriages.

The location of a large kitchen-garden in the southwest corner of the lot, where the lawn might be extended with fine effect, as in Plates XI and XIII, was made in order to place the orchard away from the side street, and the enterprise of bad boys. The vegetable-garden offers few temptations for moonlight poachers over a street-fence, but an orchard in the same place is almost irresistible. By interposing the kitchen-garden between it and the street, the fruit is safer. Were it not for this reason we would decidedly prefer to have the kitchen-garden back of the house, the orchard on the south side of the lot, and so arranged that the ground under the trees should appear to be a prolongation of the south lawn. The plan being made with reference to the protection of the orchard, sacrifices to this object Rule I, of Chapter XI – there being no length of lawn on the lot commensurate with its size. Yet the manner of grouping, in those portions of the lot which are in lawn, is such as to conceal this defect in a great degree from the eye of an observer in the street, or in the house; though it is evident enough on the paper plan.

We have alluded to the length of carriage-road on this lot as disproportioned to the size of the residence. This is so decided that we must consider the plan as an example of a fault to be avoided, rather than a plan to be followed. Not only the length of the drive is objectionable for a residence of this simple character, but also the corner entrance, which is usually the least convenient point for crossing the street-gutters and the sidewalks. Plate X shows a much more sensible entrance and carriage-way.

In other respects this plan is better; the grouping being such as would give very pleasing effects, whether looking towards the house or from it. On the south are several openings to the street, and on the north one only, connecting with private grounds on that side.

Supposing the roads, walks, orchard, and garden to have been laid out as shown by the plan, the following trees and shrubs are suggested for some of the principal places. The lines conforming in part to the forms of the groups of shrubs are intended to show the form of beds to be enriched and prepared for them.

The group at *a*, on the left of the corner entrance-way, to be composed of a weeping willow or a weeping Scotch elm in the centre, and the three best varieties of dogwood on the three points of the group; the bed to be filled, while these are growing, with spreading shrubs of low growth. The group, on the right of the same entrance, to have an American weeping elm in the centre, and at *i*, *j*, *k*, and *l*, the American and European Judas trees, the broad-leaved strawberry tree (*Enonymus latifolius*), and the dogwood (*Cornus florida*); and between them the syringas, weigelas, variegated elder, flowering currants, etc., etc.

The trees at *b* and *c* may be the double-flowering white and the red-flowering horse-chestnuts; between them and the fence a mass of large shrubs. At *d*, a weeping beech; between it and the fence plant shrubs, to be removed when the beech needs all the space; near the fence Siberian arbor-vitaes to form a concave hedge to, and across, (overarching) the side-entrance gate. At *e*, ten feet from both the walk and the drive, a pair of sassafras trees four feet apart, with an oval mass of low spreading shrubs – spireas, flowering-currants, berberries, deutzias, red-twigged dogwoods, and honeysuckles around them. At *f*, a choice selection of the most pleasing shrubs, either deciduous or evergreen; of the latter an assortment of the best rhododendrons will make a superb group. At *g*, a *Magnolia machrophylla*; *h*, nearest the house, the *Kolreuteria paniculata*; *h*, near the gate, the osage orange. At *o*, in the centre of the front, a purple beech; at *m* and *n*, groups composed of the weeping Norway spruce (*inverta*) for the centres, and the golden arbor-vitae, and the erect yew (*Taxus stricta* or *erecta*), the golden yew and the *Podocarpus japonica*, on opposite sides of them. If for this central space it is desired to make a quick mass of foliage in the place of these small groups, a weeping willow, or a group of two or three osage orange trees planted at *o*, a group of deutzias at *m*, and of weigelas or bush honeysuckles at *n*, will quickly effect it. At the left of the gateway on the right, a pair of pines, the white and Austrian; *p* and *q*, the dwarf mountain pine (*P. pumila*) and the mugho pine (*P. mugho*); *r*, the dwarf white pine, and between these, while small, plant evergreen shrubs. At *s*, is a belt of shrubs terminated by a pair of pines, the Austrian and the Bhotan. At *t*, a pair of weeping birches; at *u*, *u*, two pairs of trees, the purple-leaved and the gold-leaved sycamore-maples at one end, and the sugar and scarlet-maples at the other, each pair near together; and between the trees, while they are young, a group of deciduous shrubbery. At *v*, a *Magnolia soulangeana*; at *w*, the weeping silver-fir (*Picea pectinata pendula*); along the boundary of the lot in the rear of *w*, a belt of hemlocks broken by an occasional spur of spruce or pine trees; *x*, *x*, *x*, weeping arbor-vitaes, junipers, or other elegant slender evergreens, and at *z*, another *Magnolia machrophylla*. On so large a place there will be room around the house, and in the various groups, and along the marginal belts of trees and shrubs, to introduce a hundred things which we have not named, and a reference to the plate of symbols in connection with the ground-plan will explain what we have not touched upon.

## PLATE XIX

*Plan for a Residence of Medium Size on a Corner Lot 150 x 200 feet, with no provision for keeping a horse or carriage.*

This house-plan is the same as that on Plate XVIII, but the lot is only one-half the depth of that one, though the frontage is the same. The street on the longer side being supposed the most desirable to front upon, the division of the lot in lawn, fruit, and vegetable-garden, resembles, on a smaller scale, that of Plate XVII; though on this the direct walk to the front door is dispensed with, and only the entrances at the two front corners of the lot are used. This is rarely a desirable arrangement, but the expression aimed at in the design of this lot is extreme openness and breadth of lawn, in proportion to the size of the lot. To dispense with a walk directly from the street to the front door increases this expression, but it is not essential to it. If the members of the family who occupy the house rarely use a carriage, it is not a matter of much importance to have a direct front walk; especially if all the travel to and from the house is along the street, so that one corner gate or the other makes a nearer approach than a walk in the centre only. But if the family have often occasion to ride, the side-entrances will seem an awkward detour, and we would then by all means dispense with the walk which runs nearly parallel with the street, and have a broad straight walk to the front porch, and a smaller walk to the rear of the house, nearly as here represented. This would, of course, involve considerable changes in the plan for planting.

An alley is supposed to bound the lot on the left; a shed and cow-house and small cow-yard are therefore represented in the rear corner on that side, and an arbor-vitae hedge is to be planted inside the fence along the alley. Ten feet from the alley, and back of the front line of the house, is a row of four cherry trees, and two others are indicated on the rear part of the croquet-ground. Six standard pear trees, on the other side of the house, form a row parallel with a continuous grape-trellis which divides the lawn from the vegetable-garden. Some peach trees may be planted in the garden-square next the cow-house. The borders by the fences around the back of the lot furnish ample room for currants, raspberries, and blackberries. (The grass from the lawn, on such a place as this, if fed as cut, is more than enough to supply one cow with green food for seven months of the year; probably, together with the pail-feed from the house, enough to keep two cows).

The decorative planting of the lawn-ground may be as follows: on each side of the gateway, at *a*, plant a group of pines, white, Austrian, and Bhotan, to be clipped when they begin to trespass on the walk, and to overarch it when large enough. The group on the left of the walk, directly in front of the same entrance, should be composed of shrubby evergreen trees or shrubs, diminishing to those of small size at the point. At *b*, the weeping silver-fir. At *c, c*, fifteen feet from the front corners of the house, a pair of either of the following species, of the varieties named: of beeches, the purple-leaved and the fern-leaved; of birches, the old weeping and the cut-leaved weeping;

of horse-chestnuts, the double-white and the red-flowering; of lindens, the American basswood and the grape-leaved; of magnolias, the *machrophylla* and the *cordata*; of mountain ashes, the oak-leaved; of maples, the purple-leaved and the gold-leaved sycamore; of oaks, the scarlet (*coccinea*) on both sides; of tulip trees (whitewood), there being no distinct varieties, the same on both sides, or a tulip tree on one side, and a virgilia or *Magnolia cordata* on the other. Our own choice among these would be of birches, maples, or horse-chestnuts.

At *d*, the face of the hedge may be broken by a projecting group of yews and arbor-vitaes. At *e*, a group of rhododendrons. At *f* and *g* any one of the following deciduous species of small low trees, if grown with care and symmetry, viz.: the Indian catalpa (*C. himalayensis*) south of Philadelphia; the Chinese cypress (*Glypto-strobus sinensis*); the silver-bell (*Halesia tetraptera*); the sassafras (although rather large for the place); the dwarf horse-chestnuts, *Pavia coccinea, P. pumila pendula*, and *P. cornea superba*; the European bird cherry, *Prunus padus*; the American white-flowering and the Cornelian cherry dogwoods, *C. florida* and *C. mas*; the American and the European Judas trees; the magnolias, Chinese white (*conspicua*), and the showy-flowered (*speciosa*); the dwarf profuse-flowering mountain ash (*nana floribunda*); the weeping Japan sophora; the double scarlet-thorn (*coccinea flore plena*); the weeping larch; the Kilmarnock willow; the large-flowered rose-acacia (*grandiflora*), if trained and carefully supported when young; the American and the broad-leaved strawberry trees; the largest and most tree-like lilacs; the purple-fringe; the syringa, *zeyheri*; and the new snow-ball or viburnum, *V. machrophyllum*, are all pleasing small trees, or tree-like shrubs, any two of which will be appropriate for these two places. Our preference among them would be the weeping Japan sophoras grafted from seven to eight feet high. If evergreens are desired for these two places, we would certainly select the weeping Norway spruce (*inverta*) and the weeping silver-fir. The small group *h*, should be made up of choice small evergreens, yews, arbor-vitaes, and dwarf firs. The pair of deciduous trees at *i*, on the right, may be a catalpa and a paulonia for places south of New York, and northward, a pair of sassafras and a dogwood (*C. florida*), to make a group of three, or a pair of *Kolreuteria paniculata* only. The group *j*, on the upper side of the walk, is intended to be filled by an Austrian pine, surrounded by evergreen shrubs that will form a dense mass. At *k*, a Siberian arbor-vitae, with the erect yew, on one side, and the golden arbor-vitae on the other. At *l*, an Irish juniper.

At *m*, a collection of magnolias, beginning with the purple-magnolia nearest the house, next to it the Chinese white, then the *M. soulangeana*, and at *n*, the *M. machrophylla*, – all to be encouraged to branch as close to the ground as they will grow. At *o*, the arbor-vitae *compacta* or another purple magnolia. At *p*, the weeping beech; at *q*, a group of the following firs, beginning nearest the house with Nordmanns fir, next the Cephalonian, and last the Norway spruce. At *r*, another *Magnolia machrophylla*. At *s*, a Bhotan pine if on the north or east side, and an Austrian pine if on the south or west side of the house. The shrubbery adjoining the house may be composed of a great variety of common species, but none that attain a height of more than six feet should be planted under or in front of windows where they might eventually obstruct the views.

## PLATE XX

*A Compact House, on an In-Lot of ninety-six feet front, with ample depth, and a Lawn connecting with adjoining neighbors.*

The main house is here 36 x 40, and the rear part 20 x 32 feet. The front veranda is ten feet in width, and between it and the street the distance is ninety-six feet. The lot is one hundred and ninety-six feet in depth back to the grape-trellis that divides the lawn from the garden, and is supposed to have ample room back of this for vegetables and small fruits.

Whether or not the occupants of this place keep horse and carriage, the front and sides of the lot are designed without any reference to them.

Floral embellishment is a prominent feature of this design, and this is nearly all in front of the house. The walk with two street-entrances encloses a circle seventy-two feet in diameter, on the margin of which the flower-beds are arranged, leaving the interior of the circle in lawn, unbroken save by a large low vase for flowers in the centre. Most of the interest of the place being thus between the house and the street, where exposure to passers on the street might annoy the occupants in the care and enjoyment of their flowers and plants, it is essential that this circle should be hidden from the street except at the gateways. The reader already knows that we have no sympathy with that churlish spirit which would shut a pleasing picture out of sight from the sheer love of exclusive possession, but we have respect for that repugnance which most persons, and especially ladies, feel against a peering curiosity in their domestic enjoyments; and as the care of one's flowers and trees is one of the sweetest of domestic labors, we would protect the privacy of working hours among them to an extent that may not degenerate into a selfish exclusiveness. In this plan, as engraved, the mass of screening foliage is not as large as would be necessary, but the trees as there placed will form a sufficient protection after ten years growth to insure a reasonable privacy for the floral lawn. It will be observed that this is not effected by a hedge on the street line, but on the contrary the lawn is open except at the entrances, and one standing on the sidewalk at A, though barred from all view of the circle by the mass of evergreens opposite, may have pleasing glimpses into the place on the lines A B, A C, and across these corners into the adjoining lot lawns.

The two front gateways should be overarched with evergreen topiary arches – one side with arbor-vitae, and the other with hemlocks, firs, or pines, as the soil and exposure may make one or the other preferable. The glimpses into the grounds from under either of these arches will extend the whole length of the lawn back to the cold grape-house on the right, and from the left, back to the grape-trellis that separates the vegetable-garden from the lawn. A still longer vista may be made from the left-hand gateway by making a decorative arch in the grape-trellis at the end of the garden-walk which corresponds with the one at the end of the cold grape-house.

The evergreen group in the middle of the lot near the street may be composed as follows: in the centre two Nordmanns firs, four feet apart, on a line at right angles with the street; on each side of these a mass of hemlocks (say four on each side) for a distance of sixteen feet each way; and at each point of the group single specimens of the weeping silver-fir and the weeping Norway spruce. This will make the group about forty feet from point to point, measuring from the stems of the last-named trees.

The trees which arch the intersections of the entrance-walks with the circular-walk, may be double pairs of sassafras on one side, and one pair of kolreuterias on the other. At *c*, a weeping beech; at *g*, the Chinese cypress (*Glypto-strobus sinensis pendula*) south of New York, and north of it a group composed of the weeping Norway spruce in the centre, and the following junipers around it: the *J. repanda densa, J. oblonga pendula, J. suecica nana, J. spaeroides*; or, instead of the junipers, the following dwarf firs, viz.: the *Abies nigra pumila, A. gregoriana, A. conica, A. canadensis inverta* (Sargent's hemlock), *A. canadensis Parsoni* (Parson's hemlock), the *Picea pectinata compacta*, and the *Picea hudsonica*. At *d* and *h*, the finest pines for which the soil and location are suited; at *e*, the *Magnolia cordata*; at *f*, a group of evergreen shrubs next the fence, and a weeping silver-fir in front of them, opposite the parlor bay-window. Two small trees are indicated in front of the corners of the veranda. If small trees are used in these places, they may be of species like the *Magnolia machrophylla*, the double white-flowering horse-chestnut, and the virgilia, which develop most beautifully when branching near the ground, or, like the weeping sophora, trailing to the ground, but if large trees are chosen, they should be of sorts which lift their heads on clean stems, so that their lower branches will be above the line of view of persons standing on the floor of the house.

At the point formed by the intersection of the sidewalk with the circular-walk there should be an interesting collection of evergreens of very slender, or very dwarf character. Near the point, and two feet from both walks, plant the *Abies excelsa pygmae*; three feet from both walks, and back of the former, the *Picea pectinata compacta*; back of these, and equidistant between the walks, the *Taxus erecta*; then, a little nearer to each walk than the latter, put in a golden arbor-vitae and a golden yew, so as to make the group in the form of a Y. If the proprietor prefers to have something new and striking in this location every year, instead of waiting patiently the interesting development of these dwarfs, this point will be an appropriate place for a skillful arrangement of showy-leaved bedding-plants, but as there is ample space for these elsewhere, we would much prefer marking the intersection of the two walks with some permanent objects that may be seen in winter and summer, and which, by living and growing year after year, will at length have associations and a little history of their own, and become monumental evidences of past labors. It is well always to mark the divergence of two walks by some permanent tree or group near the inner angle of intersection, and in the case under consideration, if the group of lilliputian evergreens should seem too insignificant and tardy in their development, or (being rarities) too expensive, we would plant some spreading tree at this intersection, and recommend for that purpose the weeping birch.

From *i* and *j*, on opposite sides of the lot, the side fences should be bordered with evergreen shrubs as far as the back line of the main house, and thence to the garden may be covered with grape-vines or other small fruits, or with a continuous belt of common deciduous shrubs. Against the foundation-walls of the house we would plant a continuous line of varieties of the English ivy, even if they creep permanently no higher than the water-table. Up to that height they often make a shrubby mass of evergreen foliage, and form a pleasing background for the finer shrubs that may be grown near the house in front of them. For a running vine on brick and stone walls, and for draping windows and cornices with foliage, the American ivy or Virginia creeper is greatly superior in this country to the English ivy. We can go no further in designating the shrubs to plant near the house-walls than to merely reiterate that they should be of those flowering and fragrant varieties which are usually full-foliaged, not apt to get bare of leaves at the bottom, and which do not exceed six feet in height; in short, low, compact, or spreading shrubs.

The fruit-tree features of this place are sufficiently designated by the symbols.

There being a cold grape-house indicated, it is natural to suppose that flowers and bulbs may be forced in it, and that the care of these, together with grounds embellished with so many flowers, will involve the employment of a gardener; to whom, or to the lady of the house, we leave the selection of the flowers to be used in filling the beds on the margin of the circle, and the vase or basket in its centre.

## PLATE XXI

*A Plan for a Deep Front Yard, on an In-Lot one hundred feet wide, with the House on a terrace plateau; designed to harmonize architectural and gardenesque forms.*

This plan is a peculiar study in many respects. All the decorative portion of the grounds is in front of the house, and the depth from the street to the house-front is even greater in proportion to the width of the lot than in the preceding plan. The arrangement at the street-front is also more simple and more formal; for here we have a hedge close to the street line, a single entrance, and a long straight walk in the middle of the lot. To this extent the plan is simpler than the preceding one, but on approaching the house the style becomes more ornate and costly. The house is elevated on a wide terrace, and the steps to reach the terrace-level are fifteen feet in front of the veranda. These steps should be of stone, not less than twelve inches wide, nor more than seven inches rise, and of a length equal to the width of the main walk. Low stone copings at the side of the steps expand at the top into square pedestals for vases, and thence are continued to meet the veranda. Such copings should, where practicable, be of some warm colored stone. It will be observed that the walk at the foot of these stone steps widens out into quite an area, and at this point the design varies by an easy transition from the formal to the graceful style; the form of the front of the terrace conforming to the curves of the walks. The walks to the left and right diverge first by geometric curves, and then enter, by more pathlike lines, dense masses of shrubbery, ending at seats embowered in foliage. From these, vistas open to the most pleasing features of the ground.

The house is supposed to be designed in a half city-style, with a basement-kitchen, and all the principal windows in the front and rear only. The blank sidewalks, if of unpainted brick or stone, may be covered with the Virginia creeper, and on the side-ground back of the points shown on the plate, fruit trees may be planted. If the lot is three hundred feet deep, there will be room back of the house for the needful kitchen-yard and a pretty little vegetable-garden, or a stable and carriage-space, but hardly for both. A lot of four hundred feet in depth would be more suitable for a house thrown back so far from the front street as this, unless space were obtained in the rear of the house by a latitudinal development of the lot in the rear of other lots.

As the entire embellishment of this place lies in front of the house, and as its features are of that gardenesque character which presuppose a decided love of horticultural art in the occupants, and therefore the necessity of constant labors to be done near the street, some thorough protection of their privacy is essential, and we have here first introduced a hedge on the street line. The gateway should be rather larger than is common on foot-walks, and covered with a carefully grown hemlock arch. The hedge may be of hemlock or of Siberian arbor-vitae, and not more than six feet in height. At *a, a*, it is designed to be hollowed by a concave cut on the sides and top, so that the latter will not be more than three and a half feet high in the middle. With this arrangement there will be three glimpses into the place from the street; one under the gateway arch, and the others over the concave cuts in the hedge. The buttresses on the inside are intended to give variety in the line, and in the lights and shadows of the hedge. They are easily made with the hedge by placing two or three hedge-plants at right angles with the line of the hedge at the points where wanted.

We have called attention in another place to a peculiarity of the arrangement of shrubs and trees on this place. There are three long lines of view, each of pre-eminent interest from the different points where each is likely to be most observed. First the walk-view, as seen from the gateway looking towards the house, or from the terrace steps looking towards the gateway; the second and third, on the lines between the bay-windows and the scollops in the front hedge, ranging the whole distance over an unbroken lawn elegantly margined on both sides with flowers, shrubs, and trees. If the reader will raise this plate nearly level with the eye, and glance along the lines indicated, he will appreciate better than we can explain what we have endeavored to accomplish in this plan. It is desirable, in order to achieve the best result of this arrangement, that the character of the foliage on the two sides of the lot should be so different as to give a distinct effect to the views out of the two bay-windows. In addition to these three prominent lines of view, charming long narrow vistas may be made to give interest to the seats at the ends of the walks.

One selection of trees and shrubs for the most prominent places on this plan may be the following:

Group 1, on the left: at *a*, the weeping juniper (*oblonga pendula*); at *b*, the erect yew (*Taxus erecta*); at *c*, the golden yew (*Taxus aurea*); at *d*, the weeping Indian juniper (*J. repanda densa*); at *e*, the dwarf Swedish juniper (*J. suecica nana*).

Group 1, on the right: at *a*, the Siberian arbor-vitae; at *b*, Parson's arbor-vitae (*Thuja occidentalis compacta*); at *c*, the Nootka Sound arbor-vitae (*Thuja plicata*); at *d*, the erect yew (*Taxus erecta*); and at *e*, the dwarf silver-fir (*Picea pectinata compacta*).

Groups 2, 2, may be composed of evergreens as follows: at *a, a*, the mugho and mountain pines (*P. mugho and P. pumila*); at *b* and *c*, in one group, dwarf white pines (*P. strobus compacta*), and on the other the Chinese yews, *Cephalotaxus fortunii mascula* and *C. drupacae*. Or, of deciduous shrubs, the group may be as follows: at *a*, on the left, the *Weigela amabalis*; and at *b* and *c*, the deutzias *crenata alba* and *crenata rubra flore plena*. At *a*, on the right, the great-leaved snow-ball (*Viburnum machrophyllum*); and at *b* and *c*, the red-tartarian honeysuckle and the lilac *rothmagensis*.

Groups 3, 3, are for showy-leaved bedding-plants or roses; 4, 4, may be tailed with choice geraniums.

Figures 5, 5, 5, 5, represent a pair each of Irish and Swedish junipers.

Beds 6, 6, are for roses or showy annuals, perennials, and bulbous flowers; 7, 7, and 9, 9, represent single plants remarkable for beautiful or showy foliage; and 8, 8, are for brilliant low-blooming flowers.

Figures 10, 10, on the left of the walk, may be, one the golden arbor-vitae, and the other the *Podocarpus japonica*; or the rhododendrons *album elegans* and *gloriosum*. If of deciduous shrubs, one the purple-leaved berberry, and the other Gordon's flowering-currant; or, one the dwarf snow-ball (*Viburnum anglicum*), and the other the variegated Cornelian cherry or dogwood (*Cornus mascula variegata*); or the Chinese purple and the Chinese red magnolias; or the dwarf catalpas *himalayensis* and *kaempferi*, or any other compact shrubs or dwarf trees of constant beauty of foliage and annual blossoms; 10, 10, on the right, maybe, one the weeping arbor-vitae, and the other the common tree-box.

Figure 11, on the left, the Japan weeping sophora, or the *Magnolia cordata*; 11, on the right, the Chinese cypress (*Glypto-strobus sinensis pendula*); 12, the *Magnolia machrophylla*; 13, a pair of *Kolreuterias*.

Figure 14, wherever it occurs, suggests a weeping silver-fir (*Picea pectinata pendula*), a weeping Norway spruce (*inverta*), or some other evergreen of slender or peculiar habit; 15, 15, the golden yew and golden arbor-vitae; 16, the weeping beech, or a pair of them; 17 and 18, rhododendrons along the walks, and robust shrubs on the outside – either evergreen or deciduous; 19, 19, 19, hardy pines best suited to the locality; 20, 20, 20, borders of the finest shrubs; 21, a heavy mass of evergreens not more than eight to twelve feet high, covering and concealing the slope of the terrace, with a brilliant flower-bed on its upper or terrace level; 22, 22, suggest large low basket forms for flowers; 23, 23, are circular beds for tall flowers. The pedestals at the top of the steps to the terrace should have elegant low vases appropriately filled with beautiful plants.

The masses of dark-toned evergreens not numbered represent close plantations of hemlocks and Norway spruce, with such other evergreen trees as may best break the monotony of their colors.

## PLATE XXII

*Designs for Neighboring Homes with connecting Grounds.*

In the chapter on Neighboring Improvements we have endeavored to call attention to the great advantage that improvers of small lots may gain by planting on some common plan, so that all the improvements of the fronts of adjoining lots may be arranged to allow each of the neighbors a view of the best features of all. This plate is intended to illustrate one of the simplest forms of such neighboring improvements.

The houses themselves are such as proprietors often build in rows for the purpose of adding to the value, and increasing the sale of adjacent property, but the connection of all the fronts into one long lawn is yet seldom practiced. The elegant effect, however, which this mode of improvement lends to places which, without it, were small and cheap-looking, will add thousands of dollars to their saleable value. It gives a genteel air to the neighborhood that five times the expenditure in buildings would fail to produce, and serves by this fact alone to attract a class of refined people of small means, who might not find the common run of houses, of the cost of these, sufficiently attractive to induce them to select homes there.

Though these five houses are quite similar in size and plan, an inspection of them will show that only Nos 3 and 4 are alike. The others all differ in some respects; the corner houses especially being adapted to their superior locations and double fronts, and therefore needing to be somewhat more expensive. The main part of each is 25 x 38 feet, and the kitchen part 12 x 20, except on lot number one, where it is larger. There is an alley in the rear, upon which outbuildings are located.

The essential feature of the planting on this neighborhood plan is this: that back of a line ten or twelve feet from the front street, to the foot-step of the porches, there shall be no shrub or tree planted on any of the fronts, and only those species of flowers which do not exceed six to nine inches in height. This secures a belt of lawn varying from fifteen to forty feet in width, the entire length of the block, and leaves ample space on each lot for a good selection and arrangement of shrubs and flowers. The light dotted lines on the plan show the leading ranges of view over this common lawn. Of course only the lightest of wire fences are to be used between the lots, if any such divisions are required, and none at all ought to be necessary.

Lot 1 is entered from the side-street, under a gateway arbor. From this entrance the whole length of the block to B and E, two hundred and fifty feet, is a lawn, broken only by beds for low flowers, margined one side by the choicest groups of shrubbery, and on the other by the various architectural features of the steps, vases, porches, and verandas of the five houses, and their flowers and vines. Nothing can more strikingly illustrate the advantage of such neighboring improvements than the view from this point, embracing as it does, under one glance, all the beauty that may be created in the 'front yards' of five distinct homes, all forming parts of a single picture. Similar effects are obtained on entering the verdant gateway arch at E, on lot 5, and also from the side-streets at the points B and C. The shorter views, from the porches and best windows of each house, are all made vastly more pleasing than would be possible on a single lot. The vignette of Chapter IV is a suppositional view from the porch (A) of the house-plan 2, looking towards B.

From the front street, the in-look between the groups that border the front, is such as to make each place when opposite to it, appear to be the most important one.

Only shrubs, or shrubby trees, are to be admitted on the fronts, but on the sides, between the houses, cherry and pear trees may be planted. The flower-beds are all shown somewhat larger on these plans than they should be.

The selections of shrubs, and their arrangement in the many groups adjacent to the front street, will require a thorough familiarity with the characteristics of shrubs, and should therefore be done by an experienced gardener. Our plate is drawn on too small a scale to enable us to designate in detail the composition of all the groups and single specimens indicated on the plan, and as such groups of .places must of necessity, at first, be all arranged under the direction of one gardener, it is not desirable that we should make a suppositional list of shrubs and trees for each lot.

## PLATE XXIII

*Three Residences occupying the end of a Block two hundred feet in width, on Lots two hundred feet deep.*

Here the end of the block is supposed to have been divided into four lots, each 50 x 200 feet; the middle two lots being first occupied by a commodious double-house, and each of the side-lots subsequently improved with basement-kitchen houses, of half city, half suburban character, and the fronts of the three places kept by agreement for mutual advantage.

The house on the left the reader may recognize as similar to the one shown on Plate XV, on a lot of the same width, but it is somewhat differently placed on the lot, and the ground arrangements are different in front and rear. One plan provides for a kitchen-garden, and the other for a fruit-yard only. It will be observed that this house, and the basement-house on the other corner, have blank walls adjoining the neighbor-lots, which are not built up to the line of the fence, but leave a space, one of five feet and the other of two feet, between the wall and the lot-line. This is almost useless for planting, but we deem it essential to give the owner no excuse for that miserable shoddy architecture which constructs a cornice on one or two sides of a building, and leaves it off on sides that are equally conspicuous; on the plea, sometimes, that the owner who has built up to his line has no right to build a cornice over his neighbor's property. Though these houses indicate continuous blank walls on one side, they are not necessarily so, when this space is preserved, and if the owner of the middle lot is a reasonable man, pleasant windows and out-looks may be made from the halls of both the outer houses, and from the bed-room of the house on the right. The arrangement of rooms in the upper stories is likely also to call for quite a number of windows overlooking the middle lot, and the fact of ownership of even a very little space in front of them will make it safer for the builder to plan them. If the occupants of the three lots are in friendly accord, the high division fences as shown back of the front lines of the houses, may be dispensed with back to the rear of the same. The blank walls can be covered with the Virginia creeper, and groups of shrubbery arranged at their base to better advantage than our plan shows; the plan supposing a concert of improvements only in front of the houses.

The house on the right has the form and extent of an unusually commodious and elegant town-house; the main part being 25 x 50 feet, and the rear 20 x 34. The front-entrance is quite peculiar, and, if designed by a good architect, will be an elegant and uncommon style of porch. There is a double object in making it of this form. It being desirable to have the entrance-gate at D, where persons passing in will at once have a vista the whole length of the side-yard to the back corner of the lot (as indicated by the dotted line), thus receiving a more favorable impression of the extent and beauty of the ground than if the gate-entrance were directly in front of the front door, this location of the gateway naturally suggests a side approach to the porch. But a porch of this form is of itself desirable in such a location, by permitting a heavy mass of shrubs to be planted directly in its front, leaving the lawn in front unbroken, and making the porch appear more distant and retired from the street than it would were the steps and walk directly in front of it, in the usual mode. It also makes a convenient front-entrance to the basement at the side of the parlor bay-window.

The grounds of this group of places are quite simple in the style of planting; yet, if laid out as here indicated, the materials properly chosen and well kept, they would be noticeable for their elegance. The necessarily small scale on which these groups of houses and lots are planned, makes it impracticable to describe them in detail, especially with reference to the selections of shrubs and trees.

## PLATE XXIV

*Four Residences, occupying the end of a Block two hundred feet in width, on Lots one hundred and fifty feet deep, and representing widely different forms of Houses and Lots.*

We will here suppose that the two lots on the left, each sixty feet front, were first purchased and improved; and the next twenty-five feet were then purchased by some one who cared little for grounds, and wished merely to provide himself a good town-house, and then the remaining fifty-five feet of the block by some one who could afford a larger style of improvement, including a carriage-house and stable. Also, that numbers one and two having built their house-fronts about forty feet from the street, purchaser number three has the good taste to put his front on the same line, but number four having a much longer house is obliged to crowd forward of the line a little. It is pleasant to observe how, in this group of utterly unlike houses, the peculiarity of each adds to the beauty of the others, and all succeed, by a harmonious improvement of their grounds on a common plan, to realize a great deal of beauty for which each one pays but a small share. Suppose the city-house number three were placed twenty feet nearer the street, it would then destroy the opportunity for the fine lawn on the line A, B; its blank side-walls would be marplots of the block on both sides, and its front-porch and bay-window, which now have charming outlooks in each direction, would then have little in view but the sidewalk and the street. By placing the house back on a line with the others, the owner has therefore made a great profit for himself, and conferred an equal one on his neighbors. Let him carry the same good sense a little farther. He has not cared to have much ground, but that strip twenty-five feet in width in front of his house must, in some way, be made creditable to the neighborhood. If it were filled with trees, shrubs, or flowers, these would destroy his grass-plat and outlooks, and his neighbors would have no considerable length of grassy ground; it would be selfish, after securing pleasant views from his bay-window over his neighbors' improvements, to so plant his own lot that their views would be destroyed. We would therefore suggest to him not to plant a tree, or a shrub, in front of his steps, but to place in the centre of the space in front of the bay-window a vase for flowers, of the most beautiful and substantial form that he can afford, and make it his 'family pride' to see that the filling of the vase and of the small flower-beds in front and behind it is as perfect a piece of art as possible. The plain lawn surrounding them, and the absence of any attempt at rural effect in front of this city-house, will alone give it an air of distinguished simplicity, while these characteristics will make its lawn, and vase, and flowers, a harmonious part of the common improvement of the whole block-front. We thus see how the owner of the narrowest lot of the group holds, as it were, the key to the best improvement of the block, and by the use of generous good sense, or the want of it, can consummate or mar the beauty of a whole neighborhood of grounds.

On lot 1, the house and grounds resemble those shown on Plate VI, though they are not identical. Besides the fruit trees in the back-yard it should have no other trees, except one of small size as shown near the front corner of the veranda; for which place we recommend the *Magnolia machrophylla*. The two small trees near the corners of the front bay-window, may be the catalpas *himalayensis* and *koempferi*, and the isolated tree nearest the street, the white-flowered magnolia (*conspicua*), or a single fine specimen of weigela, deutzia, lilac, viburnum, or honeysuckle. The gateway arch should be of hemlock, with evergreen undershrubs near it.

On lot 2, but two trees are shown in front of the house. These are twenty feet in front of the main house corners. Of rapid growing deciduous trees for this place, none are better adapted than the weeping birches; of those of slower growth, the double white-flowered horse-chestnut; or of evergreens, the weeping Norway spruce and weeping silver-fir. The gateway arch should be made with hemlocks.

Lot 4 has also two trees in front of the corners of the veranda. These being but eight feet from the latter, should be of some species which makes clean stems of sufficient height to carry their branches over its roof, in order not to darken and obstruct the outlook from the veranda. For this the ginkgo tree, most of the birches, and the scarlet oak are well adapted. But if it is desired to have the veranda deeply shaded, and somewhat secluded by foliage in summer, then the magnolias *soulangeana* or *cordata*, or almost any of the hard maples and horse-chestnuts, or the beeches and lindens, will do. We decidedly prefer deciduous trees to evergreens, in places so near the pleasantest outlooks from the house as these trees are located; for the reasons that their shadows are broader and more useful in summer, and by dropping their leaves in autumn, they relieve us in winter of a shade that would be needless and sombre.

## PLATE XXV

*Two Suburban Houses with Stables and Gardens, on original Lots 100 x 200 feet, illustrating a mode of embellishment by the addition of a Lot behind other Lots.*

The reader must imagine these two houses originally built on lots of the same size as that of plan No. 2 of this plate, viz.: 100 x 200 feet, having similar lots behind them, fronting on the side-street.

The owner of the corner lot No. 1, having it in his power, and desiring to enlarge his embellished grounds, buys the lot 100 x 200 feet in the rear of the two lots, first occupied, and thus doubles the area of his ground. The carriage-house and stable which he may or may not have had before, can now be located on the part of the new lot in the rear of the stable on original lot No. 2. Around it, in the rear of the same lot, is ample room for the vegetable-garden, and a yard for the horse and cow. This leaves the entire length of the ground near the side-street clear for decorative improvement. The outside kitchen-door of the house on lot 1 is through the laundry W, where the paths connecting it with the stable and outbuildings are entirely disconnected from the pleasure-walks. The carriage-road which connects with the steps of the back veranda is for the use of the family and household friends only; the street on the main front being the place for casual callers to alight.

Had the house been originally designed for the lot as it now stands, it could doubtless have had its best rooms arranged to look out more directly on the best portions of the grounds. As it is, the parlor gets no part of the benefit of the enlargement of the place by the addition of the rear lot. But the dining-room D, by a wide window or low-glazed door opening upon the back veranda, commands a full view of the croquet and archery ground, and its surrounding embellishments; and the family sitting-room S secures a similar view with a different fore-ground, by a bay-window projected boldly towards the side-street for that purpose. The outlook from the unusually large parlor on this plan, depends mostly on the adjoining place for the fine open lawn that is in view from the bow-window, but as the finest rooms of the house on lot 2 are equally dependent on the outlook across lot 1 for their pleasing views, it is not to be supposed that the occupants of either would wish to interrupt the advantageous exchange. The extreme openness of lawn on the front of both places, and the almost total absence of shrubbery on the front of No. 1, is for the purpose of giving a generous air to both, and to maintain all the advantages of reciprocity. It would be quite natural to suppose that No. 1, which is an old place remodelled, had once had its front yard filled full of shrubs and trees, and that in the formation of the new lawn in the rear the shrubbery was mostly removed to make the lawn more open, and to stock the groups of the new plantation; and then that the flower-beds were planned to relieve its plainness, without obstructing the neighbor's views, as shrubs and trees might.

The house on lot No. 2 is 40 x 44 feet, with a kitchen-wing 18 x 24. Having the main entrance on the side, the carriage-way passes the door, on the way to the stable, without unnecessary detour, and the best rooms of the house occupy the entire front. The house is considerably smaller than that on lot No. 1, though all its rooms are of ample size; the difference between the houses being in the stately parlor and bedroom on the first floor, which the house on lot No. 1 has, and the other has not. The sitting-room and parlor of the latter, however, opening together by sliding doors, will be fully equal in effect to the single parlor in the former plan, and, in proportion to its size, the latter seems to us the best house-plan.

The details of the planting on both places we can follow no further than the plate indicates them, without drawings on a larger scale to refer to. The fronts are simple and open to a degree that may be unsatisfactory to many persons – especially near the street-front of the corner lot, but as that lot is supposed to be richly embellished with shrubbery in the pleasure-ground back of the carriage-entrance, we believe the marked simplicity of the front will tend to make the new portion of the place more interesting by the contrast which its plainness presents to the profusion of sylvan and floral embellishments of the pleasure-ground proper.

## PLATE XXVI

*A Village Block of Stores and Residences, illustrating a mode of bringing Grounds back of Alleys into connection, for Decorative Purposes, with the Residences on the Village Street.*

We desire to call the reader's attention to this elaborate study of an unusual mode of securing to homes on contracted village lots the delightful appendage of charming little pleasure grounds.

The business of small villages usually clusters on one street, and sometimes occupies but a few stores near 'the corners', and it is a common practice of thrifty and prudent village merchants to have the residence on the same lot with the store, or on an adjoining lot. As the village increases, the lots near the leading merchant's are those earliest occupied by good improvements, in stores or residences. Our plate shows a village or suburban block of two hundred feet front on the principal street, with lots one hundred and fifty feet deep to an alley.

Let us suppose that Mr Smith, the wealthiest business man of the vicinage, has purchased the one hundred feet front on the right, and erected two fine stores on the corner (one of which he occupies), and a dwelling-house on the balance of the lot. While beginning to amass wealth he was doubtless occupying a much smaller store and house, and has erected these large improvements when his means enabled him to move with considerable strength. Let us further suppose that on the completion of this fine residence, a couple of well-to-do citizens buy two adjoining lots of twenty-five feet front each and put up a pair of city houses, and that the corner fifty feet, on the left, is then improved as shown on the plate.

Mr. Smith, and those who have built after him, have all been intent on getting themselves good houses, and have not had either the leisure or the taste to give much thought to grounds for embellishment. With a business exacting all his time, and a young family to provide for, the business man has looked forward to a new store or a new house as the *ultima thule* of his ambition. But when these are acquired, and larger means and more leisure and observation of the results of culture and wealth in other places open his eyes to other refined objects of expenditure, he cannot but see, living as he does in the centre of a farming country, with open fields and pleasant shade-trees only a few squares away, how he has cramped his house, like a prisoner, between the walls of his stores and his new neighbors, and has not even play-room for his children. But the fine house is built and cannot be abandoned. The neighbors, with fine, but smaller city-houses, are in the same predicament. They are all persons in good business, with (we will suppose) the average taste of tolerably educated people for a certain degree of elegance outside as well as inside their houses.

We have represented the entire fronts of the lots as bounded by a low stone-wall and coping, making the grounds four steps (twenty-eight inches) above the level of the sidewalks, and the main floors of the houses five steps more, so that the basement-kitchens for which all the houses are planned will be mostly above the level of the ground. In addition to a fine low iron fence on the stone coping, and some elegant vases in the centre of each of the front spaces between the walks, and the vines on the porches and veranda, the three places nearest the store can have little more done to them to make them attractive homes exteriorly. The backyard of the double-house has room for a little decoration, and as the wall next to the alley has an east exposure, it is a good place for a cold grape-house, and is used accordingly. The rear arcade and bay-windows of the library and dining-rooms now have a pleasant lookout on a pretty bit of grass-plat, dotted with a vase and a few beds for low flowers; the grapery bounding the view in front, and a square rose-covered arbor marking the intersections of the walks on two sides of the fruit and vegetable square, behind the store-yards. The other neighbors follow suit with cold grape-houses along the alley; the one on the extreme left improving on the others by adding a decorative gable-entrance fronting the main street, and forming a pleasing termination to the view of the side-yard as seen from the front. These four places now have about all the out-door comforts and beauties that the lots are capable of, but after all they are city houses, on cramped city lots. The pleasures incident to the care of these bits of lawn, the filling of the vases, and the management of the vines and plants in the grape-houses, all have a tendency to beget a craving for more room; for similar pleasures and more beautiful creations on a larger scale. Mr. Smith, the owner of the stores and the double-house, has been obliged to buy the lot back of the alley (100 x 185 feet) to get room for his stable, vehicle, and man-servant. Not being in a street where property is used for business, or popular for residences, he buys it for a small part of what lots on the east street are worth, and the lot is first used for a horse and cow pasture, or run-ground, in connection with the stable. Now let us suppose Mr. Smith is one of those good specimens of business-men whose refined tastes develop as their means increase, and that he longs, and that his good family seconds the longing, for those lovely stretches of lawn flecked with shadows of trees, margined with shrubberies, and sparkling with flowers, that some friend's acre has enabled him to display; that the family envy the possession of fine croquet grounds where children, youth, and old people are alike merry in the open summer air with the excitement of the battles of the balls; that they desire some better place than the street to air the little children, and to stroll with family familiarity on fair summer days, and evenings, and sociable Sundays.

To obtain all these pleasant features of a home without going into the country, or exchanging the home in the heart of the village for a new one farther off, or giving up the convenient proximity to his business which Mr. Smith has always enjoyed, we propose to tunnel the alley, and to convert the cow-pasture-lot into a little pleasure-ground, as shown on the plan. This project, however, presupposes that the soil is naturally so gravelly as to be self-draining, so that water might never rest in the tunnel, or else that drainage for the bottom of the tunnel can be effected by a sewer in the alley beneath it, or not far off.

It may be asked – 'why tunnel rather than bridge the alley?' The reasons are conclusive in favor of the tunnel. A bridge over the alley must be high enough to allow a load of hay to pass under. The great height would make it a laborious ascent and descent. In going from one piece of embellished ground to the other it is precisely to avoid the sight of the alley that we want bridge or tunnel. But by mounting a bridge, although we thus secure clean footing at all times, which might not be the case in crossing on the ground, the alley would be more entirely in sight than if one were to cross it in the usual way, and (if the bridge were uninclosed) persons making use of it would be targets for the eyes of the neighborhood. If inclosed and roofed, its height would make it absurdly conspicuous, expensive, and liable to be carried off by winds. Whether used or not, it would stand obtrusively in sight from all directions, without the excuse for its conspicuousness which attaches to a wind-mill, which, to be useful, must stand on tip-toe to catch each wandering breeze.

The tunnel, on the other hand, is unobtrusive, out of sight of all but those who use it, private, and a cool summer retreat. It forms, when properly constructed, a novel contrast and foil to the sunny garden to which it is designed to introduce the passer. Descending into its vaulted shade, the view on emerging into a sunny pleasure-ground is made doubly charming by the contrast. Its sides should be recessed for seats, which in the hottest days of summer will have a delightful coolness, and in winter form good places for storing half-hardy box plants, bulbs, and small trees. One needs but call to mind the charming tunnels for footpaths in the New York Central Park to imagine the beauty that may be given to even such small tunnels as the ones here recommended.

If well constructed, such tunnels cannot be done cheaply. But in a case like the one under consideration, where the owner of a fine place must either sell out and improve elsewhere, or else devise some mode of utilizing the lots across the alley, the expense of a tunnel and its appropriate adjuncts, will be very small compared with the sacrifices that would be necessary to secure the same benefits by removal.

The construction of such a tunnel and its approaches requires the employment of a very good architect. To enable the reader to have a better idea of the plan, as indicated on our plate, we will give some explanations in detail. Nine feet below the surface of this alley is supposed to be deep enough for the floor of the tunnel. Seven feet clear will be high enough for the inside passage, which will leave enough earth over the top of a brick arch to protect it, and six feet will be a sufficient clear width inside. For an alley fifteen feet wide, the arch should be eighteen feet long. The steps down to it, and their flanking walls, would make a length of ten to fifteen feet more on each side – depending on the manner of the descent, and the nature of the superincumbent improvements – and likely in any case to make the entire excavation upwards of forty feet in length, including the slopes for the steps. The side-walls throughout should be double or hollow walls; the inner one of brick, nicely pointed, the outer one of stone, and both made watertight with water-lime cement. The arch over the tunnel proper should be made with great care to render it perfectly water-tight also, and if the entire filling above the arch, and on the outside of the side-walls, is made with good gravel, broken stone, or coarse sand, so as to let all surface water soak down directly to the drain below the floor of the tunnel, there will be little liability to excessive dampness or dripping water in the tunnel. The arch for the main tunnel on this plan is to have the springing points five feet from the floor, and to be that segment of a circle which will make the centre seven feet high. For stairs, broad solid stone steps are of course the best in the long run, but some expense for such work may be saved by having the slope down to the tunnel floored with a smooth water-lime cement, and a flight of plank steps put in, supported at the ends only, and high enough above the sloping cement floor to allow the latter to be readily brushed and kept clean under the plank steps. These, having the air circulating freely all around them, will not be liable to quick decay.

In the plan under consideration, the walk leading directly from the rear arcade of the double-house to the grape-house is to descend gradually for about twenty feet, so that at the front line of the latter it will be two feet below the general surface, and a step on the same line will drop eight inches more to a stone landing, from which four steps up on each side lead to the two sides of the grape-house, and ten steps down, to the floor of the tunnel. On the side towards the mansion, the inclosed porch and roof of the entrance to the tunnel being made in the construction of the grape-house, cannot be considered a part of the cost of the former, but the flanking walls, the steps, the tunnel itself, and the necessary covered porch over the exit from the tunnel on the farther side of the alley, altogether involve a considerable expenditure. The whole could probably be done in a plain style for about one thousand dollars, including a handsome inclosed porch on the upper side, but not including the pavilion shown on the left of it, which is a separate affair; though the two may be made together as one construction.

This pavilion will certainly be a desirable feature after the pleasure-ground has become sufficiently complete to make a view over it pleasing. It should have a solid wall on the alley side. The floor is raised five feet above the lawn, and the space beneath (with a floor a foot or two below the lawn and a window on the alley) may be used as the gardener's work-room. Fronting to the west as here shown, the pavilion will be a pleasant place for members of the family to retire on warm summer evenings after tea to observe the warm lights on the trees, the lengthening shadows on the lawn, and all the glories of our American sunsets. Or, if a darker seat in the summer-house in the far corner of the lot be preferred, the light of the sun upon the arches and other features of the pavilion will make a bright addition to the beauty of the view towards it.

Before describing the pleasure-ground upon which the proposed tunnel from the double-house opens, we wish to call attention to what new ambitions the spirit of emulation is likely to produce in the owners of the two city houses on the twenty-five-feet lots adjoining. They are much worse off for yard-room than Mr. Smith ever was, and his successful use of the rear lot by means of the tunnel suggests to them the purchase of the equal sized remaining lot back of their own improvements. Both want it, and they compromise by buying it together, with a view of joining in the expense of a tunnel- entrance to it. It will be seen that we have arranged for them a double-tunnel with passages four feet in width.

The new lot must be partitioned between them, so as to give each an equal area, and an equal value. This is done in a peculiar way in order to make the form and consequent effect of the improvements on each lot as different from the other as practicable. Each owner has entrance to his own tunnel through his grape-house, and the exit porches on the opposite side open upon lawns and pleasure walks that can quickly be made interesting. In connection with the double exit porch we have drawn buildings for hired men, including workshops and tool-rooms of the same width, under a roof supposed to be a continuation of the pavilion-structure on Mr. Smith's lot. Many persons who employ men-servants object to lodging them in their residences. As rooms for them may be provided more cheaply in connection with the building of this tunnel porch than if built separately, we have introduced them, but they are not essential to the plan.

We will now sketch the general features of the planting for the first described lot back of the alley. It must be borne in mind, to begin with, that this lot, 100 x 185 feet, is a small area upon which to place all the structures and gardenesque embellishments that the ground-plan indicates, and being surrounded by a high wall or fence to insure its absolute seclusion, its lawn-surface will be still further lessened by the belts of trees and shrubs that must be planted inside the walls to relieve their monotony. This limited area can be planted so as to avoid inelegant crowding only by a selection of trees of secondary size, and a very judicious choice of shrubs. But when such walled grounds are successfully treated, there is an expression of snugness and elegant privacy about them that the ladies are apt to speak of as 'delicious'. Those who have passed through dark houses on some of the narrow streets of old Paris, and emerged suddenly in great gardens behind them, which one could hardly imagine there was vacant room for within a mile of the place, or those who have been equally surprised and delighted with the brilliant gardens behind the dismal street-walls of Spanish American cities, can appreciate fully how charming such grounds as these may be made, and how the mere novelty of such a tunnel-entrance to a walled garden will give it a special charm.

We have not hitherto called attention to the path from the kitchen (under the dining-room) directly to and across the alley, to the carriage-house and stable. Between this path and the exit-porch of the tunnel, the space is to be filled with a pine tree and a dense growth of hemlocks, and an impervious screen of the latter is to be continued along the right-hand side of the path issuing from the tunnel, to be grown to a height that will conceal the stable buildings from view as one passes along by the side of them. The path connecting the stable and the main path should open from the latter under a narrow hemlock-arch. The group of evergreens on the left of the exit from the tunnel must be those which do not exceed seven feet in height, or which may readily be kept down to that height, and not interfere with the view from the arcade; say a pair of Sargent's hemlock, next to the arcade, the *Cephalotaxus fortunii mascula* next; the golden arbor-vitas in front of that, and a bed of flowers diminished to a point as shown on the plan.

At the divergence of the main paths a really elegant flower-vase should be placed; it being the first object that will engage the eye on emerging from the tunnel. Behind it a rose-bed is shown. Perhaps a fine evergreen would be better there, say the weeping silver-fir, on a line with the centre of the tunnel and the vase.

Following the main path to the right, there should be masses of strong-growing shrubs between it and the stable, to prevent the latter from being noticeable in passing. A mass of shrubs eight feet high, within two yards of the walk, will conceal an object twenty-four feet high, twenty-four feet from the walk. Of course all parts of this stable-building should be well finished, as it must be seen from nearly every part of the pleasure-ground, but if the upper parts of it – the roof-lines, cornices and upper windows – are properly designed, a view of them over the shrubs and among the tops of the environing trees will improve, rather than injure, the expression of the place. The three sunny sides of the building are also to be covered with the foliage of grape-vines. In addition to the needful shrubbery to conceal this building from too close inspection, the corner of the lot in its rear is to be stocked with cherry and pear trees. Where the walk turns toward the left, leaving the fruit-tree group, a mass of fine shrubs borders the walk on both sides; then for a short distance the lawn opens on the right to a grape-espalier, and a group of the finest rhododendrons in front of it; on the left, at *a*, is a pair of *Kolreuterias*, and beyond them another group of rhododendrons and azalias. We here come in sight of the summer-house in the corner, with its flanking of hemlocks and bright little flower-beds, and a vase opposite the walk from it. The view of the grounds from this point is intended to be the best. Passing along to the left, the tree marked *b* is intended for the weeping beech; beyond, the walks form a circle for a grand mass of bedding-plants, in a bay of evergreens. The tree *c* may be the Magnolia machrophylla; at *d*, a pair consisting of a sassafras and a white-flowering dogwood; opposite to them a group of three pines, the Bhotan, Austrian, and white. On the right (returning towards the tunnel), the wall between the pines is to be screened by a collection of small evergreens. As they will have only a north exposure until their tops are higher than the division fences, a hemlock hedge close to the fence, with a formal collection of rhododendrons and evergreen dwarfs in front of it, will be best there. The pine tree at the last turn of the walk is intended for the dwarf white (*compacta*), or a weeping Japan sophora would be well placed there.

The suppositional plantings of the other lots back of the alley we must leave to the reader; except to mention that the long wall which divides the place just described from its neighbor, offers on its south side too good an opportunity for a grape-border to be lost. We have therefore used its entire length for that purpose.

The reader will hardly fail to notice that the corner place on the left, which originally had double the width of lot of its next neighbors, and that too on a corner where bay-windows, and ground well improved on the side, gave it many advantages in point of beauty and comfort, has now no pleasure-ground that deserves the name compared with those which have been secured by means of the tunnel, in connection with the houses on the twenty-five-feet lots.

## PLATE XXVII, A & B

*Two Plans for Residences and Grounds on Lots having acute Angles formed by equally important Streets.*

These are common forms of town and suburban lots, which puzzle improvers as to how to front the house, to plan it, and to place the outbuildings, and lay out the ground so that the improvements shall look well, and the connections be the most convenient from both streets.

The two ground-plans here given show different modes of fronting a house that is nearly the same in plan on both, on the same lot; the different frontages involving a totally different style of laying out in each case, and some variations in the kitchen part of the house-plans.

The lots are one hundred and fifty feet on each of the shorter sides, and would be three hundred feet in length on the longest side if extended to a sharp point; this makes them equal in area to a parallelogram 150x 225 feet; a trifle more than three-quarters of an acre.

The carriage-house and road are of similar character in both plans, and enter from the same street. In other respects the ground-plans differ widely, and yet have some points of resemblance which the form of the boundaries renders essential. Both have been designed with care to make them valuable studies for those who have similar lots to improve. Design B has a considerable length of pleasure-walks which may be dispensed with, without marring the design for planting, and design A shows no walks on the pleasure-ground proper, though a walk could be laid out around the lawn above the house, if thought desirable, without changing the plan of its planting. The dotted lines on design B represent some of the open lines of view to and from the principal windows of the house, from the streets, and from one part to another of the grounds.

The extremely small scale of the drawings make it impracticable to give details for planting.


## PLATE XXVIII

*Plans for two Triangular Corner Lots opposite each other.*

The upper of these two lots is larger than those of Plate XXVII, and contains an acre and a half, but is of precisely the same form, and supposed to be differently circumstanced in the character of the street on its longest side; which, though used for the carriage-entrance A, and one foot-path entrance *b*, is not of sufficient importance to make it desirable to leave openings in the shrubbery on that side for views from the street to the house. The residence is more mansion-like than those on the plate referred to, and its carriage-entrance has a much more stately character. The large turn-way in front of the main entrance is larger than necessary for a turn-way merely, in order to make a broader green directly in front of the main entrance, and to give room for a grove of fine trees with which it is to be shaded. The walk from the front street at *c*, with the one before mentioned at *b*, and the kitchen entrance-gate at *d*, give the most convenient access from the streets to the house from whichever direction one comes, and leave a large area between *c* and *b*, unbroken by walks, which the plan shows to be carefully and elegantly improved; while to the right of the walk from *c*, a heavy mass of shrubbery forms a boundary between the pleasure-ground proper, and a considerable orchard, kitchen grass-plat, and vegetable-ground. The triangular space between the walk-entrance *b*, and the carriage-entrance A, should be filled with evergreens – say a Norway spruce in the centre and hemlocks around it. Between *a* and *d* is room for masses of some of the noblest shrubs. The small scale of the drawing here again forbids a further detailed enumeration of the materials for the plantation.

The lower plan is essentially different in its conditions and treatment from the three that have been noticed, though it resembles plan B of Plate XXVII in its frontage, if that plan were turned upside down. But on this plan we suppose the lot to be little more than a mere triangle – turning the corner on the left only forty feet, just far enough to include a row of fruit trees and a private entrance to the stable and carriage-house on that side by a straight road to it. It will be observed that the kitchen, carriage-house, and stable are joined, and turned into the corner of the lot in the most compact arrangement possible, and that the entire house-plan (the main part of which is 33 x 50 feet) is a model of compactness, convenience, and good connections with the several parts of the ground. The latter also affords a rare study of the elegant effect that may be produced on only two-thirds of an acre by skillful arrangement of buildings and plantings, and the abandonment of a vegetable-garden.

In most respects this plan if well studied will explain itself, but there are two inconspicuous features on this drawing which the observer may fail to catch the meaning of. First, the point where the long walk to the kitchen diverges from the one leading to the front, shows what appears like a large tree over it. This is intended to represent five trees (the trunks of which are shown by light dots on the engraving) planted in the form of a pentagon, for the purpose of making an umbrage of the character of some of those described in Chapter XIV. Where the hawthorns flourish we would make the collection of them alone, including among them the new thorn (not a true hawthorn), *Coccinea flore plena*. But the group may be well composed of many other small species of trees – taking care that when more than one species or variety is used all shall be of similar size and form, in order to make a congruous mass when grown. Second, at a point opposite the parlor bay-window a round flower-bed is shown, backed by dense evergreen foliage. On each side of this flower-bed a pair of small trees are indicated, connected by light lines. These are intended for hemlock arches of fanciful forms, to give interest to the place by their own novelty, and the pretty effect of vistas through them. The commonest bit of lawn with a glimpse of bright flowers, when seen through such arch-frames, often has a pretty effect that is quite remarkable considering the meagre materials that produce it.

## PLATE XXIX

*A first-class Suburban Residence and Plantation on a Comer Lot of 300 x 540 feet, containing 3 $^{71}/_{100}$ acres.*

This is one of those elegant places that requires a large income for its maintenance, and which most Americans who have little idea of the breadth of view that the name park implies, are apt to speak of as a private park. It is by no means a park, but it is a generous pleasure-ground for a retired citizen, with all the elegant appliances that wealth makes practicable. There is room enough here to indulge in a great variety of trees and shrubs without crowding the lawn. The latter opens generously upon the public highway in front, and connects on the right with a supposed good neighbor. The entrance-drive is simple in its character, and from the point A, the visitor in entering would command vistas the entire length of the lot over the lawn in front, and at the right, a view of the elaborate flower-garden that forms the principal feature of interest opposite the parlor bay-window. The plan directly violates one rule that is generally desirable to observe in the arrangement of trees, viz.: to plant so as to make the house the centre of the picture from the most prominent or most natural points of view. But on this plan the trees in front, and near the front of the house, when well grown, will effectually hide it from the entrance at A, and leave but partial views open from the highway to the east side of the house; while from all other points along the street towards which it fronts, it will be completely shut off by trees. This has been done for the following reason. On so large a lot it would savor of selfish exclusiveness not to have the lawn open generously to the street. But many families have a strong desire for a considerable degree of privacy in their front veranda and porch. As in this case they front to the south, not only their free use, unobserved from the street, but their comfort in the face of so much gravelled road, requires a mass of trees to shut off too open a view from the street, and to render the veranda and porch comfortable in hot weather by their cooling shadows. It being desirable for these reasons to violate the usual rule, it is better to do it entirely than by halves, and by inviting the eye, in entering, away from the front to other views around the house, the latter when seen, as it can be to great advantage from the pavilion and from several points in the pleasure-walk in the rear part of the lawn, will (if in itself pleasing) add the more to the attractions of these walks.

In concluding this series of designs, we cannot forbear to call attention again to the great advantage that a neighborhood of homes on deep lots, with narrow fronts, has over one of equal population covering an equal area in lots of less depth and more frontage. Narrow frontages enable a community to keep up fine walks and fences in their fronts with less expense to each owner, and thus to add the comforts of city streets to the rural pleasures that await those who court them in the grounds behind the gate. Depth of lots suggests a deep space between the houses and the street, which, by neighborly agreement, opening from one home to another in continuous lawn, and planted with trees and shrubs for the common benefit of all, becomes a broader expanse of embellished ground than is attainable where shallow lots force proprietors to place their residences closer to the street line. Nothing is lost by having the rear part of one's lot, which is necessarily divided by high fences, or walls, from the neighbors, in a long and narrow, rather than a shallow or squarer form. A space forty feet in width, and one hundred and twenty feet in depth behind the house, is more useful for planting, and for domestic purposes, than an area seventy feet square, though the latter is somewhat the largest. The speculative habit of cutting up suburban lands into narrow city lots 25 x 100 feet, or but little more, destroys all chance of making true suburban improvements. Such lots will only sell to citizens who are either too poor, too cockneyish, or too ignorant of their own needs, to insist on something more, and cannot be managed so as to attract that class of cultivated and intelligent people who want rurally suburban homes, and not city houses and city habits on the margin of the country.

# 16

# The Renovation of Old Places

Whatever objection may be urged against buying and renovating old houses, will not apply to the purchase of ground stocked with old trees and shrubs. Many a rickety, neglected place, is filled with choice old materials, which, with small expenditures in clearing away the superfluities, and polishing the lawn, will group at once into pleasing pictures. Such neglected places may be compared with a head of luxuriant hair all uncombed and disorderly, which needs but to be clean and arranged with taste to become a crown of beauty to the wearer.

Old yards are generally filled with mature trees of choice species, but so huddled together, and filled in with lank neglected shrubs and tangled grass, that one observes only the shiftlessness and disorder, and turns with greater pleasure to look upon a polished lawn with not a tree upon it: as in music a single note given purely and clearly is more pleasing than the greatest variety of sounds making discords together. But a week's work among these medleys of trees and shrubs – the bold cutting or digging-out of the poorest trees, the re-arrangement of the shrubbery, so that the sunlight may play with the shadows of those that remain, upon some open breadth of velvety grass – and there will stand revealed a mass of beautiful home adornments that the place bare of large trees and mature shrubs will envy. Sometimes old fruit-trees that have had an air habitually expressive of hard times and low living, with a little pruning, and extra feeding, and the well-to-do air that a new green lawn-carpet gives them, will assume a new dress of foliage, and wear it with such luxuriant grace that they become the most pleasing of trees – scarcely recognizable as the same which so lately wore a dejected air.

In renovating old grounds that are filled with mature trees and shrubs, the first thing to be decided on is the amount of clean cutting-out to be done; what had better be entirely removed in order that something better may be developed. 'Trimming-up', instead of cutting-out, is the common error of persons ignorant of the arts of sylvan picture-making; an error invariably defended with the

potent plea of—'*I* don't believe in cutting down shade trees'. It is the semblance of a good reason, and the best excuse that can be given for ignorance in an art which can only be taught by example to those who are not born with landscape mirrors in their hearts. It is only necessary, however, to show a dense grove of high-trimmed trees on one side, and then a similar grove one-third of which has been cut away to make clear openings of sunny lawn through it, and give the remaining trees room to spread their bending boughs to meet the grass, to feel the difference between art that mars, and art that reveals natural beauty.

Yet in regard to 'trimming-up' there may be occasions for some exceptional treatment. Noble growths of evergreens growing to the ground sometimes fill the grounds of a small place, obstructing the views over the lawn to a serious extent; what they conceal being a more important part of the beauty that may be developed than is their own beauty. To destroy the trees may leave too great a void; to leave them as they are is to retain the gloomy expression that results from lack of sunny lawn and bright vistas under the boughs of trees. In such cases we would trim-up old fir trees just high enough to give a clear view of the lawn under them, as shown by Fig. 44.

The reader will observe that a glimpse of quite an extent of lawn is suggested under the branches of this tree. If, however, the branches rested upon the ground, the landscape vista would be effectually shut out. The advantage of this mode of treatment is principally on small grounds, for,

FIG. 44.

were there space enough to secure ample lawn-views without it, we would by no means recommend this mode of securing them.

In choosing which to cut out, and which to retain, let it be observed that a large tree of an inferior sort may be better worth preserving than a small or thin specimen of varieties that are otherwise superior. There is no more disagreeable impertinence to the cultivated eye than the growth of slender starved saplings planted under the branches of large trees, and striving to get to the sun and sky by thrusting themselves between the limbs of their superiors. As between a sugar-maple and a black oak, for instance, the former is by far the most beautiful and desirable species in all respects, but if you have a well branched large tree of the latter and only young sapling maples, we would sacrifice the saplings of the better breed for the mature beauty of the inferior oak. There is a dignity in big trunks, and loftiness, for which the prettiness of young trees is an unsatisfactory substitute.

Everybody has heard of the countryman who went to see a city but 'could not see the town, there were so many houses!' His quaint speech ludicrously suggests the main fault of most old places; the multiplicity of their trees and shrubs conceal each other, so that they have little beauty either singly or in the mass, and they are rarely so arranged as to make the home they surround the centre of a sylvan picture. Wherever there are large trees there must be proportional breadths of unbroken lawn – open spaces from which the trees can be seen, or their beauty is of no avail. A dense forest around a home suggests the rudeness of pioneer life, not the refinement of culture. Forests breed timber, not sylvan beauty. It is the pasture-field, the park, and the brook-space, that give sun and scope and moisture to develop the sylvan pictures that painters love. Therefore in renovating over-grown places, bear in mind that the cutting away of some of your old trees may be necessary to reveal and improve the beauty of the others.

Another and different fault of many old places, resulting from the effort of uneducated planters to avoid the error of over-crowding trees and shrubs, is that of distributing them sparsely but pretty evenly all over the place. This is destructive of all picturelike effects, for it gives neither fine groups, nor open lawn, and even the single trees, however fine they may be, cannot be seen to advantage, because there are no openings large enough to see them from. This must be remedied by clearing out in some places and filling-in in others.

There is one value in the possession of thrifty saplings of sorts not especially desirable, that few persons know, and which is very rarely made use of. We refer to their usefulness as stocks upon which to graft finer varieties, and by the greater strength of their well-established roots producing a growth of the inserted sorts much more luxuriant and showy than could be obtained in twice the time by fresh plantings. The black oak is not worth preserving, unless of large size, but it can be readily grafted with the scarlet oak. White oaks in superfluous number may be grafted with the rare weeping oaks of England, or the Japan purple oak, or some of the peculiar varieties of the Turkey oak. The common chestnut (*castanea*) may be grafted with ornamental varieties of the Spanish chestnut; the common horse-chestnut or buckeye with a number of beautiful and singular varieties; the common 'thorn apple' of the woods with exquisite varieties of the English hawthorns, and the same with maples, elms, and all those trees of which grafts of novel varieties of the same species may be procured. Scions of rare varieties may be procured at our leading nurseries, or by sending through our seedsmen or nurserymen to England or France for them; for which purpose application should of course be made as early as mid-winter. These suggestions about using trees to graft upon, apply only to young trees. Large ones should not have their nobler proportions marred by such work.

Old apple-trees are not appreciated as they should be. No tree of its size has a grander spread. Their horizontal branches often have the majesty of small park-oaks. This look of low breadth and strength is expressive of its domestic character, and makes it peculiarly appropriate in proximity to residences of moderate size and cottage character. Few trees are in leaf earlier; none are more fragrant or beautiful in bloom; none bend with such a ruddy glow of useful fruit. The fall of immature fruit is an objection to all fruit trees on lawns. If the proprietor is not tidy enough to have his lawn always close mowed under them, and all insect-bitten fruit and windfalls picked or raked up as soon as they drop, then he does not deserve to have trees that are at the same time beautiful and useful. These remarks apply especially to full-grown trees. It is only after the apple-tree is from thirty to forty years old that it attains a noble expression, and its best characteristics, like those of the oak and chestnut, are developed in its old age.

We protest against doing violence to old apple-trees by cutting them to pieces to graft them with better ones. The beauty of a broad old tree is worth more than the additional value of grafted fruit will ever be. One cannot see an old apple-tree near a house thus marred, without thinking that the owner is either beauty-blind, or so penurious that he grudges the old tree its room upon the lawn unless he can make it pay ground-rent.

Apple or other low branching trees that have become decrepit from age or insects, can be turned to pleasing use by cutting off their branches several feet from the main trunks and training vines over them. The pipe-vine or birthwort (*Aristolochia sipho*), with its luxuriant mass of large heart-shape leaves, makes a superb show on supports of this kind. Almost any of our twining or creeping vines are beautiful enough in such places, and few more so than the common hop, but running roses, though often used in this way, are the least suitable. Trees whose tops are not sound enough to be thus used, may often be sawed off from one to three feet above the ground, and used for bases of rustic flower-vases or baskets; provided they stand in places where it is appropriate to have flower-vases.

Old shrubs of any of the standard species, if of large size, even though unshapely, may often be turned to good account in the places where they stand, by using them as centres for groups of smaller shrubs. Sometimes their very irregularity of outline will make them picturesque objects to stand conspicuously alone on the lawn. Often a shrub of noble size has been hid by inferior shrubs and trees crowding it, which may all be removed to bring it into full relief. The beauty of full and well grown single specimens of our most common shrubs is as little known as though they were the most recent introductions from Japan. Not one American in a thousand, even among those most observant of sylvan forms, has ever seen a perfectly grown bush-honeysuckle, lilac, snow-ball, or syringa, though every suburban home in the land is filled with them. Growing either in crowded clumps, or under trees, or in poor uncultivated sodden soil, we have learned to love them merely for their lavish beauty of bloom, and have not yet learned what breadth and grace of foliage they develop when allowed to spread from the beginning, on an open lawn.

There are no worse misplantings in most old grounds than old rose-bushes, whose annual sprouts play hide-and-seek with the rank grass they shelter – roses which the occupants from time immemorial have remembered gratefully for their June bloom, till their sweetness and beauty have become associated with the tangled grass they grow in. There is no reason for having a lawn broken by such plants. Rose-bushes do better for occasional transplantings, and their bloom and foliage is always finer in cultivated, than in grassy ground. Mass them where they can be cultivated and enriched together. Plate XXXI shows many forms for rose-beds, and by using care in keeping the strongest growers nearest the centre, varieties enough may be displayed in one snug bed to spoil a quarter-acre lawn planted in the old way – 'wherever there is a good open space' – precisely the space that should not be broken by anything, least of all by such straggling growers as roses.

Do not be in haste to decide where the shrubs you dig up shall be planted again. When the air and sun have been let in to the roots and tops of the best large trees and shrubs, and the lawn is completed about them, it may be that the effect of your lawn, and the trees that shadow it, will be nobler it you omit altogether all the smaller shrubs. Large trees and shrubs are robbed of half their beauty if they have not a fair expanse of unbroken lawn around them.

**Vines on Old Trees** – Some evergreens, the balsam-fir for instance, and the hemlock when it is old, become gloomy-looking trees. The black oak and red oak have also a similar expression, though entirely different in form. If such trees stand where more cheerful and elegant trees are needed, the desired improvement may be made by enriching the ground near their trunks, and planting at their base, on both sides, such vines as the Chinese wistaria and the trumpet-creeper, which will cover them to their summits in a few years with a mass of graceful spray and luxuriant leafage. The Chinese wistaria is probably better adapted to cover lofty trees than other climbers, but the trumpet-creeper, Virginia-creeper, the native varieties of the clematis, and the Japan and Chinese honeysuckles, may all be used. The wild grape-vine is admirable for filling up trees of thin and straggling growth, such as the oaks before named. The hardy grape, known as the Clinton, is well adapted to this use, while very good wine can be made of its fruit. Perhaps no flowering vine excels it in luxuriance of foliage-drapery, but its prolific fruitage renders it necessary to bestow a good deal of time in gathering the clusters scattered among the branches of a lofty tree. There is no question that the value of the fruit will far more than pay for the labor, but unless picked clean every year it may disfigure both the tree and the lawn. Whether the birds will insure against any damage of this kind we have not had the means of learning.

An exquisite example of the effect of such planting is an old hemlock at 'Cottage Place', Germantown, PA. The tree is three feet in diameter and eighty feet high. At a little distance it cannot be recognized as a hemlock, so completely is its lofty summit crowned with a magnificent drapery of the waving foliage of the Chinese wistaria. A root of the wistaria was planted on each side of the trunk. Their stems are now from six to eight inches in diameter.

In conclusion, it may be safely said that new places rarely afford a skillful planter such opportunities for making quick and beautiful effects at small cost as old places of similar extent. Our town suburbs would in a half dozen years be more beautiful than most persons can conceive possible, even without the addition of a single new home, provided all the old homes could feel the renovating hands of true artists in home-grounds, and be kept up in the same spirit. The metamorphosis of such places, from cluttered aggregations of superfluities, to gleaming lawns, smilingly introducing the beholder to beautiful trees and flowers that luxuriate in the new-made space and sun around them, is too great not to inspire those who have profited by the change to preserve the beauty that may so easily be brought to light.

**Old Houses** – Old places which have houses 'just good enough not to move off or tear down', are greatly undervalued by most purchasers. It is not quite in the scope of this work to put in a plea for old houses, but we must confess to a very loving partiality for them when tastefully renovated. No one, however, but an architect who is known to have a tasteful faculty for such adaptations should be employed to direct the work. (The attention of the reader is commended to Vaux' *Villas and Cottages*, page 205, for some valuable remarks on this subject).

There is a thoughtless prejudice in the minds of most Americans against all things which are not span-new, and we have met men of such ludicrous depravity of taste in this respect, as to cut down fine old trees in order to have room to plant some pert and meagre little nurslings of their own buying! Although houses do not grow great by age, like trees, yet, where strongly built at first, and afterwards well occupied, they acquire certain quaint expressions which are the very aroma of pleasing homes; which nothing but age can give a home, and this beauty of some old houses should be as lovingly preserved as that of the aged apple, maple, or elm trees around them.

# 17
# Flowers and Bedding Plants, and Their Settings

We are the sweet flowers Bom of sunny showers,
(Think whene'er you see us, what our beauty saith),
Utterance mute and bright,
Of some unknown delight,
We All the air with pleasure by our simple breath:
All who see us, love us:
We befit our places;
Unto sorrow we give smiles, unto graces—races.
See (and scorn all duller Taste) how heaven loves color;
How great Nature clearly joys in red and green;
What sweet thoughts she thinks,
Of violets and pinks,
And a thousand flushing hues made solely to be seen ;
See her whited lilies Chill the silver showers,
And what a red mouth is her rose, the woman of her flowers.

'Chorus of Flowers', *Leigh Hunt*.

As all vegetable productions, from the greatest trees to the minute mosses, are equally flowering plants, it is to be understood that the subject of flowers, as here treated, is limited to observations on annuals, perennials, and bedding plants.

Considering such flowers as the finishing decorations of a home, as accessory embellishments rather than principal features, it is desired to suggest the places where they may be put with the best effect rather than to give descriptions of even a small number of their almost innumerable variety. The immense collections of our leading seedsmen, and their beautifully illustrated catalogues, give a bewildering sense of the folly of attempting to know, much less to grow, a hundredth part of those which are reputed desirable, and they also force upon us the wise reflection that the good growth and skillful arrangement of a few species only, will produce effects quite as pleasing as can be attained with the greatest variety.

Annuals, perennials, and bedding plants are used in three tolerably distinct modes, viz.: First, in narrow beds bordering a straight walk to a main entrance, or skirting the main walk of a kitchen-garden. Second, in a variety of beds of more or less symmetrical patterns, grouped to form a flower-garden or parterre, to be an object of interest independent of its surroundings. Third, as adjuncts and embellishments of a lawn, of groups of shrubs, of walks and window views, to be planted with reference to their effect in connection with other things.

On large and expensively kept grounds all these styles may be maintained in appropriate places respectively. But on small lots the first or the last mode should be adopted, though sometimes both may be desirable.

The simplest and rudest mode of planting in the first style, is to border a walk closely with a continuous bed from two to four feet wide, filled with flowering plants of all sizes and shapes and periods of bloom, here overhanging the walk with unkempt growth, like weeds, there leaving a broad barren spot where spring-flowers have bloomed and withered. Fortunately this mode is becoming less common, and the pretty setting of a margin of well-cut grass is better appreciated than formerly.

Flower-beds cut in the grass have a more pleasing effect than when bordered by gravel-walks. When made as marginal embellishments of straight walks, they should rarely be cut nearer than two feet from the side of the walk if they are of much length parallel with it, but where the openings between the beds are frequent, or the beds are in circles or squares with their points to the walk, one foot of grass between their nearest points and the walk will answer. Narrow beds of formal outlines or geometric forms of a simple character, are preferable to irregular ones. All complicated 'curlecue' forms should be avoided. Plate XXX shows a variety of shapes for flower-beds on straight walks. Such beds must, of course, be proportioned in size and form to the dimensions of the lawn in which they are cut. They should never be planted where there is not a space of open lawn back of them equal at least in average width to the distance across the walk from one bed to another. Being close to the eyes of all those who use the walks, they must be planted and kept with a care that is less essential in beds seen from a greater distance. This style of cultivation necessitates far more labor than the third, which we have adopted in most of the plans for suburban lots. To keep a great number of small beds filled through the summer with low blooming flowers, and their edges well cut, is expensive, and, if they are also planned so that the grass strips between them must be cut with a sickle, few gentlemen of moderate means will long have the patience to keep them with the nice care essential to their good effect.

The border-beds shown on Plate XXX are all arranged so that a rolling lawn-cutter may be used easily by hand between them. These plans are especially adapted to places with straight main walks, where the gentleman or lady of the house is an enthusiastic florist. Walk No. 1 shows a row of round beds from two to three feet in diameter on each side; the alternate circles to be filled with bushy single plants from one and a half to two feet high, and the others with low bedding flowers that do not exceed six inches in height. Nos 2, 3, and 4 are narrow strips, and circles or squares alternated. Such slender evergreens as the Irish juniper, clipped tree-box, and some of the many dwarf firs, may be used with good effect in some of these circles, but must not be too frequent. The beds at the sides of walks 5 and 6, require more lawn-room on each side, and will look best filled, each, with a single color of the lowest bedding-plants. The same remark will apply to the beds on walks 8 and 11. Walks 7 and 10 have larger beds suitable for filling with plants of different colors and heights. The former is intended to be bordered, between the beds, with square boxes filled with plants from the conservatory, and back of them, in the circles, clipped dwarf evergreens; the latter (10) is to have the small circles next the walk occupied by a succession of pot-plants in bloom, set in larger pots buried in the grass to receive them, so that the former can be taken up and put one side when the grass is to be cut.

Flower-beds which are not more than two feet in width, and on the borders of walks, should have no plants in them more than eighteen inches high, including the height of the flower-stalks, and plants from six to fifteen inches in height have the best effect. In wider beds, by placing the low growing sorts in front, or on the outside edges of the beds, the higher show to good advantage behind them.

In sowing flower-seeds, which are intended to cover a bed, put them in drills across the bed so that a hoe may be used between the plants when they appear.

To make a fine display throughout the season, in beds for low flowers, it is necessary to have at least two sets or crops of plants; one from bulbs, such as snow-drops, crocuses, jonquils, hyacinths, and tulips, all of which may be planted in October, to bloom the following spring; while the bedding-plants for the later bloom, such as verbenas, portulaccas, phlox drummondii, etc., etc., are being started. The bulbs of the former should remain in the ground till June and July to ripen, but the summer blooming plants can be planted between the bulbs, so that the latter can be removed without disarranging the former. Persons having good hotbed frames, or a greenhouse to draw from, may make more brilliant beds by more frequent changes, but two crops, if well managed, will be quite satisfactory.

Few persons are aware of the grand displays that may be made in a single season by the use of those annuals, perennials, and bedding-plants which grow quickly to great size. Proprietors commencing with bare grounds can make them very effective temporary substitutes for shrubbery. Many species, especially those half-hardy plants of recent introduction, which are remarkable for the great size, or rich colors of their leaves, are large enough to form, by themselves, groups of considerable size and beauty, from midsummer till frost. Of these, the different varieties of the ricinus (castor-bean plants) are the most imposing in height, breadth, and size of leaves. The tree ricinus, *R. borboniensis arboreus*, grows in one season to the height of fifteen feet; the *R. sanguineous*, ten feet; the silver-leaved, *R. africanus albidus*, eight feet, and the common castor-oil bean, *R. communis*, five feet. These are all great spreading plants. The *arunda donax* is a tall plant resembling the sugar-cane, grows rapidly to the height of ten feet, and takes up but little room horizontally. The magnificent cannas are of all sizes, from two to seven feet in height, and mass well either in beds by themselves, or with low plants of lighter- colored foliage in front of them, and the *arunda donax* or the Japanese striped maize behind them. The Japanese striped maize is a curiously beautiful species of corn from four to six feet in height, with leaves brightly striped with white and green. The hollyhocks are noble perennials greatly neglected. Few plants make so showy a display massed in beds, to be seen at a little distance. Height, three to six feet. The *wigandia caracasana* is a very robust bedding-plant which attains the height of six feet, and is remarkable for the size and beauty of its leaves. The *Nicotea atro purpurea grandiflora* is also noticeable for the robust beauty of its foliage, to which is added the charm of showy dark-red blossoms. The beauty of the gorgeous-leaved *colleus verschafelti* is pretty well known. In the open sun, and in rich moist soil, each plant will form a compact mass of foliage two feet in height and breadth. It also makes a brilliant border for the larger plants. The larger geraniums can also be used for the same purpose, and sweet peas, the larger cenotheras, the *lillium giganteum*, and many others, are good taller plants to place behind them. While masses of shrubs usually display their greatest floral beauty in the spring and early summer, these grand annuals and semi-tropical plants attain their greatest luxuriance of leaf and bloom at the season's close. The brilliantly colored or variegated-leaved plants, most of which are half-hardy, require to be propagated and grown in pots in the greenhouse, but flourish in the open ground during the summer months with great luxuriance, and are among the brightest and most interesting features of suburban lawns. We have named but few out of many of the plants suitable for forming showy masses or conspicuous single specimens. Descriptive lists of all which are valuable may be found in the illustrated catalogues of the great florists and nurserymen.

Fig. 45, drawn to the scale of one-sixteenth of an inch to one foot, is a design for a group of small beds to border a straight short walk on each side, and opposite each other. A low broad vase for flowers occupies the centre; the beds 2, 2, to be filled with brilliant bedding bulbs for a spring bloom, and such plants as verbenas, *phlox drummondii*, and portulaccas for the summer and autumn bloom. The larger beds 3 and 4 (which would be better if finished with a small circle at their points), will have a good effect filled first with bedding-bulbs like the former, and afterwards with a variety of geraniums diminishing in size towards the point of the bed; or roots of the great Japan lily, *Lillium auratum*, may be planted in the widest part of the beds to show their regal flowers above the masses of the geraniums. If such a variety of greenhouse flowers is greater than the planter wishes to procure, these larger beds, two on each side of the walk, may be filled very showily with petunias in one, dwarf perennial poppies in another, dwarf salvias in

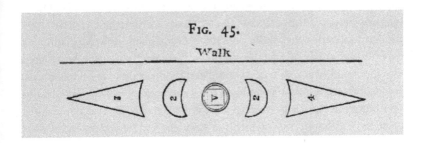

FIG. 45.

Walk

another, and coxcombs or pinks in another. The vase, if a broad one, may have a plant of Japanese striped maize for its centre, two *colleus verschafelti*, and two mountain-of-snow geraniums alternated around it, and around the edge of the vase the *vinca elegantissima*, the *lobelia erinus paxtoni*, the *tropaeolium*, or some half a dozen other drooping plants of brilliant foliage and blossoms which a florist may name.

Fig. 46 is a group of five small beds on the outside of a circular walk. No. 1 may be filled with four canna plants of sorts from three to four feet high; the beds 2, and 2, one with Lady Pollock geranium, and the other with some one gorgeous-leaved plant of about the same size 3 and beds 3 and 4 with brilliant trailing flowers.

Fig. 47 is a group of beds requiring more space, and adapted to the inner side of a curved walk where there is considerable depth of lawn behind. V is a large low vase. The circular extremities *a, a, a*, may be filled with compact specimens of curious-leaved plants like the Lady Pollock, or mountain-of-snow geranium, *colleus verschafelti, iresene herbstii*, etc., etc.; or they may be more permanently occupied by such very dwarf evergreens as the *Abies nigra pumula*, the garden boxwood, or the *Andromeda floribunda*. The narrow parts of the two beds next to the walks should be occupied by some shrubby little annuals or perennials which do not exceed nine inches in height, and the balance of the beds filled with plants increasing in size towards the vase, none of which, however, should be higher than the top of the vase. The rear bed should be filled in a similar manner, and being further from the walk, may be occupied with showy plants of coarser foliage than the front beds. By an error in the drawing the circular front of the back bed is made further from the vase than the side ones. It should be made larger in the direction of the vase, and have its corners truncated like the others.

Fig. 48 is a circular series of eight beds formed on an octagonal plan, with a large vase for flowers in the centre, a width of four feet in lawn around the vase, and the beds, five feet in length, radiating as shown. The plan is suitable for an open space, to give interest to a window view, or to face a porch where the entrance-walk runs parallel with the house. So many different plants may here be used with good effect, that whichever we may name, may be bettered by a more skillful florist. Yet we will suggest for the widest part of these beds, stools of the eight finest Japan lilies, to be surrounded by fall planted bulbs that bloom in April and May, which can be removed by the first of June; these to be followed by such plants as gladiolus and tuberoses, on the ends

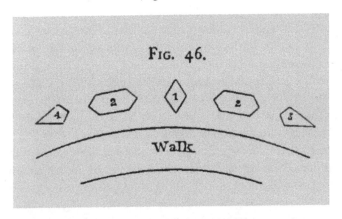

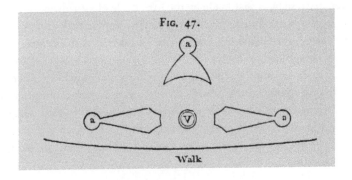

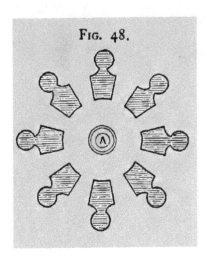

nearest the vase, and by the finest eight varieties of compact geraniums in the outer circles. Or the beds may be planted with an entirely fresh variety of flowers every year.

Fig. 49 is a group of flower-beds suitable to place at the end of a walk or at the intersection of diverging walks. A rustic or other vase is here, also, the centre of the group, with four or five feet of lawn around it. The beds *a*, *a*, should be filled with flowers that do not exceed six or nine inches in height. The beds *b*, *c*, and *d*, are large enough to allow of considerable variety in their composition. The two smaller ones should have no plants that grow higher than two feet, while in the middle of the bed *d*, and in the trefoil end, may be planted those which grow from three to five feet in height.

Fig. 50 (drawn to a scale of one-twelfth of an inch to one foot) requires a larger space such as that made by the turn circle of a roadway, or a place where a walk or road describes the segment of a circle with an open lawn on the inside of the curve. A tree might be planted at the centre, where a vase is designated, and these beds could be formed around it for half a dozen years or more, or until the shade from its branches renders the location unsuitable for the growth of flowers. If a tree be not preferred, then the single vase, or a large basket-vase with a smaller vase rising out of it, would be the most appropriate centerpiece for such a group. The four principal beds are about twelve feet in length on their middle lines,

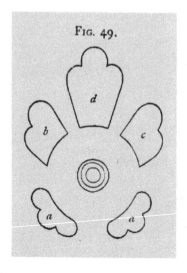

FIG. 49.

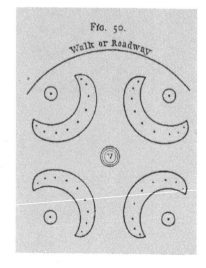

FIG. 50.

Walk or Roadway

and two and a half feet in greatest diameter. The dots show places for nine robust and compact plants, which may be from four to five feet in height in the centre, and diminish to one foot at each end. Where good plants can be obtained from a greenhouse, we recommend for the centre of one bed the *Canna coccinea vera*, or the *C. Lindleyana*, which grow to five feet in height, to be flanked with pairs, divided one on each side, of the following varieties, viz.: the *C. limbata major*, four feet high; the *C. bicolor de Java*, three feet; *C. flaccida*, three feet; *C. compacta elegantissima*, two feet, and *C. augustifolia nana pallida*, one foot. Many other varieties will do just as well as the ones named, provided they are of a size to diminish symmetrically from the centre to the ends of the bed. For the centre of another bed the *Nicoteana atro-purpurea grandiflora*, a noble, large-leaved plant, that grows five feet in height, and bears panicles of dark-red blossoms; next to this on either side a plant of *Canna gigantea splendidissima*, three feet, then a pair of *Acanthus mollis*, three feet; next the *Amaranthus bicolor*, two feet, and for the ends, the Lady Pollock geranium, one to two feet. For the centre of a third bed the *Wigandia caracasana* may be used, being another of the splendid leaved plants recently introduced. It grows to the height of six feet. This may be flanked on either side with the *Ricinus communis*, four to five feet high; next to these a mass of hollyhocks of stocky growth; next the *Mirabilis* (four o'clock), and on the points the *Colleus verschafelti*. In the centre of the fourth bed may be a stool of Japanese striped maize, five to six feet high; next on either side a plant of the striped-leaved *Canna zebrina*, five feet high; next, and in the centre-line of the bed, the *Lillium auratum*, with the *Lillium longiflorum* near the edge of the bed; next the *Salvia argentia*, three feet, and for the ends of the bed the *Amaranthus melancholicus ruber*, one to two feet high. The four outside circles may be filled respectively with the *Colleus verschafelti*, of gorgeous crimson and purple leaves; the mountain-of-snow geranium, with white foliage and scarlet flowers; the *Amaranthus bicolor*, with green and crimson leaves, and the Lady Pollock geranium with variegated leaves. The vase for a group of beds of this size should be large, and well filled in the centre with gay-leaved plants, with more delicate foliage drooping over its sides. If such groups are made without a vase in the centre, we suggest in place of it, the planting of an *Arunda donax* within a circle of Japanese maize, the bed to be about three feet in diameter, and well enriched; or the Irish juniper may be planted as a permanent and more formal centre.

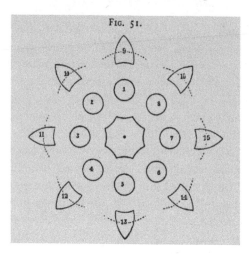

Fig. 51 is a design for a number of beds occupying so great a space that it would constitute a flower-garden. The centre bed is supposed to be cut within a circle of four feet radius, so that it will be eight feet in diameter from point to point. The eight circular beds surrounding it are each three and a half feet in diameter, and laid out so that their centres are on a circle eight feet from the main centre. The inside ends of the outer circle of beds are segments of circles struck from the centres of the small beds, and may be made of any form that the surrounding features of the place suggest. The most elegant feature for the centre of the central bed would be a broad shallow vase two feet in height, and four in breadth, on top, elevated on a pedestal two feet high, which should be concealed by a dense mass of shrubby flowering plants around it; the sides of the vase to be draped with pendulous plants overhanging its sides, and its centre filled with plants of a tropical appearance. Next in elegance to the large vase-centre would be a basket-bed similar to the one shown in the engraving at the end of this chapter. This would require a different style of planting. Supposing its base to be four feet in diameter, there would be a margin of two feet all around it for low trailing flowers. The design for a basket-vase is intended for an open lawn, and shows a collection of plants quite different from what would be best for the design under consideration. Here we would have for its centre a single group of the *Canna sanguinea chatei*, surrounded by a circle of Japanese maize; next a circle of *Salvia argentea*, and for the outside border the Lady Pollock geranium inter-planted with some of the slender, drooping, light-leaved plants, named farther on in this chapter, for the decoration of vases.

If this central bed is to have neither a pedestal-vase nor basket- vase, it may still be made the most conspicuous point of interest in the parterre with plants alone. It is desirable that the lawn should rise gently towards it on all sides, and that the bed be raised in the centre as much as may be without making the earth liable to be washed upon the lawn. In the centre, if this flower-garden is intended to be permanent, we would plant the remarkable variety of the European silver fir, known as the *Picea pectinata pendula*, or the variety of the Norway spruce, known as the *Abies excelsa inverta*, shown in Fig. 52, and around it a circle of the tallest Japan lilies; next a circle of the mountain-of-snow geranium alternated with gladioli, and for the outside of the same bed, the *Colleus verschafelti*, alternated with the Lady Pollock geranium. Some years will be required to grow the evergreens named to the size that will make them appropriate centres for such a parterre. If a showy bed is required the first season without the use of either vase, basket, or evergreen tree-centre, the following plants may be suggested to effect it, viz.: for the centre, the *Canna gigantea auriantica*, ten feet high; around it on a circle eighteen inches from the centre, the *Canna sanguinea chatei*, six feet high, to be planted one foot apart in the circle; next on a circle one foot further out, the *Salvia argentea*, or the mountain-of-snow geranium, to be planted one foot apart in the circle; for the next circle, one foot from the same, the *Amaranthus melancholicus ruber*, a plant of deep-red foliage from one to two feet high, and for the edge of the bed the fern-like low white-leaved *Centaurea gymnocarpa*; or if plants of the latter are too expensive to use freely, make a border of the common Indian pink, or the blue lobelia. These plants, if successfully grown, will make a magnificent bed from midsummer till frost. For a display in the first half of the season, early blooming bulbous flowers must be relied upon. We have thus far considered only the central-bed of the group shown in Fig. 51, and have suggested various modes of treating it which would be equally applicable to a round bed of the size named, were it disconnected with the surrounding beds. For the small circular-beds, each alternate one may have a cluster of the Japanese striped maize in its centre; the other four beds might have in their centres the *Canna flaccida*, the *Nicotiana atropurpurea grandiflora*, the *Canna gigantea splendidissima*, and the *Wigandia caracasana*. Around their edges may be planted any well-foliaged flowering plants which do not exceed nine inches in height, and a different species in each bed. The outside tier of beds are for low bedding flowers or annuals, which should not exceed fifteen inches in height for the centres, or more than six inches near the borders.

Fig. 52 represents a circular-bed with one of the pendulous firs mentioned in a preceding page, in its centre, and such tall growing brilliant flowers as the Japan lilies and gladiolii next to it; a circle of petunias around them, and creeping plants near the margin.

The common firs are often planted to form centres for such beds, but they soon grow to such over-shadowing size as to be quite unsuitable. The weeping silver fir, and weeping Norway spruce, however, are pendulous to such a degree that they make but slow additions to their breadth. If their central stems or leaders are kept vertical by tying to a stake or straight twig bound to the stem below, and the side branches trimmed back whenever they show a tendency to the normal form, the appearance shown in the cut may be preserved for many years. Where these varieties of the fir are not to be had, the Irish juniper, or the hemlock, may be substituted. The former of those trees is almost monumental in its slender formality, but is pleasing in color and delicate foliage. The latter, if trimmed back every spring in April or May, but not afterwards during that season, will exhibit during the rest of the year the most airy outline of pendulous spray. The trimming in the spring must not be done so as to leave a solidly conical hedge-like form, but

Fig. 52.

with some irregularity, imitating within slender limits the freedom of outline natural to the hemlock; the idea being to produce by artificial means the appearance of one of nature's abnormal varieties or sports, which will bear the same relation to the common form of the hemlock that the pendulous fir in the cut bears to its family.

The last cut of this chapter, already alluded to, is a form of basket-vase now little used, which we recommend as an appropriate embellishment for a lawn, when filled with suitable plants. Such basket forms may be made either of rustic woodwork, of terra-cotta, or of iron, and need have no bottom; or at least only rims around the bottoms on the inside sufficient to prevent them from settling into the ground unevenly. When filled with earth they form simply raised beds to be planted with such things as the taste of the owner may choose. The basket form simply gives an artistic relief to the bed, and at the same time is so low that it does not obtrusively break the views over a small lawn, like those tall vases of a garish complexion which are often seen in lonely isolation, thrust forward 'to show'. All vases of classic forms need to be supported by architectural constructions of some kind, nearby, which harmonize with them in style; or else to be so embowered with the foliage of the plants they bear, and by which they are surrounded, in the summer months at least, that they will gleam through leaves and flowers like the face of a beautiful woman seen through a veil. The variety of forms and sizes for basket-beds is illimitable; they may be suited to almost any spot where a flowerbed is desirable, and can be made cheaply, or with costly art, as the surroundings may suggest. We venture, however, to warn their makers not to put arch-handles over them. A basket form is chosen because it is pretty and convenient, but it does not follow that the bed of flowers should make any pretence to be in fact a real basket of flowers. The transparency of the deception makes it ridiculous.

Rustic vases made of crooked joints and roots of trees, and twigs with or without their bark, have become quite common, and are often made so strongly and skillfully as to be pleasing works of art. Strength, durability, and firmness on their bases are the essential qualities which they must have. Any constructions of this kind which suggest flimsy wood, or bungling carpentry, or rotting bark, or want of firmness at the base, though they may be planted to give a pretty effect at first, soon become rickety nuisances. But those which are 'strongly built, and well', are certainly more likely to have a pleasing effect on common grounds than little plaster, iron, or stone vases, and cannot so easily be used amiss. All rustic constructions of this kind will last much longer, and look cleaner, if the wood is obtained when the bark will peel readily, and made up with no bark upon it. The first effect is certainly less rustic, but sufficiently so to harmonize with the surroundings of a suburban home, and after a few years the advantages of the barkless constructions are very evident.

There is a frequent fault in the use of vases, whether rustic or classic, that mars all their beauty wherever they are placed. We refer to the want of care in keeping their tops level, and their centres vertical. A house 'out of plum' is not more unsightly than a vase awry.

The plants used with good effect in rustic vases are those which have large and showy or curiously marked leaves, for the centres, surrounded by delicate-leaved drooping or trailing plants. The gorgeous crimson-leaved *Colleus verschafelti* is a deserved favorite for vases of good size, being a rank grower and developing its greatest beauty in exposures open on all sides to the sun. The following are some of the plants recommended by Henderson, in his book of Practical Floriculture, for the central portions of small baskets, and will answer also for small vases: 'The *Centaurea Candida*, a plant of white, downy leaves, of compact growth; Tom Thumb geranium, scarlet, dwarf, and compact, blooming all summer; *Sedum sieboldii*, a plant of light glaucus foliage and graceful habit,' and for large baskets the following: 'Mrs. Pollock geranium, foliage crimson, yellow and green, flowers bright scarlet; *Centaurea gymnocarpa*, foliage fern-like, whitish gray, of a peculiar graceful habit; *Sedum sieboldii* variegation, glaucus green, marbled with golden yellow; *Achyranthes gilsonii*, a beautiful shade of carmine foliage and stem; *Alyssum dentatum* variegation, foliage green and white, with fragrant flowers of pure white; *Altemanthera spathula*, lanceolate leaves of pink and crimson; pyrethrum or golden feather, fern-like foliage, golden yellow.' For plants to put around the edge of a small basket or vase, and to fall pendant from its sides, he recommends the following: '*Lobelia erinus paxtoni* an exquisite blue, drooping eighteen inches; *Tropceolum* (ball of fire), dazzling scarlet, drooping eighteen inches; *Lysimachia numularia*, flowers bright yellow, drooping eighteen inches; *Linaria cymbalaria*, inconspicuous flowers but graceful foliage.' For the edging or pendant plants of a large basket he recommends the following, which are also suitable for the edging of a vase: '*Maurandia barclayana*, white or purple flowers; *Vinca elegantissima aurea*, foliage deep green, netted with golden yellow, flowers deep blue; *Cerastium tomentosum*, foliage downy white, flowers white; *Convolvulus mauritanicus*, flowers light blue, profuse; *Solatium jasminoides variegatum*, foliage variegated, flowers white with yellow anthers: *Geraniumpeltatum elegans*, a variety of the ivy-leaved, with rich glossy foliage and mauve-colored flowers: *Panicum variegatum*, a procumbent grass from New Caledonia, of graceful habit of growth, with beautiful variegated foliage, striped white, carmine, and green.' These are mostly half-hardy conservatory plants, and if the proprietor has no conservatory they must be purchased, when wanted, of the florists, or they may be started by a skillful lady-florist in her own window. Nearly every lady of refined taste longs to have a conservatory of her own. But a building, or even an entire room, built for, and devoted to plants alone, is an expensive luxury. Those who have well-built houses heated by steam, or other good furnaces, may easily have a plant-window in a sunny exposure in which the plants required to bed in open ground the following summer may be reared, and beautiful well-grown plants may be obtained from the commercial florists to keep the window gay with blossoms and foliage at a price greatly below the cost for which amateurs can raise them in their own conservatories. These remarks are not designed to discourage the building of private conservatories by those who can afford them – far from it – but rather to suggest to those who cannot afford them, not to be envious of those who can.

**Roses** – We have not previously mentioned the Rose, among flowers and bedding plants, for the reason that, being the queen of flowers, more than ordinary attention is usually considered due to her. Besides, her royal family are so numerous, so varied and interesting in their characters, and have been the subject of so many compliments from poets, and biographical notices from pens of distinguished horticulturists, that it would be presumption to attempt to describe, in a few brief paragraphs, the peculiar beauties and characteristics of the family; still less of all its thousand members. The mere fact of royalty, however, has attracted such numbers of admirers and chroniclers of their beauty, that, in failing to do justice to them by any observations of our own, there is a satisfaction in knowing that scores of their devoted admirers have written lovingly and sensibly of them, and from their pages, we may glean and present such general information concerning the relative rank, characters, and habits of the various roses as comes within the scope of a work on the arts of arrangement, rather than a floral manual of classification or culture.

In all the languages of civilized nations volumes have been written on the history, the poetical and legendary associations, the classification, and the culture of the rose; so that, whoever desires to be especially well informed on any branch of knowledge pertaining to roses will seek among the books in his own language for the special and full information he desires. As roses come properly under the head of shrubs, we shall, under that head, give so much on the subject as may be necessary in connection with the embellishment of suburban places, together with a plate of designs for rose-beds, of a great variety of sizes and forms, with various selections of roses that may be used to advantage in filling them. We will only add here what has before been mentioned in connection with the subject of arrangement, that the planting of rose-bushes, as isolated small shrubs on a lawn, is almost always a misplacement. There are a few sorts, especially some of the wild bush-roses, which form fine compact bushes, sufficiently well foliaged to be pleasing all the summer months when not in bloom, but the greater part of the finest roses, particularly the perpetuals which make a straggling and unequal growth, produce a far finer effect when planted pretty snugly in masses. A practice of planting each root of a sort by itself, like so many hills of potatoes, is quite necessary in commercial gardens where they are grown for sale, and each of a hundred varieties must be kept distinct from every other, so that it may be distinguished readily, and removed for sale without injury to the others, but this is market-gardening, not decorative, and the least interesting of all modes of cultivating the rose. Decidedly, the prettier way in small collections is to learn first what is the comparative strength of growth and height of the several plants which are to make up one's collection, and then to distribute the smaller sorts around the larger, so that all may be seen to advantage, and made to appear like a single bush, or symmetric group. As it is desirable to know each sort when out of flower and leaf, labels, fastened with copper wire, can remain attached to the stems near the base as well when in groups as when separate.

It must not be understood that we favor great formality of outlines in a group, or what is called a lumpish mass, but only that the general outline of bush or group shall be symmetrical, and that it shall contain a sufficient mass of foliage in itself to allow the straggling spray, which gives spirit to its outline, to be relieved against a good body of foliage. However formally a rose-bed is laid out, the free rambling growth of the plants will always give a sprightly irregularity of outline sufficient to relieve it from all appearance

of primness. It is as unnatural to force the rose into formal outlines as to suppress the frolicksomeness of children, but in both cases the freedom natural to each may be directed, and made to conform, to the proprieties of place and occasion. Allusion has previously been made to the bad taste of conspicuous pieces of white-painted carpentry very generally used as supports for running roses. The simpler and more inconspicuous such supports are made, provided they are substantial, the better.

# 18

# The Philosophy of Deep Drainage and Cultivation In Their Relation to the Growth of Trees, and the Successful Culture of Those which are Half-Hardy; Together with Suggestions for Protecting Young Trees in Winter and Summer

A large portion of the gross weight of all soils is water. If we dry any soil perfectly, the residuum of weight will bear a very small proportion to the average weight of the soil in its natural condition. Water, therefore, occupies a large part of the texture of what we call solid earth. When we draw the water from any soil by drains, the space occupied by the water in the earth is supplied by air. Thorough draining, therefore, airs the soil to whatever depth it drains off the water. The air transmits heat and cold less rapidly than water by direct conduction, so that, if air occupies the place of water in the interstices of the soil, the latter will feel all changes of temperature more slowly. Deep drainage, therefore, tends to equalize the temperature of the earth's surface, and to neutralize the effect of great and sudden changes in the air above. It is impossible to drain a subsoil too thoroughly from beneath, because the capillary attraction of the earth is always sufficient to draw up from below all the moisture that is essential to most forms of vegetable life, and in addition to the moisture thus drawn from below, the earth, when the air can circulate freely in it, has the power when dry to absorb a vast amount of moisture from the air, as well as to yield it up to the air by evaporation when it holds an excess. To all general observations like these, the reader's intelligence will of course suggest exceptions; as of trees and plants which thrive best where their roots are immersed in water, and which make water their element rather than earth; but the fact holds good as to the great mass of beautiful trees, shrubs, and plants – that they will thrive best, and bear the winter's cold and the summer's heat and drought with least injury, in the most deeply drained soils. If this is true as a general rule, it is plain that for trees which are peculiarly sensitive to either extreme, there is greater need of deep drainage than for any other.

The airing of the soil, which deep draining secures, acts in two ways for the benefit of all vegetation: first, by equalizing the temperature of the soil in consequence of the non-conducting power of air; secondly, by exposing the deeper soil to the contact of air, it becomes changed in character, and undergoes a constant process of fertilization by the action of air upon it. It is being oxygenized. Anyone familiar with farming operations in new countries, knows that when virgin soils are first turned over, there are, usually, only a few inches of dark soil on the surface. If the plow turns a furrow five or six inches deep, it will generally show a much lighter color than the surface which is turned under, but in a few years of continued culture this lighter-colored soil becomes as dark as the original surface. By the combined action of the sun and air it has all become equally oxygenized. If such ground were repeatedly plowed without growing a crop from it, and so as to permit no growth of vegetation to be turned under, it would still, for a time, gain rapidly in fertility, by the mere chemical changes produced by the sun and air. What plowing effects quickly by the direct exposure of the upper soil to these elements, deep draining and the consequent airing of the soil effects slowly, and less thoroughly, in subsoils through which the air is induced to permeate. Imperceptibly, but surely, the earth beneath our feet is being warmed and fertilized by the action of the air upon it, whenever we invite the air in, by drawing the water out. This increased warmth and richness of the subsoil invites the roots of trees deeper and deeper in proportion as it approximates in character to the warmth and oxygenation of the surface-soil. To have a deeply aired soil, therefore, is to encourage trees to root farther down, and away from the trying changes of winter and spring temperature that weaken or kill semi-tropical trees and shrubs, and often impair the vitality of young trees of hardy species.

**Earth Heat** – Next in importance to deep drainage, therefore, is deep tillage. It supplements drainage by often repeated exposure of a certain depth of soil to the action of the air and sun, by which its oxygenation is carried on more rapidly than it can possibly be when not so exposed.

The earth grows warmer as we go down. If its temperature were tested in winter, we should find an increasing warmth with each foot of depth below the frost. The more porous and dry the soil, the less depth it will freeze, and the more rapid the increase of temperature below the frost line. This explains why gravelly subsoils make warm soils, and suggests that deep drainage is the most efficient means of providing for trees an equable 'bottom heat'.

In the northern States the range of earth-freezing is from one to three feet deep. It is not always deepest where the cold is greatest; for where a considerable altitude makes the winters more severe, the greater snow-falls are likely to husband the earth's warmth as with a feathery blanket, so that the soil may be frozen no deeper at Utica than at Philadelphia. But when the surface protection is the same, altitude and latitude tell quickly on the climate in its effect on trees.

Roots at the surface of the ground are either torpid in their icy encasement, or alternately thawed-out or frozen-in during four or five months. Those a foot below the surface are ice-bound not much more than half this time; those two feet below, a third, and those three feet below, not at all. All the roots which are just under the frost-line during any part of the winter, are in no colder soil than the winter surface-soil of the Gulf States. Whether six inches or three feet under the surface, where the ground is not frozen, the roots maintain some action.

The younger and smaller a tree or shrub, the nearer its roots are to the surface, and all its fluctuations and severities of temperature; and therefore the greater need of guarding against them. The analogy between animals and plants is greater than most persons suppose. 'Keep your feet warm and dry, and you will not be likely to take cold', is a trite piece of advice, because it is so true and so useful. Now if we can keep the plants' feet warm and dry, or at least save them from the greatest extremes of cold and wet, we do them the same kindness that we do the children by wrapping their feet in wool and leather protections.

The roots of trees and shrubs during the first five years of their growth are mostly in that part of the soil which is frozen in the northern States from one to three feet deep every winter. Some rapid-growing trees, as the yellow locust and the silver poplar, send down their roots to a great depth very soon after planting. We have seen roots of the locust that had penetrated a marly clay and were as large as pipe-stems at a depth of six feet below the surface, from trees only three years planted. This power of quick and deep rooting in the subsoil is probably the reason why the locust tree, with its tropical luxuriance and extreme delicacy of foliage, is able to endure a degree of cold that many less succulent and hardier looking trees cannot bear.

**Deep Roots as Conductors of Heat to the Tops of Trees** – The deep roots have an influence in maintaining an equilibrium of temperature in the tree that is little understood. They are direct conductors from the even warmth of the unfrozen subsoil, to the trunk and branches which are battling with frigid air, and winds that strive to rob them of their vital heat. All winter long this current of heat is conducted by the deep roots to the exposed top. The greater the cold, the greater the call on these roots to maintain the equilibrium, and consequently their usefulness in this respect is in proportion to the extremes of temperature above ground which the tree may be required to resist, and the proportion of roots which are below the frost-line. Surface roots are the summer-feeding roots – multiplying their myriads of fibres, each one a greedy mouth, when spring opens and the leaves need them, and there is always a perfect proportion between their abundance and vigor, and the luxuriance of the foliage above them. Surface manuring promotes a rank growth of these roots, and of the foliage, and should only be used for young trees and shrubs which are unquestionably hardy, or for the less hardy which are already deeply rooted, but not for young trees of doubtful hardiness. These must first be provided with the bottom heat that deep drainage and a well-aired subsoil provides, until they are deeply rooted.

As newly planted trees have not the means of keeping themselves warm in winter by means of their deep roots, it follows that they must be nursed in some way so that they will maintain a vigorous life until they are thus provided.

Trees or shrubs of half-tropical habit, by which we mean those that flourish in our southern States without protection, and which may be so carefully managed as to develop their beauties healthily in the northern States, of course need this careful nursing more than any other, and not only to guard them against winter's excesses, but to give them the most equable ground temperature at all seasons. Most trees in their native localities grow in deep shades, and the soil over their roots is rarely heated by the direct rays of the sun, however powerful its heat upon their tops. The very luxuriance of vegetation forms a bower of shade for the soil; so that in forests the roots of trees are in a soil that is comparatively equable in temperature and moisture. When trees from such localities are grown on open lawns, they are naturally disposed to branch low, in order to cover their roots from the heat of the summer sun by the shade of their own boughs. The magnolias and rhododendrons are marked examples of trees and shrubs which are cultivated most successfully in deeply drained soils, but at the same time are ill-at-ease in ground where the soil over their roots is bared to the scorching summer heat. In the case of evergreen trees, their low-branching keeps the ground under them cool and shady in summer, and also protects the roots in winter, acting as a blanket to hold the radiation of the earth's heat, and to hold the snow which makes another blanket for the same purpose. A well-cut lawn is some protection to the roots of trees, but it interferes with that active oxygenation of the soil which deep- culture produces, and while it acts as a shield against the scorching effect of the summer sun on bare earth, and as a mulch to counteract, in a slight degree, the rapid changes of temperature on the surface-roots, it at the same time reduces the vitality and power of resistance to cold in the tree, by preventing the deep soil from becoming well aired and oxygenized, as it is under high culture. Under the sod of a lawn, therefore, the roots of trees will be nearer the surface than in ground under cultivation, and will have less power to resist cold, so far as deep roots enable them to resist it.

If a tree is planted in a thoroughly drained soil which is to be cultivated, instead of one which is to be covered with lawn, it may be set several inches deeper, so that the main roots need not be injured by the spade, while they will be kept in warm soil by the occasional turning under of the surface which has been under the direct action of the sun's rays. The roots at the depth of ten inches, in a soil which is spaded annually, and well cultivated, will be as well aired, and have as warm feeding ground, as in a similar soil two inches below an old sod. This cultivation, therefore, gains for the tree a summer and winter mulching of eight inches in depth above its rootlets; a great gain in winter, and equal to several degrees of more southern latitude.

Half-hardy trees should therefore not only be planted in ground drained most deeply and thoroughly, but also where the ground may be deeply cultivated until they are rooted in a warm subsoil below the action of frosts – say ten years. Trees which eventually grow to considerable size may, when young, be centres or parts of groups of shrubs that also require high culture, and when the tree begins to over-top the shrubs, the latter should be gradually removed. But it must be constantly borne in mind that all trees, and especially those of doubtful hardiness, need a full development of low side-branches when young, and no shrubbery should remain near enough to them to check this side-growth. When all the excess of shrubbery around the tree is removed, and the latter is supposed to have become sufficiently established to be able to dispense with deep culture, and have the ground under its branches converted into lawn, then two or three inches in depth of fresh soil should be added all around the tree, as far as the roots extend; and for half-hardy trees, an autumn mulching with leaves or evergreen boughs should never be omitted at any age of the tree. The subject of mulching will be treated again in this chapter.

**Protection from Winds** – The effect of protection from the winds is nearly the same for delicate trees as for delicate human beings. 'Keep out of a strong draught of air' is a common admonition given to those who are healthy, as well as to invalids, and this, too, when only the pleasant breath of summer is to be guarded against. Now when we reflect that trees have not the power of warming themselves by exercise, but must stand with suffering patience the coldest blasts of winter, with no more covering on body and limbs than sufficed them in genial summer air, how thoughtless and heartless of us to expect any of them, least of all the denizens of semi-tropical forests, to laugh with blossoms, and grow fat with leaves, after being exposed to all the rigors of a northern winter. Ought we not to be most thankful that even the hardened species of northern zones can bear the vicissitudes of our climate? And if semi-tropical trees can also be made to thrive by kindly protection, should we grudge them the care which their delicacy demands?

Much as our horticultural writers have endeavored to impress the importance of protection from winds, by means of walls of hardy evergreen trees, few persons have had the opportunity of observing how great the benefits of such protection. Houses, outbuildings, and high fences may generally be so connected by such hedges and screens as to form warm bays and sheltered nooks where many trees and shrubs of novel beauty may be grown, which, in exposed situations, would either die outright or eke out a diseased and stunted existence. This remark applies with most force to the smaller trees and shrubs for which constructive protections against winds may be erected with no great expense; or verdant walls may be grown within a few years. Yet larger trees like the *Magnolia machrophytta* and the Bhotan pine (*P. excelsa*) may be so protected in their early growth that the health and vigor acquired during the first ten years of careful attention to their needs will enable them to resist vicissitudes of climate which trees of the same species, less judiciously reared, would die under. Vigor of constitution in animals is not alone a matter of race and family, but also to a considerable degree the result of education and training. Delicate youths who nurse their strength, and battle with their own weakness by obeying the laws of health that intelligence teaches them, often become stronger at middle age than those of robust organization who early waste their vigor by careless disregard of those laws. By studying the nature of trees we may effect similar results with similar care.

Winter protection from winds must be effected principally by hardy evergreens. Of these the Norway spruce is one of the most rapid in its growth. In itself a beautiful object, it may be massed in pleasing groups, or compact belts, or close cut colossal hedges. The white pine in sandy soils has a still more rapid growth, and is, therefore, suited to form the highest screens. The American and the Siberian arbor-vitaes are naturally so hedge-like in form that the sight of them at once suggests their usefulness; while the rambling and graceful young hemlock is readily trained into verdant screens of exquisite beauty.

The relative growth of these trees is about in the following order: The white pine planted from the nursery should attain the height of twenty feet in ten years, and forty feet in twenty years. The Norway spruce grows with about the same rapidity, but its growth being relatively less in breadth at the top, its summit gives less check to winds. The hemlock may attain about two-thirds the size of the pine in the same time; while the arbor-vitaes just named may be relied on to make about a foot of growth per year. These facts suggest to intelligent planters the service these trees may be made to render in the capacity of protectors of the weaker species of trees and shrubs.

The warming power of evergreen trees in winter is not fully appreciated. They are like living beings, breathing all the time, and keep up, and give off their vital heat in the same manner. In a dense forest the cold is never so intense as on an adjoining prairie, and the difference between the temperature of even a small grove of evergreens, and open ground nearby, is often great enough to decide the life or death of sensitive shrubs and trees. In our chapter on the Characteristics of Trees will be found some interesting facts concerning this quality of trees and plants.

Deep drainage, deep culture, and protection from winds are the three great means to give trees a healthy and rapid development, and to acclimatize those which are not quite hardy. It has also been suggested that certain trees and shrubs need to be protected from the sun, as well as from cold and wind. This fact will be noted in the descriptions of them.

We now come to the special treatment of newly planted trees, premising that the general conditions just given have been complied with.

**Mulching** – Mulch signifies any substance which may be strewn upon the ground to retain its moisture for the benefit of the roots which it covers, or to serve as a non-conductor of the coldness or the heat of the air, and to retain the natural warmth of the earth beneath. Mulching may be done in a great variety of ways, and for different purposes. Summer mulching is intended to protect the soil from too rapid drying under the direct rays of the sun. Winter mulching is designed to prevent the sudden and excessive freezing of the earth.

Leaves are the natural mulch for forest trees. At the approach of winter, observe how all the trees disrobe their branches to drop a cover of leaves upon their roots. The winds blow them away from the great trunks which are deep rooted and need them least, to lodge among the stems and roots of the underbrush which need them most. Leaves being the most natural cover for roots are the best. But they cannot be used to advantage in summer in well-kept grounds because of the difficulty of retaining them in place, and their unsightly effect when blown about on a lawn. In autumn, however, they should be gathered, when most abundant, for a winter mulch, and can be retained in place by heavy twigs over them. The twigs and leaves together catch the blowing snow and thus make a warm snow blanket in addition to their own protection. For summer mulching, saw-dust (not too fresh) and 'chip-dirt', are good and tidy protections. Old straw is excellent, but is unsightly and too disorderly when blown by winds to be satisfactory in neatly kept places, and when used too freely harbors mice. Tan-bark is a favorite summer mulch, and very good if not put on too thick. Evergreen leaves and twigs are admirable for either summer or winter mulching, but especially for winter, on account of the snow that accumulates in them. Massed to the depth of a foot, the ground beneath them will hardly feel the frosts. Trees or shrubs which are hardy enough to be forced into a rank growth without making their new wood too succulent and tender to bear the following winter, may be mulched with short manure, but trees of doubtful hardiness must not be thus stimulated. If used at all it should be in autumn, for winter service, and raked off in spring, to be replaced by cooler materials during the growing season.

In addition to the mulching required over the roots of young trees and shrubs in winter, it is necessary to cover the trunk, and sometimes the entire tops of those which are half-hardy with some protection. The stems of young trees may be covered with straw bound around them, or with matting, or strong brown paper. Small tree-tops and spreading shrubs may be carefully drawn together with straw cords, and bound up as completely in straw and matting as bundles of trees sent out from a nursery. As such masses are likely to catch the snow, and offer considerable resistance to the wind, it is absolutely necessary in all cases after a subject has been thus bound, that strong stakes be driven nearby, and the bound-up branches securely fastened to them until the binding is taken off in the spring. The following cuts, illustrating a mode of protecting peach trees, to secure their fruit-buds from injury in winter, also illustrates the mode of protecting the tops for other purposes.

In the case of the peach tree a strong cedar post is supposed to be deeply set for a permanent fixture at the same time the tree is planted, and that the latter grows up around it as shown by Fig. 53. At the approach of winter the branches which can be most conveniently bound together are prepared like nursery bundles as shown by Fig. 54, and when done are secured by cords to the central post as shown by Fig. 55. In addition to this straw binding, earth from beyond the branches is banked up around the stem, as shown in the same cuts. This mode of protection is especially adapted to the fruit-yard. It would not be admissible to have permanent posts or stakes in the embellished parts of grounds, but a similar mode of protection can be employed by the use of strong stakes to be driven when wanted, and removed in the spring.

Tender vines, and pliable-wooded bushes, may be turned down on the approach of winter, and laid flat upon the ground or lawn, where there is room. If in cultivated ground, there is no better protection than a covering of several inches of earth. If standing upon a lawn they may be either covered with earth in the same way, if it can be brought from a convenient distance, or may be pinned down and covered from four to twelve inches deep with evergreen boughs or twigs.

Very tender plants must of course be covered more deeply than hardier ones, and the cover should be removed gradually in the spring. It is advisable to mark the exact place where each vine or branch is laid, so that in uncovering, in the spring, it may not be injured by the spade.

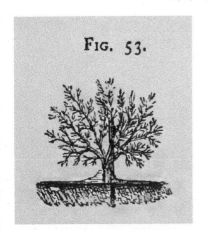

FIG. 53.

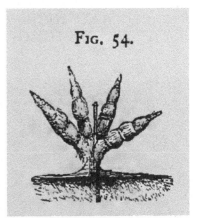

FIG. 54.

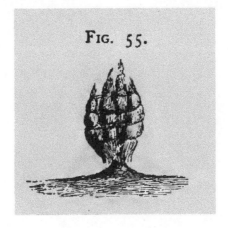

FIG. 55.

# A KEY TO THE SYMBOLS USED IN
# THE FOLLOWING DESIGNS

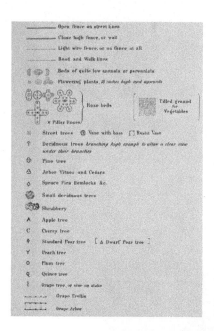

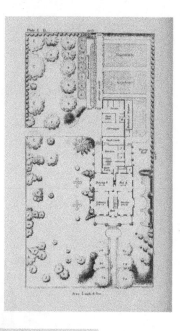

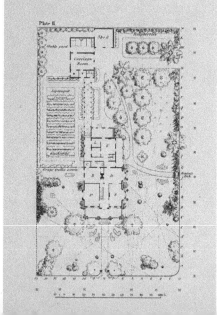

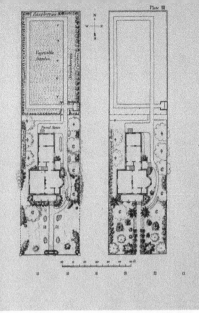

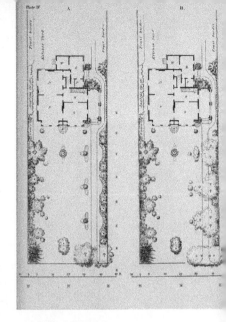

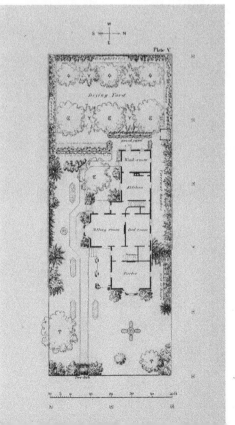

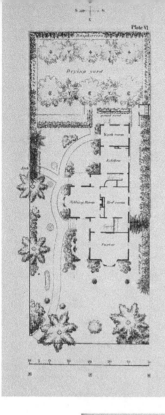

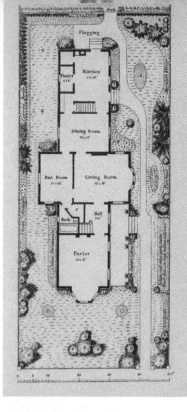

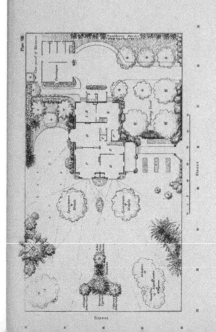

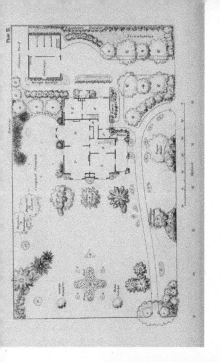

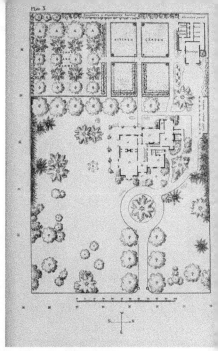

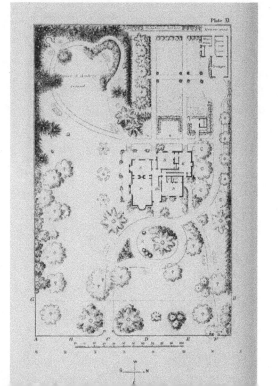

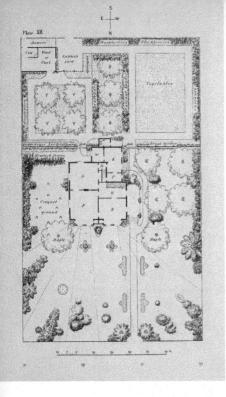

Plate XII.

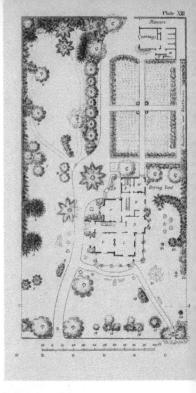

Plate XIII.

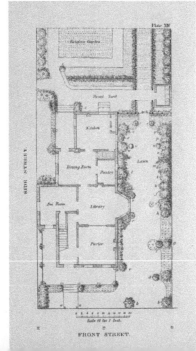

Plate XIV.

FRONT STREET.

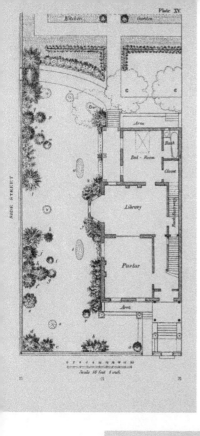

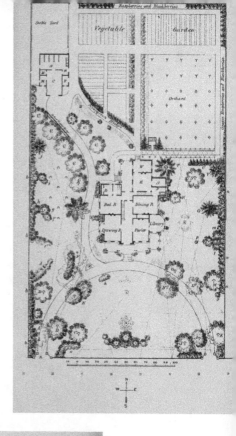

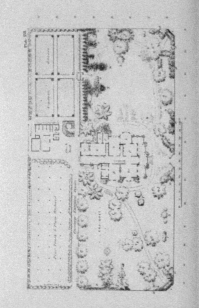

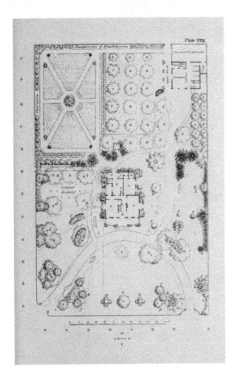

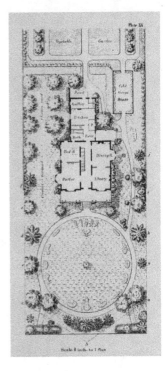

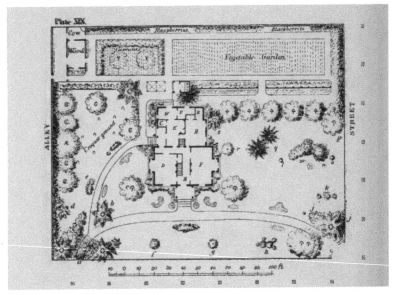

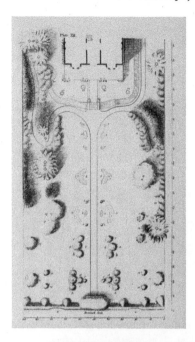

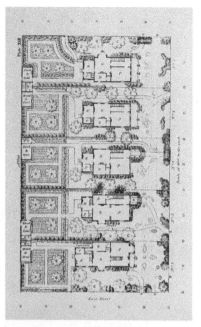

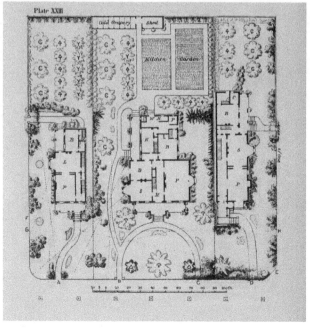

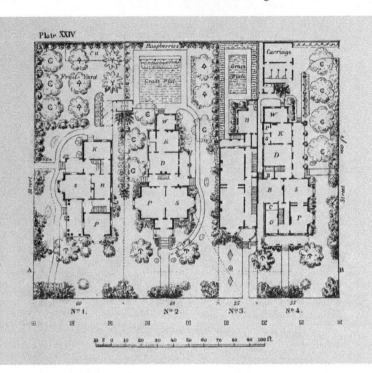

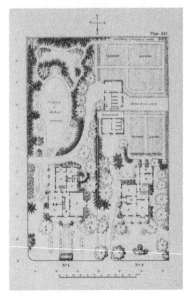

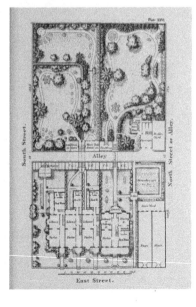

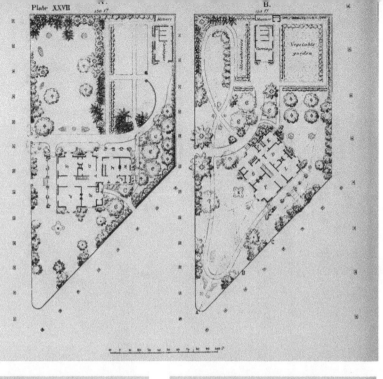

Plate XXVII

Plate XXVIII

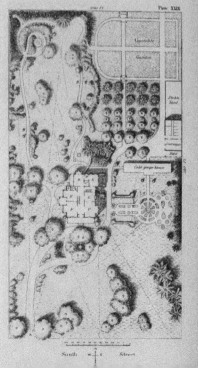

Plate XXIX

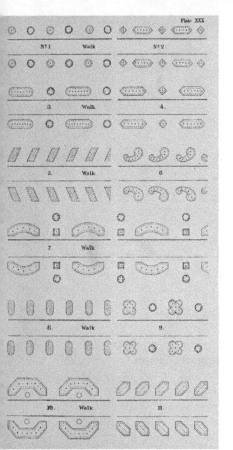

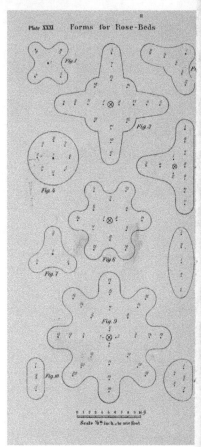